Processing and Analyzing Financial Data with R

Marcelo S. Perlin (marcelo.perlin@ufrgs.br)

2017-05-01

Processing and Analyzing Financial Data with R

by Marcelo S. Perlin

Proof reader:	Proof Reading services
Cover designer:	Rubens Lima (Capista)
Publisher:	Independently published
ISBN:	978-85-922435-5-5

History of editions:
- First edition: 2017-05-01

Contents

Preface

Since you are reading this book, you are likely a financial analyst looking for alternative and more efficient ways to process your financial data, an undergraduate or graduate student in its first steps regarding scientific research, or an experienced researcher, looking for new tools to use in your work. In all cases, this book is for you. The objective of this work is to introduce the reader to the use of R as a computational tool for data analysis, with a special emphasis on empirical research in finance. With this book, you will learn how to load financial data into R, manipulate the information in a way that makes sense to your problem and build the content of a report with tables and figures.

The material in this book started as class slides from my work as a teacher and researcher. By watching students learning and using R in the classroom, I frequently observe the positive impact this knowledge has in their careers. They can do complex data tasks with their computer, providing better and more comprehensive analysis to help the decision making process in their organizations. They spend less time doing repetitive and soul-crushing data chores and more time thinking about their analysis. This book attempts to go beyond the classroom and reach a bigger and more diversified audience.

Another motivation for writing this book is my personal experience using code from other researchers. Usually, the code is not well-organized, lacks clarity, and, possibly, only works in the computer of its author! After being constantly frustrated, I realized the work needed to figure out the code of other researchers would take more time than writing the procedure myself. These cases hurt the development of science, as one of it basic principles is the **reproducibility** of experiments. For the case of a computer intensive field, such as empirical finance, the underlying research code should run without effort in other people's computers. As researchers are expected to be good writers, it should also be expected that their code is in a proper format and readable by other people. Unfortunately, this is not usual.

With this book, I will tackle this problem by presenting a code structure focused on scientific reproducibility, organization, and usability.

In this book, we will not work on the advanced uses of R. The content will be limited to simple and practical examples of using the software to construct research focused on the area of Finance. One of the challenges of writing this book was defining the boundary between introductory and advanced material. Wherever possible, I gradually dosed the level of complexity. For readers interested in learning advanced features of the program and its inner workings, I suggest the work of Venables et al. (2004), Teetor (2011) and Wickham (2014).

The book includes the following chapters:

- **Chapter 1 - Introduction** - Introduces the reader to the use of R as a programming platform designed to solve data related problems in finance. In this chapter, we will present the steps for installing the required software and the reasons why you should adopt it.

- **Chapter 2 - Basic Operations** - Discusses the basic commands in R and the features of RStudio. These are common operations and form the groundwork of using the software. It includes the topics of objects creation, international and local format, using auto-complete features of RStudio and many more.

- **Chapter 3 - Basic Classes** - Presents the most used classes of objects in R, including numeric types, factors, text and Dates. In this chapter you'll learn how to use the basic classes to represent information about your data problem and the possible manipulations for each type of object.

- **Chapter 4 - Data Structure Classes** - Discusses the use of more advanced objects that structure the basic classes in an efficient way. Most importantly, we will discuss the use of *dataframes*, a powerful and flexible object that will represent our whole dataset.

- **Chapter 5 - Financial Data and Common Operations** - In this chapter we will discuss the origin and content of the most used types of financial data, including data from financial markets, project assessment and financial statements. Common operations with this data, such as the calculation of returns, are also discussed.

- **Chapter 6 - Importing and Exporting Data from Local Files** - This chapter presents the most common functions for importing and exporting data from different file extensions such as *.csv*, *.RData*, *.xlsx*.

- **Chapter 7 - Importing Financial Data from the Internet** - This part of the book presents the most popular packages available in CRAN for importing financial data using the web. Base on these packages we will access the trade history of stocks, the US yield curve, financial statements and others.

- **Chapter 8 - Creating and Saving Figures with `ggplot2`** - Here we will learn to use functions from package `ggplot2` to create visualizations of our financial datasets, including the most common cases in finance, time series and statistical plots.

- **Chapter 9 - Programming and Data Analysis with R** - In this chapter we will learn the programming capabilities of R, including the use of functions, loops and conditional statements. A special emphasis is given for using R's functions in the manipulation of financial datasets. Package `dplyr` is also presented as an alternative and efficient way of processing financial information.

- **Chapter 10 - Financial Econometrics with R** - Presents the use of six common econometric models for financial research. It includes linear, GLM, panel data, Arima, Garch and markov switching models. For each type of model, we will learn how to simulate, estimate and forecast. Whenever appropriate, we will also learn to use R in the calculation of related statistical tests.

- **Chapter 11 - Writing Research Scripts** - Discusses the structure of a research script, including stages and folder organization. Three replicable examples of financial research scripts are presented. This includes an analysis of the performance of international stock indices, a study for the performance of a forecasting algorithm and an analysis of high frequency trade data.

I'm a fan of open source code. All the code used in the book, including examples separated by chapters, is available on the Internet. I also maintain a personal website with details of my work as a researcher and a *blog* (*R and Finance*), where I write about the use of R on specific problems among other things. All web addresses are given below:

Book site: https://sites.google.com/view/pafdr/home

Personal page: https://sites.google.com/site/marceloperlin/

Blog *R and Finance*: https://msperlin.github.io/

A suggestion, before you read the book, go to the book website and look at the related links page. There, you will find all internet addresses highlighted in the text, including the links for the installation of R and RStudio.

I hope you enjoy this book and find it useful.

Good reading!

Marcelo S. Perlin

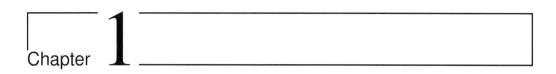

Chapter 1

Introduction

In the digital era, information is abundant and cheap. From the ever-changing price of financial contracts to the unstructured data of social media websites, the high volume of information we observe in the workplace creates a strong need for data analysis. A company or organization benefits immensely when it can create a bridge between raw information from its environment and making strategic decisions. Undoubtedly, this is a prolific time for professionals skilled in using the right tools for acquiring, storing, and analyzing data.

In particular, datasets related to Economics and Finance are widely available to the public. International and local institutions, such as central banks, national research agencies, financial exchanges, and many others, provide their data publicly, either by legal obligation or to foment research. Whether you are looking into statistics for a particular country or a company, most information is just a couple of clicks away. By analyzing this information efficiently, you'll be able to offer valuable insights to your team.

Technological advancements were accompanied by a decrease in computational cost. Today, home computers can process massive amounts of data in a short while, making it accessible to anyone. The methods applied to the data have also advanced in complexity. While in the past, a simple spreadsheet can do the job; today, the situation is different. For areas of knowledge with practical applications, such as Economics and Finance, it is expected that a graduate student or a data analyst has learned at least one programming language that allows him to do his work in an efficient manner. Learning how to program is becoming a requisite for the job market.

In this setup, the role of R, a programming language aimed to solve computational problems involving data analysis, shines. In the following sections, we will explain what R is and why you should use it .

1.1   What is R

R is a programming language specially designed to resolve statistical problems and allow the graphical display of data. R is a GNU version of S, a programming language originally created in Bell Laboratories (formerly AT&T, now Lucent Technologies). The base code of R was developed by two academics, **Ross Ihaka** and **Robert Gentleman**, resulting in the programming platform we have today. For anyone curious about the name, the letter R was chosen due to the common first letter of the name of their creators.

Today, R is almost synonymous to data analysis, with a large user base and defined packages that extend its use. It is likely that researchers from various fields, from Economics to Biology, find in R significant preexisting code that facilitates their analysis. In the business side, large and established companies, such as *Google* and *Microsoft*, already adopted R as the internal language for data analysis. R is maintained by **R Foundation** and the **R Consortium**, a collective effort to fund projects for extending the programming language.

1.2   Why Choose R

Learning a new programming language requires a lot of time and effort. Perhaps you're wondering why you should opt for R and invest time in learning it. Here are the main arguments.

First, **R is a mature, stable platform, continuously supported and intensively used in the industry**. When choosing R, you will have the computational background not only for an academic career in scientific research, but also to work as a data analyst in private organizations. If you are a student, learning R will create more options for your future career. Also, the strong support from the community means it is very unlikely the R platform will ever fade away or be substituted for something else. Depending on your career choices, R might be the only programming language you ever need to learn.

Learning R is easy. My experience in teaching R allows me to say students, even those with no programming experience, have no problem learning the language and using it to create their own code. The language is intuitive and certain rules and functions can be extended to different cases. For example, function `print` is used to show the contents of an object on the screen. You can use it for any kind of object as it adapts to the class of the object. So, by learning it one time, you'll be able to apply it in many different scenarios. Once you understand how the program works, it is easy to discover new features starting from a previous logic. This generic notation facilitates the learning process.

The engine of R and the interface of RStudio creates a highly productive environment. The graphical interface provided by RStudio facilitates the use of R and increases productivity. By combining both, the user has at his disposal many tools that facilitate the use of the platform.

R is compatible with different operating systems and it can interface with different programming languages. If you need to use a code in other programming language, such as *C++, Python, Julia*, it is easy to integrate it with R. Therefore, the user is not restricted to a single language and can use features and functions from other platforms. The possibility of using other programming languages within R is part of its functionalities.

R is free! The main software and all its packages are free to use. For most packages, the user's license gives you freedom to use and modify the code freely in your work. This supports the adoption of the R language in a business environment, where obtaining individual and collective licenses of commercial software can cause a high financial cost. Not surprisingly, R is used in a large number of companies.

1.3 What Can You Do With R and RStudio?

R is a fairly complete programming language and any computational problem can be solved based on it. Given the adoption of R for different areas of knowledge, the list is extensive. With finance, I highlight the following possibilities:

- Import, export, process, and store financial data based on local files or the internet;

- Substitute and improve data intensive tasks from spreadsheet like software;

- Develop routines for managing and controlling investment portfolios and executing financial orders;

- Implementation of various possibilities of empirical research through statistical tools, such as econometric models and hypothesis testing;

- Create dynamic *websites* with the `Shiny` package, allowing anyone in the world to use a financial tool created by you;

- Create an automated process of developing technical financial reports with package `knitr`;

- Write a technical book with `bookdown`;

- Write and publish a blog about finance with `blogdown`;

Besides the previously highlighted uses, public access to packages developed by users further expands these capabilities. The CRAN website offers a *Task Views* panel for the topic of Finance. On this page, you can find the main packages available to perform specific operations in Finance. This includes importing financial data from the internet, estimating econometric model, calculation of different risk estimates, among many other possibilities. Reading this page and the knowledge of these packages is essential for those who intend to work in Finance. It is worth noting, however, this list contains only the main items. The complete list of packages related to Finance is much larger than shown in *Task Views*. The link to the CRAN site is available on the book page. In this book, we will cover many packages from the task view in finance.

1.4   Installing R and RStudio

Before going further, let's install the required software on your computer. R is installed on your operating system like any other program. The most direct and practical way to install it is to go to R website and click the *Download* link in the left side of the page, as shown in Figure 1.1.

The R Project for Statistical Computing

Getting Started

[Home]

Download

CRAN

R Project

About R
Logo
Contributors
What's New?
Reporting Bugs
Development Site
Conferences
Search

R is a free software environment for statistical computing and graphics. It compiles and runs on a wide variety of UNIX platforms, Windows and MacOS. To **download R**, please choose your preferred CRAN mirror.

If you have questions about R like how to download and install the software, or what the license terms are, please read our answers to frequently asked questions before you send an email.

News

R version 3.3.3 (Another Canoe) has been released on Monday 2017-03-06.

- **useR! 2017** (July 4 - 7 in Brussels) has opened registration and more at http://user2017.brussels/
- Tomas Kalibera has joined the R core team.
- The R Foundation welcomes five new ordinary members: Jennifer Bryan, Dianne Cook, Julie Josse, Tomas Kalibera, and Balasubramanian Narasimhan.

Figure 1.1: Initial page for downloading R

The next screen gives you a choice of mirror to download the installation files. The CRAN repository (*R Comprehensive Archive network*) is mirrored in various parts of the world to improve the access speed. You can choose one of the links from the nearest location to you. If undecided, just select the mirror *0-Cloud*, as show in

Figure 1.2.

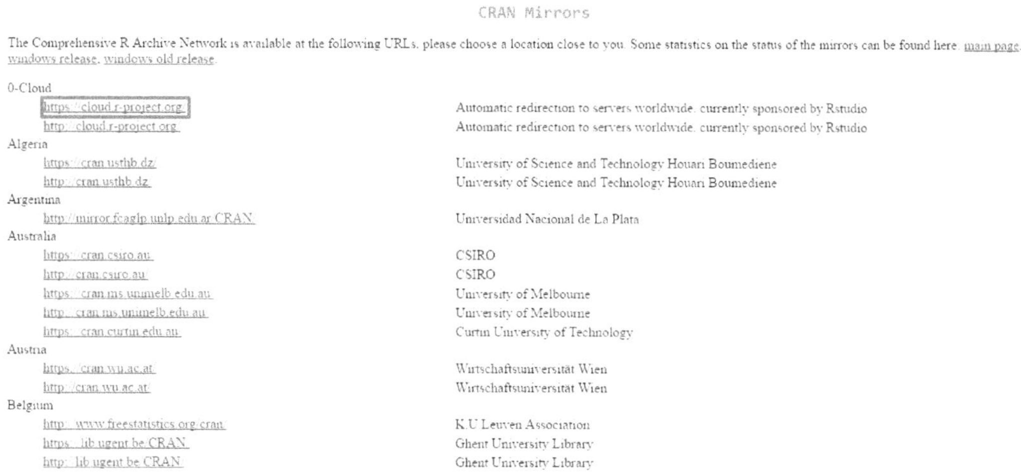

CRAN Mirrors

The Comprehensive R Archive Network is available at the following URLs, please choose a location close to you. Some statistics on the status of the mirrors can be found here. main page. windows release, windows old release.

0-Cloud
- https://cloud.r-project.org/   Automatic redirection to servers worldwide, currently sponsored by Rstudio
- http://cloud.r-project.org/   Automatic redirection to servers worldwide, currently sponsored by Rstudio

Algeria
- https://cran.usthb.dz/   University of Science and Technology Houari Boumediene
- http://cran.usthb.dz/   University of Science and Technology Houari Boumediene

Argentina
- http://mirror.fcaglp.unlp.edu.ar/CRAN   Universidad Nacional de La Plata

Australia
- https://cran.csiro.au/   CSIRO
- http://cran.csiro.au/   CSIRO
- https://cran.ms.unimelb.edu.au/   University of Melbourne
- http://cran.ms.unimelb.edu.au/   University of Melbourne
- https://cran.curtin.edu.au/   Curtin University of Technology

Austria
- https://cran.wu.ac.at/   Wirtschaftsuniversität Wien
- http://cran.wu.ac.at/   Wirtschaftsuniversität Wien

Belgium
- http://www.freestatistics.org/cran   K.U.Leuven Association
- https://lib.ugent.be/CRAN   Ghent University Library
- http://lib.ugent.be/CRAN   Ghent University Library

Figure 1.2: Choosing the CRAN mirror

The next step involves selecting your operating system. This is likely to be *Windows*. Due to the greater popularity of this platform, from now on, we will focus on installing R in Windows. The instructions for installing R in other operating systems can be easily found online. Regardless of the underlying platform, using R is about the same. There are a few exceptions, especially when R interacts with the file system. In the content of the book, special care was taken to choose functions that work the same way in different operating systems. A few exceptions are highlighted throughout the book. So, even if you are using Mac or Linux, you can take full advantage of the material presented here .

After clicking the link *Download R for Windows*, as in Figure 1.3, the next screen will show the following download options: *base*, *contrib*, *old.contrib* and *RTools*. Among the *download* options, the first (*base*), should be selected. It contains the basic installation of R in *Windows*. If the user is interested in creating and distributing their own R packages, it is necessary to install *RTools*. For most users, however, this should not be the case, so I suggest ignoring this program. The links to *contrib* and *old.contrib* relate to files for the current and old releases of R packages. You should not worry about it for now. We will discuss the use of packages in the next chapter.

After clicking the link *base*, the next screen will show the link to the *download* of the R installation file (Figure 1.5). After downloading the file, open it and follow the steps in the installation screen. At this time, no special configuration is required. I suggest keeping all the default choices and simply hit *accept* in the displayed dialogue screens. After the installation of R, it is strongly recommended to install RStudio, which will be addressed next .

Figure 1.3: Choosing the operating system

Figure 1.4: Installation options

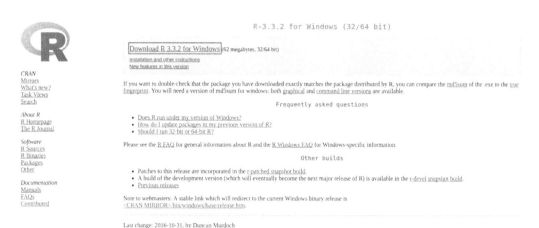

Figure 1.5: Downloading R

The base installation of R includes its own *GUI* (graphical user interface) that facilitates the use of the program. However, this native interface has several limitations. RStudio is a software that substitutes the original interface and makes the access to R more practical and efficient. One way to understand this relationship is with an analogy with cars. While R is the engine of the programming language, RStudio is the body and instrument panel, which significantly improve the user experience. Besides presenting a more attractive look, RStudio also adds several features that make the life of a programmer easier, allowing the creation of projects and packages, creation of dynamic documents (*Sweave/knitr*), among others. As an example, the book you are reading was written in RStudio with package `bookdown`.

The installation of RStudio is simpler than that of R. The files are available in RStudio website, provided in the book site. After accessing the page, click *Download RStudio* and then *Download RStudio Desktop*. After that, just select the installation file relative to the operating system on which you will work. This option is probably *WINDOWS Vista 7/8/10*. Note that, as well as R, RStudio is also available for alternative platforms.

I emphasize that using RStudio is not essential to develop programs in R. Other interface software are available and can be used. However, in my experience, RStudio is the interface that offers the widest range of features for the language and is widely used, which justifies its choice.

1.5   Resources in the Web

The R community is vivid and engaging. There are many authors, such as myself, that constantly release material about R in their blogs and are happy to discuss it. It includes package announcements, posts about data analysis in real life, curiosities, rants and tutorials. R-Bloggers is a website that aggregates these blogs in a single place, making it easier for anyone to access and participate. I strongly recommend to sign up for the R-Bloggers feed in RSS, Facebook or Twitter. Not only you'll be informed of what is happening in the R community, but also learn a lot by reading other people code and articles.

Learning and using R can be a social experience. Several conferences and user-groups are available in many countries. You can find the complete list in this link. I also suggest looking for local groups in Facebook. These may not be registered in the previous link.

1.6   Structure and Organization

This book presents a practical approach to the use of R in finance, accompanied by R code, which will show and illustrate the functionality of the program. To get the most out of this book, I suggest you first seek to understand the code shown, and only then, try using it on your own computer.

Learning to program in a new language is like learning a foreign spoken language: the use in day-to-day problems is imperative to create fluency. All the code and data used in this book is available in the book webpage. I suggest you test the code on your computer and *play* with it, modifying the examples and checking the effect of changes in the outputs. Whenever you have a computational problem, try using R for solving it. You'll stumble and make mistakes at first. But I guarantee that, soon enough, you'll be able to write complex data tasks effortlessly.

Throughout the book, every demonstration of code will have two parts: the R code and its output. The output is nothing more than the result of the commands in the program screen. All inputs and outputs code will be marked in the text with a special format. See the following example:

```r
# create a list
x <- list('abc', 1:5, 'dec')

# print list
print(x)
```

```
## [[1]]
```

```
## [1] "abc"
##
## [[2]]
## [1] 1 2 3 4 5
##
## [[3]]
## [1] "dec"
```

For the previous chunk of code, lines `x <- list('abc', 1:5, 'dec')` and `print(x)` are actual commands given to R. The program output is the on-screen presentation of the contents of object `x` with the predecessor symbol `##`. This symbol is used for any code output. Notice also that inline comments are set with the symbol `#`. Anything in the right side of `#` is not evaluated by R. These comments serve as written notes about the code.

Code can also be spatially organized using new lines. This is a common procedure around arguments of functions. The next chunk of code is equivalent to the previous, and will run the exact same way. Notice how we used a new line to vertically align the arguments of function `list`. You'll soon see that, throughout the book, this type of vertical alignment is constantly used.

```
# create a list
x <- list('abc',
          1:5,
          'dec')

# print list
print(x)
```

```
## [[1]]
## [1] "abc"
##
## [[2]]
## [1] 1 2 3 4 5
##
## [[3]]
## [1] "dec"
```

The code also follows a well-defined structure. One decision in writing computer code is how to name objects and how to structure it. It is recommended to follow a clear pattern, so it is easy to maintain over time and be used and understood by others. For this book, a mixture of the author's personal choices with the coding style suggested by Google (link on the book website) was used. The reader, however, may choose the structure he finds more efficient and aesthetically pleasing. Like many things in life, this is a choice.

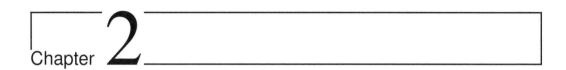

Chapter **2**

Basic Operations in R

Before you start developing your code, you need to understand how to work with R and RStudio. This includes work patterns, language components, basic commands and RStudio shortcuts. Understanding the software and how to take advantage of the platform is essential for the development of data-based research scripts. This is the main chapter for those who are not familiar with R or other programming languages.

In this section, we will go through the initial steps from the point of view of someone who has never worked with R and possibly never had contact with another programming language. Those already familiar with the program will not find novel information here and therefore, I suggest you skip to the next section. It is recommended, however, that you at least check the topics discussed here so that you can confirm your knowledge about the features of the program.

2.1 Working With R

The greatest difficulty a new user experiences when starting to develop routines in R is the format of work. Our interaction with computers has been simplified over the years and we are currently comfortable with the *point&click* format. That is, if you want to perform some operation on the computer, just point the *mouse* to the specific location on the screen and click the button that performs the operation. Visual cues and a series of steps in this direction allows the execution of complex tasks. But, be aware that this form of interaction is just one layer above what actually happens on the computer. Behind all these *clicks*, there is a command being executed. Any common task such as opening a *pdf* file, a spreadsheet document, directing a *browser* to a web page has an underlying call to a command. This command was created by the program developer to run within your operating system.

While this visual and motor interaction format has its benefits in facilitating and popularizing the use of computers, it is not flexible and effective when working with computational procedures. By knowing the commands available to the user, it is possible to create a file containing several instructions in sequence and, in the future, simply request that the computer **execute** this file using the recorded procedures. There is no need to do a "scripted" point&click operation. You need to spend some time creating the program but, in the future, it will always execute the recorded procedure in the same way. In the medium and long term, there is a significant gain in productivity between the use of a *script* (sequence of commands) and a *point&click* type of interface. Going further, the risk of human error in executing the procedure is almost nil because the commands and their sequence are recorded in the text file and will always be executed in the same way. This is one of the main reasons why programming languages are popular in science. All steps of data based research can be replicated.

In the use of R, the ideal format of work is to merge the use of the mouse with commands. R and RStudio have some functionality with the *mouse*, but their capacity is optimized when we perform operations using code. When a group of commands is performed in a smart way, we have an R script that should preferably produce something important to us at the end of its execution. In Finance, this can be the updated value of an investment, the calculation of the risk of a portfolio, the historical performance of an investment strategy, the result of an academic research, among many other possibilities.

Like other software, R allows us to import data and export files. We can use code to import a dataset stored in a local file (or the web), do an analysis of this data and save the results to later import it into a technical report. In fact, we can use RStudio to write a dynamic report, where code and content are integrated, using *knitr* and *Sweave* (Leisch, 2002). For example, the book you're reading was written using *knitr* and the `bookdown` package (Xie, 2016). The book is compiled with the execution of the R codes and their outputs are recorded in the scope of the text. All figures and data tasks in the book can be updated with the execution of a simple command. Needless to say that by using the capabilities of R and RStudio, you will work smarter and faster.

2.2   Objects in R

In R, everything is an object, and each type of object has its properties. For example, the daily market closing prices of a stock can be represented as a numerical vector, where each element is a price recorded at the end of a trading day. Dates and times related to these prices can be represented as text (*string*) or one of the `datetime` classes. Finally, we can represent the price data and the dates together by storing them in a single object of type *dataframe*, which is nothing more than a table with rows and columns. These objects are part of the R ecosystem, and it is through their manipulation that we take full advantage of the software.

While we represent data as objects in R, a special type is a `function`, which stores a pre-established procedure that is available to the user. R has an extremely large number of functions, which enable the user to perform a wide range of operations. For example, the basic commands of R, available in the package `base`, adds up to a total of 1217 functions. Each function has its own name and a programmer can write their own functions. For example, the `mean` function is a procedure that calculates the average values of a vector. If we wanted to calculate the average value of the sequence `1, 2, 3, 4, 5`, simply insert the following command in the *prompt* (left bottom of RStudio) and press *enter*:

```
mean(1:5, na.rm = TRUE)
```

```
## [1] 3
```

The `:` symbol used above creates a sequence starting at 1 and ending at 5 (more details about this operator in a later section). Note that the `mean` function is used with start and end parentheses. These parentheses serve to highlight the entries (*inputs*), that is, the information sent to the function to produce something. Note that each entry is separated by a comma, as in `MyFct(input1, input2, input3, ...)`. We also set option `na.rm = TRUE`. This is a specific directive for the `mean` function to ignore elements of type `NA` (*not available*), if they exist. This specific type of object will also be discussed in a future chapter.

Functions are at the heart of R and we will dedicate a large part of this book to them. You can use the available functions or write your own. You can also publish your functions and let other people use your code. In a later chapter, we will learn how to use functions to do data analysis in an efficient way.

2.3 International and Local Formats

Before beginning to explain the use of R and RStudio, it is important to highlight some rules of formatting numbers, Latin characters and date formats.

- **decimal:** Following an international notation, the decimal point in R is defined by the period symbol (.), as in `2.5` and not comma, as in `2,5`. In some countries, this might not be the case. This difference can create a lot of confusion and errors at the beginning. Some software, such as Microsoft Excel, does the conversion automatically when the data is imported. This, however, is generally an exception. As a general rule of using R, only use commas to separate the inputs of a function. Under no circumstances should the comma symbol be used as the decimal point separator. Always give priority to the international format because it will be compatible with the vast majority of data. Other researchers may experience some difficulty in understanding your code if you use your local notation for the decimal.

- **Latin characters:** Due to its international standard, R has problems understanding Latin characters, such as the cedilla and accents. If you can avoid it, do not use these characters in the names of your variables or files. In character objects (text), you can use them without problems as long as the encoding is correctly specified (e.g. UTF-8, Latin1). Given that, it is recommended that the R code be written in the English language. This automatically eliminates the use of Latin characters and facilitates the usability of the code by people outside of your country.

- **date format:** Dates in R are formatted according to the YYYY-MM-DD pattern, where YYYY is the year in four numbers, MM is the month and DD is the day. An example is 2017-05-05. This may not be the case in your country. When importing local datasets, make sure that the dates are in this format or do a conversion. Again, while you can work with your local format of dates in R, it is best advised to use the international notation. The conversion between one format and another is quite easy and will be presented in a future chapter.

If you want to learn more about your local format in R, use the following command by typing it in the prompt and pressing enter:

```
Sys.localeconv()
```

```
##      decimal_point     thousands_sep           grouping
##                "."               ""                 ""
##   int_curr_symbol   currency_symbol mon_decimal_point
##              "BRL"              "R$"                ","
## mon_thousands_sep      mon_grouping      positive_sign
##                "."            "\003"                 ""
##      negative_sign    int_frac_digits        frac_digits
##                "-"               "2"                "2"
##      p_cs_precedes     p_sep_by_space      n_cs_precedes
##                "1"               "1"                "1"
##     n_sep_by_space       p_sign_posn        n_sign_posn
##                "1"               "3"                "3"
```

The output of `Sys.localeconv()` shows how R interprets decimal points and the thousands separator, among other things. As you can see from the previous output, this book was compiled using the Brazilian notation for currency but uses the dot point for decimals. As mentioned before, it is good policy to follow international notation, especially for the decimal point. If necessary, you can change your local format to the US/international notation using the following command.

```
Sys.setlocale("LC_ALL", "English")
```

A note, however, is that you'll need to run this command every time that R starts or incorporate it in the initialization of the software.

2.4 Types of Files in R

Like any other programming platform, R has a file ecosystem and each type of file has a different purpose. In the vast majority of cases, however, the work will focus mostly on two types: *.R* and *.RData* files. Next, I provide a description of various file extensions. The items in the list are ordered by importance. Note that we omit graphic files such as *.png*, *.jpg*, *.gif* and data storage files (*.csv*, *.xlsx*, ..) among others, as they are not exclusive to R.

- **Files with the extension *.R*** : text files containing several instructions for R. These are the files that will contain the sequence of commands that configures the main script and subroutines of the data research. Examples: My-Research.R, My_Functions.R.

- **Files with extension *.RData***: files that store data in R native format. These files are used to save (write) objects created in different sessions. For example, you can use a *.RData* file to save a table after processing and cleaning up the raw database. This file can be later loaded for a subsequent analysis. Examples: My_data.RData, Research_Results.RData.

- **Files with extension *.Rmd*, *.md* and *.Rnw***: represent files used for editing dynamic documents related to the *Rmarkdown* and *markdown* formats. The use of these files allows the creation of documents where text and code output are integrated. This is an advanced topic and will not be covered in this book. For those interested, I suggest reading Baumer et al. (2014) and a tutorial at this link. Example: My_Report.Rmd.

- **Files with extension *.Rproj***: contain files for editing projects in RStudio, such as a new package, a *shiny* application or a book. This is also an advanced topic and will not be dealt with here. While you can use the functionalities of RStudio projects to write R scripts, it is not a necessity. For those interested in learning more about this functionality, I suggest the RStudio manual. Example: MyProject.Rproj.

2.5   Explaining the RStudio Screen

After installing the two programs, R and RStudio, open RStudio by double clicking
its icon. It should be noted that R also has an interface program and this often causes
confusion. You should find the correct shortcut for RStudio by going through your
software folders. In Windows, you can search for RStudio using the *Start* button.

After opening RStudio, the resulting window should look like Figure 2.1.

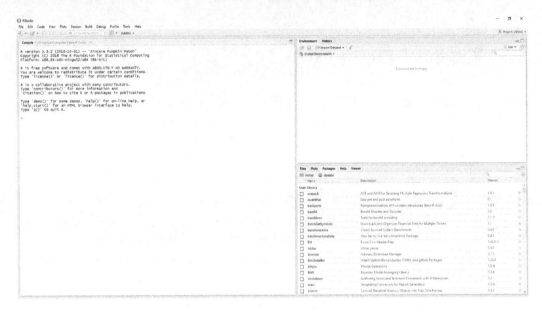

Figure 2.1: The RStudio screen

Note that RStudio automatically detected the installation of R and initialized your
screen on the left side.

If you do not see something like this on the screen of RStudio:

```
R version 3.3.3 (2017-03-06) -- "Another Canoe"
Copyright (C) 2017 The R Foundation for Statistical Computing
Platform: x86_64-w64-mingw32/x64 (64-bit)


R is free software and comes with ABSOLUTELY NO WARRANTY.
You are welcome to redistribute it under certain conditions.
Type 'license()' or 'licence()' for distribution details.


R is a collaborative project with many contributors.
Type 'contributors()' for more information and
'citation()' on how to cite R or R packages in publications.
```

```
Type 'demo()' for some demos, 'help()' for on-line help, or
'help.start()' for an HTML browser interface to help.
Type 'q()' to quit R.
```

then R was not installed correctly. Repeat the installation steps in the previous chapter and confirm the startup message on the lower left side of RStudio.

As a first exercise, click *file*, *New File*, and *R Script*. A text editor should appear on the left side of the screen. It is there that we will enter our commands, which are executed from top to bottom, in the same direction that we normally read text. A side note, all *.R* files created in RStudio are just text files and can be edited in other editors as well. It is not uncommon for experienced programmers to use a specific software to write code and another to run it. The resulting screen should look like the following:

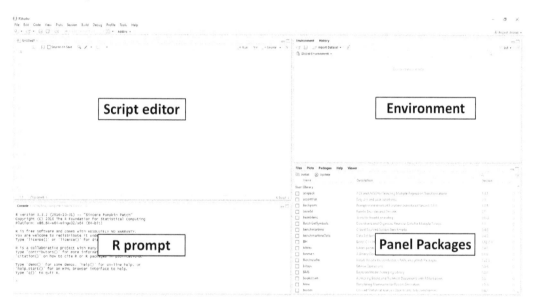

Figure 2.2: Explaining the RStudio screen

The main items/panels of the RStudio screen in Figure 2.2 are:

- **Script Editor:** located on the left side and above the screen. This panel is used to write scripts and functions;

- **R prompt:** located on the left side and below the script editor. It displays the *prompt* of R, which can also be used to give commands to R. The main function of the prompt is to test code and display the results of the commands entered in the script editor;

- **Environment:** located on the top-right of the screen. Shows all objects, including variables and functions currently available to the user. Also note a *History* panel, which shows the history of the commands previously executed by the user;

- **Panel Packages:** shows the packages installed and loaded by R. Here you have four tabs: *Files*, to load and view system files; *Plots*, to view pictures; *Help* to access the help system and *Viewer* to display dynamic and interactive results, such as a web page.

As an introductory exercise, let's initialize two objects in R. Inside the prompt (lower left side), insert the following commands and press *enter* at the end of each. The <- symbol is nothing more than the result of joining < (less than) with the - (minus sign). The ' symbol represents a single quotation mark and, in the computer keyboard, it is found under the escape (*esc*) key.

```
# set x
x <- 1
```

```
# set y
y <- 'My humble text'
```

If done correctly, notice that two objects appeared in the *environment* panel, one called x with a value of 1, and another called y with the text content "My humble text". Notice how we used specific symbols to define objects x and y. The use of double quotes (" ") or single quotes (' ') defines objects of the class `character`. Numbers are defined by the value itself. As will be discussed later, each object in R has a class and each class has a different behaviour. After sending the previous commands to R, the *history tab* has been updated.

Now, let's show the values of x on the screen. To do this, type the following command:

```
# print contents of x
print(x)
```

```
## [1] 1
```

The `print` function is one of the main functions for displaying values in the *prompt* of R. The text displayed as [1] indicates the index of the first line number. To verify this, enter the following command, which will show a lengthy sequence of numbers on the screen:

```
# print a sequence
print(50:100)
```

```
##  [1]  50  51  52  53  54  55  56  57  58  59  60  61  62  63
## [15]  64  65  66  67  68  69  70  71  72  73  74  75  76  77
```

```
## [29]   78  79  80  81  82  83  84  85  86  87  88  89  90  91
## [43]   92  93  94  95  96  97  98  99 100
```

In this case, we use the : symbol in 50:100 to create a sequence starting at 50 and ending at 100. Note that on the left side of each line, we have the values 1, 15, and 29. These represent the index of the first element presented in the line. For example, the fifteenth element of 50:100 is 64.

2.6   Running Scripts from RStudio

Now, let's combine all the previously typed codes into a single file by copying and pasting all commands into the editor's screen (upper left side). The result looks like Figure 2.3.

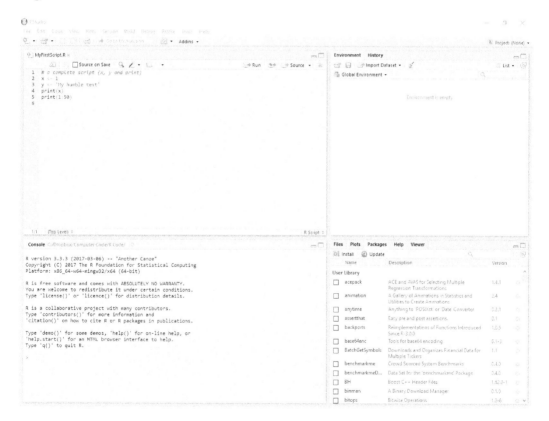

Figure 2.3: Example of a R script

After pasting all the commands in the editor, save the *.R* file to a personal folder where you have read and write permissions. One possibility is to save it in the **My Documents** folder with a name like 'MyFirstRScript.R'. This saved file, which at the moment does nothing special, records the steps of a simple algorithm that creates several objects and shows their content. In the future, this file can take an expressive size by containing all stages of the data analysis such as importing data, cleaning it, performing the data analysis and exporting tables and figures.

In RStudio, there are some predefined and time-saving shortcuts for running code from the editor. To execute an entire script, simply press `control + shift + s`. This is the *source* command. With RStudio open, I suggest testing this key combination and checking how the code saved in a *.R* file is executed. The output of the script is shown in the prompt of R. The result in RStudio should look like Figure 2.4.

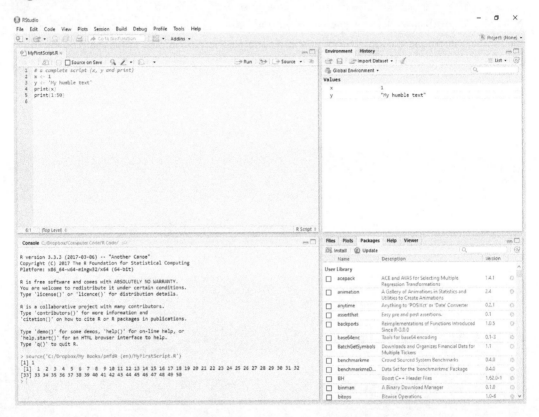

Figure 2.4: Example of a R script after execution

Another very useful command is code execution by the lines. In this case, the whole file is not executed, but only the line where the cursor is located. For that, just press `control + enter`. This shortcut is very useful in developing scripts because it allows each line of the code to be tested before running the entire program. As an example of usage, point the cursor to the `print(x)` line and press `control + enter`. As you will notice, only the line `print(x)` was executed. Therefore, before running the whole script, you can test it line by line and check for possible errors.

Next, I highlight these and other RStudio shortcuts, which are also very useful.

- **control + shift + s**: executes (source) the current RStudio file;
- **control + shift + enter**: executes the current file with echo, showing the commands on the prompt;
- **control + enter**: executes the selected line, showing on-screen commands;
- **control + shift + b**: executes the codes from the beginning of the file to the current line where the cursor is;
- **control + shift + e**: executes the codes of the lines where the cursor is until the end of the file.

My suggestion is to use these shortcuts from day one. They greatly facilitate the use of the program. For those who like to use the *mouse*, an alternate way to execute code is to click the *source* button in the upper-right corner of the text editor. If you want to set your own shortcuts in RStudio, go to option, "Tools" and "Modify Keyboard Shortcuts". One suggestion here is to set the *source* command to F5, which is used by several other software as an "execute" shortcut.

If you want to run code in a *.R* file within another *.R* file, you can use the `source` command. For example, imagine that you have a main script with your data analysis and another script that performs some support operation such as importing data to R. These operations have been dismembered as a way of organizing the code.

To run the support *script*, just call it with function `source` in the main script, as in the following code:

```
# execute import script
source('import-data.R')
```

In this case, all code in `import-data.R` will be executed. This is equivalent to manually opening file `import-data.R` and hitting *control + shift + s*.

2.7 Testing and Debugging Code

The development of code follows a cycle. At first, you will write a command line on a script, try it using *control + enter* and check the output. A new line of code is written once the previous line worked as expected. A moving cycle is clear, writing code is followed by line execution, followed by result checking, modify and repeat if necessary. This is a normal process. You need to make sure that every line of code is correctly specified before moving to the next one.

When you are trying to find an error in a preexisting script, R offers some tools for controlling and assessing its execution. This is specially useful when you have a long and complicated script. The simplest and easiest tool that R and RStudio offers is code breakpoint. In RStudio, you can click in the left side of the script editor and a red circle will appear, as in Figure 2.5.

```
1   # set x
2   x <- 1
3
4   # set y
5   y <- 'My humble text'
6
7   # print contents of x
8   print(x)
```

Figure 2.5: Example of breakpoint in an R script

This red circle indicate a code breakpoint that will force the code to stop at that line. You can use it to test existing code and check its objects at a certain part of the execution. When the execution hits the breakpoint, the prompt will change to `Browse[1]>` and you'll be able to try new code of verify the content of the objects. From the Console, you have the option to continue the execution to the next breakpoint or stop it. The same result can be achieved using function `browser`. Have a look:

```
# set x
x <- 1

# set y
browser()
y <- 'My humble text'

# print contents of x
print(x)
```

The practical result is the same as using RStudio's red circle, but it gives you more control for the case of several commands in the same line.

2.8   Creating Simple Objects

One of the most basic and most used commands in R is the creation of objects. As shown in previous sections, you can define an object using the `<-` command, which is verbally translated to *assign*. For example, consider the following code:

```
# set x
x <- 123

# set x, y and z in one line
my.x <- 1 ; my.y <- 2; my.z <- 3
```

We can read this code as *the value 123 is assigned to x*. The direction of the arrow defines where the value is stored. For example, using 123 -> x also works, although this is not recommended as the code becomes less readable. Also notice that you can create objects within the same line by separating the commands using a semi-colon.

The use of an arrow symbol <- for object definition is specific to R. The reason for this choice was that, at the time of conception of the *S* language, keyboards with a key that directly defined the arrow symbol were available and used. This means that the programmer only had to hit one key in the keyboard in order to set the arrow symbol. Modern keyboards, however, do not have this format any more. If you find it troublesome to use this symbol, you can use shortcuts as well. In *Windows*, the shortcut for the the symbol <- is alt plus -.

You can also use the = symbol to define objects such as in x = 123, but the use of = with this specific purpose is not recommended. The symbol of equality has a special use within the definition of function arguments. This case will be better explained and demonstrated in future section.

The name of the object is important in R. With the exception of very specific cases, the user can name objects as he likes. This freedom, however, can be a problem. It is desirable to always give short names that make sense to the content of the script and which are simple to understand. This facilitates the understanding of the code by other users and is part of the suggested set of rules for structuring code. Note that all objects created in this book have nomenclature in English and specific formatting, where the white space between nouns are replaced by a dot, as in my.x <- 1 and name.of.file <- 'my_file.csv'.

R executes the code looking for objects available in the environment, including functions. Be aware that R is case sensitive, that is, object m is different than M. If we try to access an object that does not exist, R will return an error message and stop the execution. Have a look:

```
print(z)
```

```
## Error in print(z): object 'z' not found
```

The error occurred because object z does not exist in the current environment. If we create a variable z as z <- 321 and repeat the command print(z), we will not have the same error message.

2.9   Creating Vectors

In the previous examples, we have created simple objects such as `x <- 1` and `x <- 'abc'`. While this is sufficient to demonstrate the basic commands in R, in practice, such commands are very limited. A real problem of data analysis will certainly have a greater volume of information.

One of the most used procedures in R is the creation of atomic vectors. These are objects that can have several elements. All elements of an atomic vector must have the same class, which justifies its *atomic* property. An example would be the representation of a series of daily stock prices as an atomic vector of the class `numeric`. Once you have a vector, you can manipulate it anyway you want.

Atomic vectors are created in R using the `c` command, which comes from the verb *combine*. For example, if we wanted to combine the values 1, 2 and 3 in one object, we could do it with the following command:

```
# create numeric atomic vector
x <- c(1,2,3)

# print it
print(x)
```

```
## [1] 1 2 3
```

This command works the same way for any other class of object, such as *character*:

```
# create character atomic vector
y <- c('text 1', 'text 2', 'text 3', 'text 4')

# print it
print(y)
```

```
## [1] "text 1" "text 2" "text 3" "text 4"
```

The only restriction on the use of the `c` command is that all elements must have the same class. If we insert data from different classes in a call to `c()`, R will try to mutate all elements into the same class following its own logic. If the conversion of all elements to a single class is not possible, an error message is returned. Note the following example, where numeric values are set in the first and second element of `x` and a character in the last element.

```
# a mixed vector
x <- c(1, 2, '3')

# print result of forced conversion
```

```
print(x)
```

```
## [1] "1" "2" "3"
```

The values of x are all of type `character`. The use of `class` command confirms this result:

```
# print class of x
class(x)
```

```
## [1] "character"
```

2.10 Knowing Your Environment

After using various commands, further development of the script requires you to understand what objects are available and what is their content. You can find this information simply by looking at the upper right screen of RStudio. However, there is a command that shows the same information in the prompt. In order to know what objects are currently available in R's memory, you can use command `ls`. Note the following example:

```
# set some objects
x <- 1
y <- 2
z <- 3

# print all objects in the environment
print(ls())
```

```
## [1] "x" "y" "z"
```

The objects x, y and z were created and are available in the current working environment. If we had other objects, they would also appear in the output to `ls`. Notice that object returned from `ls` is a `character` vector.

To display the content of each object, just enter the names of objects and press **enter** in the *prompt*:

```
# print objects by their name
x
```

```
## [1] 1
```

```
y
```

```
## [1] 2
```

```
z
```

```
## [1] 3
```

Typing the object name on the screen has the same effect as using the `print` command. In fact, when executing the sole name of a variable in the prompt or script, R internally passes the object to the `print` function.

In R, all objects belong to a class. As previously mentioned, to find the class of an object, simply use the `class` function. In the following example, `x` is an object of the class `numeric`, `y` is a text (`character`) object and `my.fct` is a function object.

```
# set objects
x <- 1
y <- 'a'
my.fct <- function(){}

# print their classes
print(class(x))
```

```
## [1] "numeric"
```
```
print(class(y))
```

```
## [1] "character"
```
```
print(class(my.fct))
```

```
## [1] "function"
```

Another way to learn more about an object is to check their textual representation. Every object in R has a textual representation and we can find it with function `str`:

```
# print the textual representation of a vector
print(str(1:10))
```

```
##  int [1:10] 1 2 3 4 5 6 7 8 9 10
## NULL
```

This function is particularly useful when trying to understand the details of a more complex object, such as a `dataframe`. We will learn more about using function `str` for learning the contents of a `dataframe` in chapter 6.

2.11 Displaying and Formatting Output

So far, we saw that you can show the value of an R object on the screen in two ways. You can either enter its name in the prompt or use the `print` function. Explaining it further, the `print` function focuses on the presentation of objects and can be customized for any type. For example, if we had an object of a class called `MyTable` to represent a specific type of table, we could create a function called `print.MyTable` that would show a table on the screen with a special format for the rows and column names. Function `print`, therefore, is oriented towards presenting objects and the user can customize it for different classes. The `base` package, which is automatically initialized with R, contains several `print` function for various kinds of objects.

However, there are other specific functions to display text in the prompt. The main one is `cat` (*concatenate and print*). This function takes a text as input, processes it for specific symbols and displays the result on the screen. Function `cat` is more powerful and customizable than `print`.

For example, if we wanted to show the text, `The value of x is equal to 2` on screen using a numerical object, we could do it as follows:

```
# set x
x <- 2


# print customized message
cat('The value of x is', x)


## The value of x is 2
```

You can also customize the screen output using specific commands. For example, if we wanted to break a line in the screen output, we could do it through the use of the reserved character `\n`:

```
# set text with break line
my.text <- ' First Line,\n Second line'

# print it
cat(my.text)


##  First Line,
##  Second line
```

Note that the use of `print` would not result in the same effect as this command displays the text as it is, without processing it for specific symbols:

```
print(my.text)
```

```
## [1] " First Line,\n Second line"
```

Another example in the use of specific commands for text is to add a *tab* space with the symbol \t. See an example next:

```
# set text with tab
my.text <- 'A->\t<-B'

# concatenate and print it!
cat(my.text)
```

```
## A->    <-B
```

We've only scratched the surface on the possible ways to manipulate text output. Other ways to manipulate text output based on specific symbols can be found in the official R manual, available on the book website.

2.11.1 Customizing the Output

Another way to customize text output is using specific functions to manipulate objects of the class **character**. For that, there are two very useful functions: **paste** and **format**.

Function **paste** *glues* a series of objects together. It is a very useful function, and will be used intensely for the rest of the examples in this book. Consider the following example:

```
# set some text objects
my.text.1 <- 'I am a text'
my.text.2 <- 'very beautiful'
my.text.3 <- 'and informative.'

# paste all objects together and print
cat(paste(my.text.1, my.text.2, my.text.3))
```

```
## I am a text very beautiful and informative.
```

The previous result is not far from what we did in the example with the **print** function. Note, however, that the **paste** function adds a space between each text. If we did not want this space, we could use function **paste0** as in:

```
# example of paste0
cat(paste0(my.text.1, my.text.2, my.text.3))
```

```
## I am a textvery beautifuland informative.
```

Another very useful possibility with the `paste` function is to insert a text or symbol between the junction of texts. For example, if we wanted to add a comma (,) between each item to be pasted, we could do this by using the input option `sep` as follows:

```
# example using the argument sep
cat(paste(my.text.1, my.text.2, my.text.3, sep = ', '))
```

```
## I am a text, very beautiful, and informative.
```

If we had an atomic vector with all elements to be glued in an single object, we could achieve the same result using the `collapse` argument. See an example next.

```
# set character object
my.text <-c('I am a text', 'very beautiful', 'and informative.')
```

```
# example of using the collapse argument in paste
cat(paste(my.text, collapse = ', '))
```

```
## I am a text, very beautiful, and informative.
```

Going forward, command `format` is used to format numbers and dates. It is especially useful when we create tables and we want to present the numbers in a visually appealing way. By definition, R presents a set number of digits after the decimal point:

```
# example of decimal points in R
cat(1/3)
```

```
## 0.3333333
```

If we wanted only two digits on the screen, we could use the following code:

```
# example of using format on numerical objects
cat(format(1/3, digits=2))
```

```
## 0.33
```

Likewise, if we wanted to use a scientific format in the display, we could do the following:

```
# example of using scientific format
cat(format(1/3, scientific=TRUE))
```

```
## 3.333333e-01
```

Function `format` has many more options. If you need your numbers to come out in a specific way, have a look at the help manual for this function. It is also a generic function and can be used for many types of objects.

2.12   Finding the Size of Objects

In the practice of programming with R, it is very important to know the size of
the objects being used. Here, size means the number of individual elements. This
information serves not only to assist the programmer in checking possible code
errors, but also to know the length of iteration procedures such as *loops*, which will
be treated in a later chapter of this book.

In R, the size of an object can be checked with the use of four main functions:
`length`, `nrow`, `ncol` and `dim`.

Function `length` is intended for objects with a single dimension, such as atomic
vectors:

```
# create atomic vector
x <- c(2,3,3,4,2,1)

# get length of x
n <- length(x)

# display message
cat('The size of x is ', n)
```

```
## The size of x is  6
```

For objects with more than one dimension, such as matrices, use functions `nrow`,
`ncol` and `dim` (dimension) to find the number of rows (first dimension) and the
number of columns (second dimension). See the difference in usage below.

```
# create a matrix
M <- matrix(1:20, nrow = 4, ncol = 5)

# print matrix
print(M)
```

```
##      [,1] [,2] [,3] [,4] [,5]
## [1,]    1    5    9   13   17
## [2,]    2    6   10   14   18
## [3,]    3    7   11   15   19
## [4,]    4    8   12   16   20
```

```
# calculate size in different ways
my.nrow <- nrow(M)
my.ncol <- ncol(M)
my.n.elements <- length(M)
```

```
# display message
cat('The number of lines in M is ', my.nrow)
```

```
## The number of lines in M is   4
```

```
cat('The number of columns in M is ', my.ncol)
```

```
## The number of columns in M is   5
```

```
cat('The number of elements in M is ', my.n.elements)
```

```
## The number of elements in M is   20
```

The `dim` function shows the dimension of the object, resulting in a numeric vector as output. This function should be used when the object has more than two dimensions. In practice, however, such cases are rare. An example is given next:

```
# get dimension of M
my.dim <- dim(M)
```

```
# print it
print(my.dim)
```

```
## [1] 4 5
```

In the case of objects with more than two dimensions, we can use the `array` function to create the object and `dim` to find its size. Have a look in the next example:

```
# create an array with three dimensions
my.array <- array(1:9, dim = c(3,3,3))
```

```
# print it
print(my.array)
```

```
## , , 1
##
##      [,1] [,2] [,3]
## [1,]    1    4    7
## [2,]    2    5    8
## [3,]    3    6    9
##
## , , 2
##
##      [,1] [,2] [,3]
## [1,]    1    4    7
## [2,]    2    5    8
```

```
## [3,]     3     6     9
##
## , , 3
##
##        [,1] [,2] [,3]
## [1,]     1     4     7
## [2,]     2     5     8
## [3,]     3     6     9
```

```
# display its dimensions
print(dim(my.array))
```

```
## [1] 3 3 3
```

An important note here is that the use of the functions, `length`, `nrow`, `dim` and `ncol` are not intended to discover the number of letters in a text. This is a common mistake. For example, if we had a `character` type of object and we use the `length` function, the result would be the following:

```
# set text object
my.char <- 'abcde'
```

```
# print result of length
print(length(my.char))
```

```
## [1] 1
```

This occurred because the `length` function returns the number of elements in an object. In this case, `my.char` has only one element. To find out the number of characters in the object, we use the `nchar` function as follows:

```
# find the number of characters in an character object
print(nchar(my.char))
```

```
## [1] 5
```

2.13   Selecting the Elements of an Atomic Vector

After creating an atomic vector of a class, it is possible that the user is interested in only one or more elements of it. For example, if we were updating the value of an investment portfolio, our interest in a vector containing stock prices is only for the latest price. All other prices were not relevant to our analysis and therefore could be ignored.

The selection of *pieces* of an atomic vector is called indexing and it is accomplished with the use of square brackets ([ ]). Consider the following example:

```
# set x
my.x <- c(1, 5, 4, 3, 2, 7, 3.5, 4.3)
```

If we wanted only the third element of `my.x`, we use the bracket operator as follows:

```
# get third element of x
elem.x <- my.x[3]

# print it
print(elem.x)
```

```
## [1] 4
```

The procedure of indexing also works with vectors. If we are only interested in the last and penultimate values of `my.x`, we use the following code:

```
# get last and penultimate value of my.x
piece.x.1 <- my.x[ (length(my.x)-1):length(my.x) ]

# print it
print(piece.x.1)
```

```
## [1] 3.5 4.3
```

A cautionary note. **A unique property of the R language is that if a non existing element is accessed, the program returns the value `NA` (*not available*).** See the next example code, where we attempt to obtain the fourth value of a vector with only three components.

```
# set object
my.vec <- c(1,2,3)

# print non-existing fourth element
print(my.vec[4])
```

```
## [1] NA
```

It is important to know this behaviour because the lack of treatment of these errors can lead to problems that are difficult to identify in more complex code. In other programming languages, attempting to access non-existing elements generally returns an error and cancels the execution of the rest of the code. In the case of R, given that access to non-existent elements does not generate an error or *warning* message, it is possible that this will create a problem in other parts of the script as `NA` objects are contagious. That is, anything that interacts with `NA` will also become

NA. The user should pay attention every time that NA values are found unexpectedly. An inspection in the length and indexation of vectors may be required.

The use of indices is very useful when you are looking for items of a vector that satisfy some condition. For example, if we wanted to find out all values in my.x that are greater than 3, we could use the following command:

```
# find all values in my.x that are greater than 3
piece.x.2 <- my.x[my.x>3]

# print it
print(piece.x.2)
```

```
## [1] 5.0 4.0 7.0 3.5 4.3
```

It is also possible to index elements by more than one condition using the logical operators & and | (or). For example, if we wanted the values of my.x greater than 2 and lower than 4, we could use the following command:

```
# find all values of my.x that are greater than 2 and lower then 4
piece.x.3 <- my.x[ (my.x>2) & (my.x<4) ]
print(piece.x.3)
```

```
## [1] 3.0 3.5
```

Likewise, if we wanted all items that are lower than 3 or greater than 6, we use:

```
# find all values of my.x that are lower than 3 or higher than 6
piece.x.4 <- my.x[ (my.x<3)|(my.x>6) ]

# print it
print(piece.x.4)
```

```
## [1] 1 2 7
```

Moreover, logic indexing also works with the interaction of different objects. That is, we can use a logical condition in one object to select items from another:

```
# set my.x and my.y
my.x <- c(1,4,6,8,12)
my.y <- c(-2,-3,4,10,14)

# find all elements of my.x where my.y is higher than 0
my.piece.x <- my.x[ my.y > 0 ]

# print it
print(my.piece.x)
```

```
## [1]   6   8  12
```

Looking more closely at the indexing process, it is worth noting that, when we use a data indexing condition, we are in fact creating a variable of the `logical` type. This object takes only two values: **TRUE** and **FALSE**. Have a look in the code presented next, where we create a `logical` object, print it and present its class.

```
# create a logical object
my.logical <- my.y > 0

# print it
print(my.logical)
```

```
## [1] FALSE FALSE  TRUE  TRUE  TRUE
```

```
# find its class
class(my.logical)
```

```
## [1] "logical"
```

2.14   Removing Objects from the Memory

After creating several variables, the R environment can become full of content that's already been used and is dispensable. In this case, it is desirable to clear the memory to erase objects that are no longer needed. Generally, this is accomplished at the beginning of a script, so that every time the script runs, the memory will be cleared before any calculation. In addition to cleaning the computer's memory, it also helps to avoid possible errors in the code. In most cases, cleaning the working environment should be performed only once at the beginning of the script.

For example, given an object x, we can delete it from memory with the command `rm`, as shown next:

```
# set x
x <- 1

# print all available objects
ls()
```

```
##  [1] "elem.x"       "M"            "my.array"
##  [4] "my.char"      "my.dim"       "my.engine"
##  [7] "my.fct"       "my.logical"   "my.n.elements"
## [10] "my.ncol"      "my.nrow"      "my.out.width"
## [13] "my.piece.x"   "my.str"       "my.text"
```

```
## [16] "my.text.1"       "my.text.2"       "my.text.3"
## [19] "my.vec"          "my.x"            "my.y"
## [22] "my.z"            "n"               "piece.x.1"
## [25] "piece.x.2"       "piece.x.3"       "piece.x.4"
## [28] "stay.quiet"      "x"               "y"
## [31] "z"
```

```
# remove x
rm('x')
```

```
# print again all available objects
ls()
```

```
## [1]  "elem.x"         "M"               "my.array"
## [4]  "my.char"        "my.dim"          "my.engine"
## [7]  "my.fct"         "my.logical"      "my.n.elements"
## [10] "my.ncol"        "my.nrow"         "my.out.width"
## [13] "my.piece.x"     "my.str"          "my.text"
## [16] "my.text.1"      "my.text.2"       "my.text.3"
## [19] "my.vec"         "my.x"            "my.y"
## [22] "my.z"           "n"               "piece.x.1"
## [25] "piece.x.2"      "piece.x.3"       "piece.x.4"
## [28] "stay.quiet"     "y"               "z"
```

Note that after executing the command rm('x'), the value of x is no longer available in the output of ls(). In practical situations, however, it is desirable to clean up all the memory used by all objects created in R. We can achieve this goal with the following code:

```
rm(list=ls())
```

The term list in rm(list=ls()) is a function argument of rm that defines which objects will be deleted. The ls() command shows all the currently available objects. Therefore, by chaining together both commands, we erase all current objects available in the environment. As mentioned before, it is good programming policy to always start the script by clearing the memory. However, you should only wipe out all of R's memory if you have already saved the results of interest or if you can replicate them.

2.15   Displaying and Setting the Working Directory

Like other programming platforms, **R always works in a directory**. If no directory is set, a default value is used when R starts up. It is based on the current directory that R searches for files to load data or other R scripts. It is in this directory that R saves any output we want if we do not explicitly define an address on the computer. This output can be a graphic file, text or a spreadsheet like file. A good programming policy is to change the working directory to the same place where the *script* is located. In chapter 11 we discuss the topic of file and folder organization.

To show the current working directory, use function `getwd`:

```
# get current dir
my.dir <- getwd()
```

```
# display it
print(my.dir)
```

```
## [1] "C:/Dropbox/My Books/pafdR (en)/Edition 2/Book Content"
```

The result of the previous code shows the folder in which this book was written and compiled. As you can see, the book files are saved in a subfolder of my Dropbox directory. From the path, you should also realize that I'm working in a Windows OS. The root directory `C:/` gives that information away.

The change of working directory is performed with the `setwd` command. For example, if we wanted to change our working directory to *C:/My Research/*, simply type in the *prompt*:

```
# set where to change directory
my.d <- 'C:/My Research/'
```

```
# change it
setwd(my.d)
```

As for simple cases such as the above, remembering the directory name is easy. In practical cases, however, the working directory can be in a deeper directory of the file system. In this situation, an efficient strategy to locate the path is to use a file explorer, like Windows *explorer*. To do so, open the *explorer* application and navigate to the location where you want to work with your *script*. Place the cursor in the address bar and select the whole path. Press *control + c* to copy the address to the clipboard. Go back to your code and paste it in. **An important step here: Windows uses the backslash to set addresses on the computer, while the R uses the forward slash**. If you try to use backslashes, an error is displayed on the screen. See the following example.

```
# set directory (WRONG WAY)
my.d <- 'C:\My Research\'
```

```
cat("##Error: '\\M' is an unrecognized escape in character string")
```

This message means that R was not able to understand the use of backslashes. This is a reserved symbol for macros and should not be used anywhere in a code. Therefore, after copying the address, modify all backslashes to forward slashes, as in the following code:

```
# set directory (CORRECT WAY)
my.d <- 'C:/My Research/'

# change dir
setwd(my.d)
```

You can also use double backslashes \\ but this is not recommended as it is not compatible with other operating systems.

Another important information here is that you can also use relative paths. For example, if you are working in a folder that contains a subdirectory called Data, you can enter this subfolder with the code:

```
# change to subfolder
setwd('Data')
```

Another possibility is to go to a previous level of directory using .., as in:

```
# change to previous level
setwd('..')
```

So, if you are working in the directory C:/My Research/ and execute the command setwd('..'), the current folder becomes C:/, which is one level above C:/My Research/.

Another, more modern, way of setting the directory is to use RStudio API functions. This is a set of functions that only work inside RStudio and provides information about current file, project and many more. To find out the path of the current R script being edited in RStudio and set the working directory to there, you can write:

```
my.path <- dirname(rstudioapi::getActiveDocumentContext()$path)
setwd(my.path)
```

This way, the script will change the directory to its own location, no matter where you copy it. Be aware, however, that this trick only works in RStudio script editor and within a saved file. It will not work from the prompt.

2.16   Cancelling Code Execution

Whenever R is running some code, a visual cue in the shape of a small red circle in the right corner of the *prompt* will appear. If you read it, the text shows the *stop* word. This button is not only an indicator for running code but also a shortcut for cancelling its execution. Another way to cancel an execution is to point the mouse to the *prompt* and press the *escape (esc)* button from the keyboard.

To try it out, run the next chunk of code in RStudio and cancel its execution using *esc*.

```
for (i in 1:100) {
  cat('\nRunning code (please make it stop by hitting esc!)')
  Sys.sleep(1)
}
```

In the previous code, we used a `for` loop to display the message `'\nRunning code (please make it stop by hitting esc!)'` every second. For now, do not worry about the code and functions used in the example. We will discuss the use of loops in chapter 9.

2.17   Code Comments

In R, comments are set using the hash tag symbol `#`. Anything after this symbol will not be processed by R. This gives you freedom to write whatever you want within the script. An example:

```
# this is a comment (R will not parse it)
# this is another comment (R will not parse it)


x <- 'abc' # this is an inline comment
```

Comments are a way to communicate any important information that cannot be directly inferred from the code. In general, you should avoid using comments that are too obvious or too generic. For example:

```
# read csv file
df <- read.csv('MyDataFile.csv')
```

As you can see, it is quite obvious from line `df <- read.csv('MyDataFile.csv')` that the code is reading a .csv file. The name of the function already states that. So, the comment was not a good one as it did not add any new information to the user. A better approach at commenting would be to set the author, description of script and better explain the origin and last update of the data file. Have a look:

```
# Script for analyzing a dataset
# Author: Mr data analyst (dontspamme@emailprovider.com)
# Last script update: 2017-03-10
#
# File downloaded from www.sitewithdatafiles.com/data-files/
# The description of the data goes here
# Last file update: 2017-03-10
df <- read.csv('MyDataFile.csv')
```

So, by reading the comments, the user will know the purpose of the script, who wrote it and the date of the last edit. It also includes the origin of the data file and the date of the latest update. If the user wants to update the data, all he has to do is to go to the referred website and download the new file. If the datafile is updated, a new date should be placed in "Last file update".

Another use of comments is to set sections in the code, such as in:

```
# Script for analyzing a dataset
# Author: Mr data analyst (dontspamme@emailprovider.com)
# Last script update: 2017-03-10
#
# File downloaded from www.sitewithdatafiles.com/data-files/
# The description of the data goes here
# Last file update: 2017-03-10
...


# Clean data
# - remove outliers
# - remove unnecessary columns


...


# Report results
# - remove outliers
# - remove unnecessary columns


...
```

This way, once you need to change a particular part of the code, you can look for the related section in the comments. If you share code with other people, you'll soon realize that comments are essential and expected. They help transmit information that is not available from the code. A note here, throughout the book you'll see that the code comments are, most of the time, a bit obvious. This was intentional as clear and direct messages are important for new users, which is part of the audience of this book.

2.18 Looking for Help

A common task in the use of R is to seek help. Even advanced users often seek instructions on specific tasks, whether it is to better understand the details of some functions or simply to study a new procedure. The use of the R help system is part of everyday routine with the software.

You can get help by using the *help* panel in RStudio or directly from the *prompt*. Simply enter the question mark next to the object on which you want help, as in **?mean**. In this case, object **mean** is a function and the use of the **help** command will open a panel on the right side of RStudio.

In R, the help screen of a function is the same as shown in Figure 2.6. It presents a general description of the function, explains its input arguments and the format of the output. The help screen follows with references and suggestions for other related functions. More importantly, examples of usage are given last and can be copied to the prompt or script in order to accelerate the learning process.

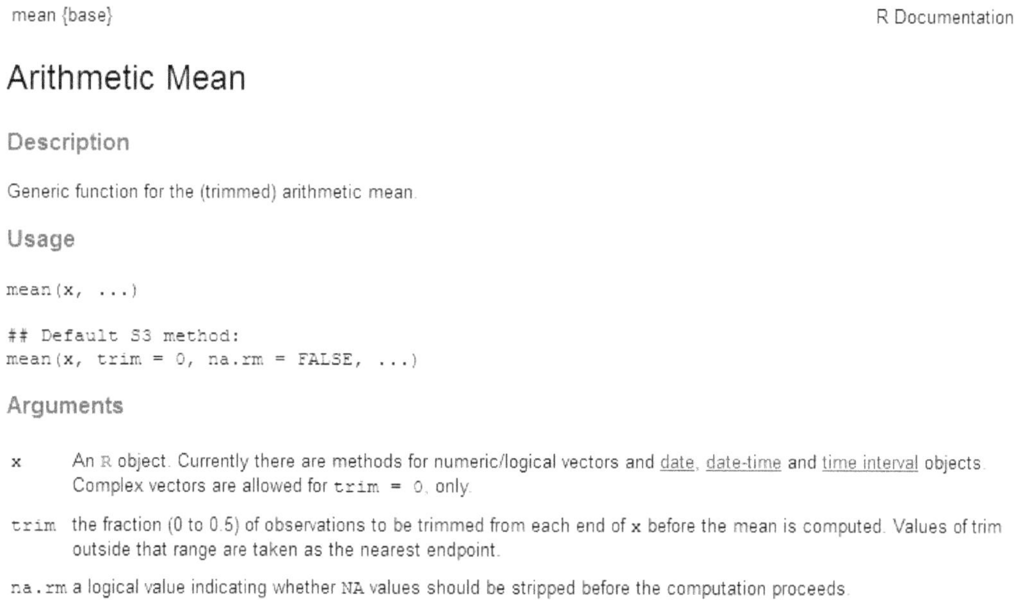

mean {base}   R Documentation

Arithmetic Mean

Description

Generic function for the (trimmed) arithmetic mean.

Usage

```
mean(x, ...)

## Default S3 method:
mean(x, trim = 0, na.rm = FALSE, ...)
```

Arguments

x   An R object. Currently there are methods for numeric/logical vectors and date, date-time and time interval objects Complex vectors are allowed for trim = 0. only.

trim   the fraction (0 to 0.5) of observations to be trimmed from each end of x before the mean is computed. Values of trim outside that range are taken as the nearest endpoint.

na.rm a logical value indicating whether NA values should be stripped before the computation proceeds.

Figure 2.6: Help screen for function mean

If we are looking for help for a given text and not a function name, we can use double question marks as in **??"standard deviation"**. This operation will search for the occurrence of the term in all packages of R and it is very useful to learn how to perform a particular task. In this case, we looked for the available functions to calculate the standard deviation of a vector.

As a suggestion of usage, the easiest and most direct way to learn a new function is trying out the examples in the manual. This way, you can see which type of input objects the function expects and what type of output it gives. Once you have it working, read the help screen to understand if it does exactly what you expected and what are the options for its use. If the function performs the desired procedure, you can copy and paste the code example for your own *script*, adjusting where necessary.

Another very important source of help is the Internet itself. Sites like stackoverflow and specific *mailing lists*, whose content is also on the Internet, are a valuable source of information. If you find a problem that could not be solved by reading the standard help files, the next logical step is to seek a solution using your error message or the description of the problem in search engines. In many cases, your problem, no matter how specific it is, has already occurred and has been solved by other users. In fact, it is more surprising not to find the solution for a programming problem on the internet, than the other way around.

2.19   R Packages

One of the greatest benefits of using R is its package collection. A package is nothing more than a group of procedures aimed at solving a particular computational problem. R has at its core a collaborative philosophy. Users provide their codes for others to use. And, most importantly, **all packages are free**. For example, consider a case where the user is interested in accessing data about historical inflation in the USA. He can install and use a R package that is specifically designed for importing economic statistics for a country.

Every function in R belongs to a package. When R initializes, packages `stats`, `graphics`, `grDevices`, `utils`, `datasets`, `methods` and `base` are loaded by default. Almost every function we have used so far belongs to the package `base`. R packages can be accessed and installed from different sources. The main being **CRAN** (*The Comprehensive R Archive network*), **R-Forge** and **Github**. The quantity and diversity of R packages increases every day. At the time of the publication of this book, the author of this book has six packages available on CRAN:

- GetHFData - Allows direct access to high frequency financial transaction data from Bovespa (Brazilian Financial Exchange);

- GetTDData - Enables access to prices and yields of bonds issued by the Brazilian government;

- RndTexExams - Enables the creation and correction of single choice exams with randomized content;

- BatchGetSymbols - Package for easy access to daily data from Yahoo! Finance and Google Finance;

- Predatory - Package to identify predatory journals based on the Beall site data;

- pafdR - Provides code, data and exercises for this book.

CRAN is the official repository of R and it is built by the community. Anyone can send a package. However, there is an evaluation process to ensure that the certain strict rules about code format are respected. For those interested in creating and distributing packages, a clear and easy to learn material on how to create and send packages to CRAN is presented on the site R packages. Complete rules are available on the CRAN website. The suitability of the code to CRAN standards is the developer's responsibility. By personal experience, sending and publishing a package on CRAN demands a significant amount of work, especially in the first submission. After that, it becomes a lot easier. Don't be angry if you package is rejected. My own packages were rejected several times before entering CRAN. Listen to what the maintainers tell you and try fixing all problems before resubmitting. If you're having issues that you cannot solve or find a solution in the Internet, look for help in the R-packages mailing list. You'll be surprised at how accessible and helpful the R community can be.

The complete list of packages available on CRAN, along with a brief description, can be accessed at the packages link on the R site. A practical way to check if there is a package that does a specific procedure is to load the previous page and search in your *browser* for a keyword. If there is a package that does what you want, it is very likely that the keyword is used in the description of the package.

Another important source for finding packages is Task Views. There you can find the most important packages for a given area of expertise. See the *Task Views* screen in Figure 2.7.

Unlike CRAN, R-Forge and Github have no restriction on the code sent to their repository and, because of this, these repositories tend to be chosen by developers. Responsibility in the use, however, is with the user. In practice, it is very common for developers to maintain a development version on Github or R-Forge and the official version in CRAN. When the development version reaches a certain stage of maturity, it is then sent to CRAN.

The most interesting part of this is that the packages can be accessed and installed directly from the prompt using the internet. To find out the current amount of

CRAN Task Views

Bayesian	Bayesian Inference
ChemPhys	Chemometrics and Computational Physics
ClinicalTrials	Clinical Trial Design, Monitoring, and Analysis
Cluster	Cluster Analysis & Finite Mixture Models
DifferentialEquations	Differential Equations
Distributions	Probability Distributions
Econometrics	Econometrics
Environmetrics	Analysis of Ecological and Environmental Data
ExperimentalDesign	Design of Experiments (DoE) & Analysis of Experimental Data
ExtremeValue	Extreme Value Analysis
Finance	Empirical Finance
Genetics	Statistical Genetics
Graphics	Graphic Displays & Dynamic Graphics & Graphic Devices & Visualization
HighPerformanceComputing	High-Performance and Parallel Computing with R
MachineLearning	Machine Learning & Statistical Learning
MedicalImaging	Medical Image Analysis
MetaAnalysis	Meta-Analysis
Multivariate	Multivariate Statistics
NaturalLanguageProcessing	Natural Language Processing
NumericalMathematics	Numerical Mathematics
OfficialStatistics	Official Statistics & Survey Methodology
Optimization	Optimization and Mathematical Programming
Pharmacokinetics	Analysis of Pharmacokinetic Data
Phylogenetics	Phylogenetics, Especially Comparative Methods
Psychometrics	Psychometric Models and Methods
ReproducibleResearch	Reproducible Research
Robust	Robust Statistical Methods

Figure 2.7: Task View screen

packages on CRAN, type and execute the following commands in the prompt:

```
# get matrix with available packages
df.cran.pkgs <- available.packages()

# find the number of packages
n.cran.packages <- nrow(df.cran.pkgs)

# print it
print(n.cran.packages)
```

```
## [1] 10503
```

If asked about which mirror to use, simply select the one closest to you. Currently (2017-05-05 14:14:58), there are 10503 packages available on the CRAN servers. We can see some details of the first three packages in `df.cran.pkgs` with function `print` and some indexing:

```
# print information about the first three packages
print(df.cran.pkgs[1:3, ])
```

```
##          Package   Version Priority
## A3       "A3"      "1.0.0"  NA
## abbyyR   "abbyyR"  "0.5.1"  NA
## abc      "abc"     "2.1"    NA
##          Depends
## A3       "R (>= 2.15.0), xtable, pbapply"
```

```
## abbyyR "R (>= 3.2.0)"
## abc    "R (>= 2.10), abc.data, nnet, quantreg, MASS, locfit"
##         Imports                              LinkingTo
## A3      NA                                   NA
## abbyyR "httr, XML, curl, readr, plyr, progress" NA
## abc    NA                                   NA
##         Suggests                             Enhances
## A3      "randomForest, e1071"                NA
## abbyyR "testthat, rmarkdown, knitr (>= 1.11)" NA
## abc    NA                                   NA
##         License                 License_is_FOSS
## A3      "GPL (>= 2)"            NA
## abbyyR "MIT + file LICENSE"     NA
## abc    "GPL (>= 3)"            NA
##         License_restricts_use OS_type Archs MD5sum
## A3      NA                     NA      NA    NA
## abbyyR NA                     NA      NA    NA
## abc    NA                     NA      NA    NA
##         NeedsCompilation File
## A3      "no"              NA
## abbyyR "no"              NA
## abc    "no"              NA
##         Repository
## A3      "https://cloud.r-project.org/src/contrib"
## abbyyR "https://cloud.r-project.org/src/contrib"
## abc    "https://cloud.r-project.org/src/contrib"
```

In short, object `df.cran.pkgs` displays the names of packages, its current version, its dependencies, along with various other information.

You can also check the amount of locally installed packages in R with the `installed.packages` command:

```
# find number of packages currently installed
n.local.packages <- nrow(installed.packages())

# print it
print(n.local.packages)
```

```
## [1] 367
```

In this case, the computer on which the book was written has 367 packages currently installed. This value is probably different from yours. Give it a try!

2.19.1   Installing Packages from CRAN

To install a package, simply use the command `install.packages`. You only need to do it once for each new package. As an example, we will install a package called `quantmod` that will be used in future chapters.

```
# install package quantmod
install.packages("quantmod")
```

That's it! After executing this simple command, package `quantmod` and all of its dependencies will be installed and the functions related to the package will be ready for use once the package is loaded in a script. Note that we defined the package name in the installation as if it were text with the use of quotation marks (" "). If the installed package is dependent on another package, R detects this dependency and automatically installs the missing packages. Thus, all the requirements for using the installed package will already be satisfied and everything will work perfectly. It is possible, however, that a package has an external dependency. As an example, package `RndTexExams` depends on the existence of a LaTeX installation. These cases are usually announced in the description of the package and an error informs that a requirement is missing. External dependencies for R packages are not common, but they do happen.

2.19.2   Installing Packages from Github

To install a package hosted in Github, you must install the *devtools* package, available on CRAN:

```
# install devtools
install.packages('devtools')
```

After that, load up the package `devtools` and use the function `install_github` to install a package directly from Github. In the following example, we install the development version of the package `ggplot2`, whose official version is also available at CRAN:

```
# load up devtools
library(devtools)

# install ggplot2 from github
install_github("hadley/ggplot2")
```

Note that the username of the developer is also included. In this case, the *hadley* name belongs to the developer of `ggplot2`, Hadley Wickham. Throughout the book, you will notice that this name appears several times. Hadley is a prolific and competent developer of several R packages and currently works for RStudio.

2.19.3 Loading Packages

Within a script, use function `library` to load a package, as in the following example.

```
# load package quantmod
library(quantmod)
```

After running this command, all functions of the package will be available to the user. In this case, it is not necessary to use " " to load the package. If the package you want to use is not available, R will throw an error message. See an example next, where we try to load a non-existing package called `unicorn`.

```
library(unicorn)
```

```
## Error in library(unicorn): there is no package called 'unicorn'
```

Remember this error message. It will appear every time a package is not found. If you got the same message when running code from this book, you need to check what are the required packages of the example and install them using `install.packages`, as in `install.packages('unicorn')`.

If you use a specific package function and do not want to load all functions from the package, you can do it through the special symbol `::`, as in the following example.

```
# example of using a function without loading package
fortunes::fortune(10)
```

```
##
## Overall, SAS is about 11 years behind R and S-Plus in
## statistical capabilities (last year it was about 10 years
## behind) in my estimation.
##    -- Frank Harrell (SAS User, 1969-1991)
##       R-help (September 2003)
```

In this case, we use the function `fortune` from the package `fortunes`, which shows on screen a potentially funny phrase chosen from the R mailing list. For our example, we selected message number 10. One interesting use of the package `fortune` is to display a different message every time R starts. As mentioned before, you can find many tutorials on how to achieve this effect by searching on the web for "customizing R startup".

Another way of loading a package is using the `require` function. A call to `require` has a different behaviour than a call to `library`. When using `library`, if the package is not found in the local libraries, it returns an error. This means that the script stops and no further code is evaluated. As for `require`, if a package is not found, it returns an object with value `FALSE` and the rest of the code is evaluated. So, in order to avoid code being executed without its explicit dependencies, it is advised to always use `library` for loading package in scripts.

The use of `require` is left for loading up packages inside of functions. If you create a custom function that requires procedures from a particular package, you must load the package within the scope of the function. For example, see the following code, where we create a new function called `my.fct` that depends on the package `quantmod`:

```
my.fct <- function(x){
    require(quantmod)

    df <- getSymbols(x, auto.assign = F)
    return(df)
}
```

In this case, the first time that `my.fct` is called, it loads up the package `quantmod` and all of its functions. Using `require` inside a function is good programming policy because the function becomes self contained, making it easier to use it in the future. This was the first time where the complete definition of a function in R is presented. Do not worry about it now. We will explain it further in chapter 9.

2.19.4   Upgrading Packages

Over time, it is natural that the packages available on CRAN are upgraded to accommodate new features, correct bugs and adapt to changes. Thus, it is recommended that users update their installed packages to a new version over the internet. In R, this procedure is quite easy. A direct way of upgrading packages is to click the button *update* located in the package panel, lower right corner of RStudio, as shown in Figure 2.8.

The user can also update packages through the prompt. Simply type command `update.packages()` and hit *enter*, as shown below.

```
# update all installed packages
update.packages()
```

The command `update.packages` compares the version of the installed packages with the versions available in CRAN. If it finds any difference, the new versions are downloaded and installed. After running the command, all packages will be

Figure 2.8: Updating R packages

synchronized with the versions available in CRAN.

2.20   Using Code Completion with *tab*

A very useful feature of RStudio is *code completion*. This is an editing tool that facilitates the search of names for objects, packages, function arguments and files. Its usage is very simple. After you type any first character, just press the *tab* (left side of keyboard, above *capslock*) and a number of options will appear. See Figure 2.9 where, after entering the *f* letter and pressing *tab*, a window appears with a list of object names that begins with that letter.

This also works for packages. To check it, type `library(r)` in the prompt or editor, place the cursor in between the parentheses and press *tab*. The result should look something like Figure 2.10, shown next.

Note that a description of the package or object is also offered by the code completion tool. This greatly facilitates the day to day work as the memorization of package names and R objects is not an easy task. The use of the *tab* decreases the time to look up names, also avoiding possible coding errors.

The use of this tool becomes even more beneficial when objects and functions are named with some sort of pattern. In the rest of the book, you will notice that objects tend to be named with the prefix *my.*, as *my.x*, *my.num*. Using this naming

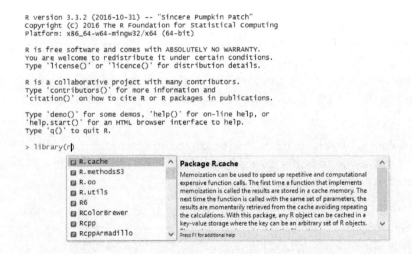

Figure 2.9: Usage of autocomplete for object name

```
R version 3.3.2 (2016-10-31) -- "Sincere Pumpkin Patch"
Copyright (C) 2016 The R Foundation for Statistical Computing
Platform: x86_64-w64-mingw32/x64 (64-bit)

R is free software and comes with ABSOLUTELY NO WARRANTY.
You are welcome to redistribute it under certain conditions.
Type 'license()' or 'licence()' for distribution details.

R is a collaborative project with many contributors.
Type 'contributors()' for more information and
'citation()' on how to cite R or R packages in publications.

Type 'demo()' for some demos, 'help()' for on-line help, or
'help.start()' for an HTML browser interface to help.
Type 'q()' to quit R.

> library(r
```

Figure 2.10: Usage of autocomplete for packages

rule (or any other) facilitates the lookup for names of objects created by the user. You can just type *my.*, press *tab*, and a list of all objects previously created by the user will appear.

You can also find files and folders on your computer using *tab*. To try it, write the command `my.file <- ""` in the prompt or a script, point the cursor to the middle of the quotes and press the *tab* key. A screen with the files and folders from the current working directory should appear, as shown in Figure 2.11. You can use the keyboard arrow keys to navigate.

Figure 2.11: Usage of autocomplete for files and folders

The use of autocomplete is also possible for finding the name and description of function arguments. To try it out, write `cat()` and place the mouse cursor inside the parentheses. After that, press *tab*. The result should be similar to Figure 2.12.

By using *tab* inside of a function, we have the names of all arguments and their description. This is the same information found in the help files.

Summing up, using code completion will make you more productive. You'll find names of files, objects, arguments and packages much faster. Use it whenever possible.

2.21 Interacting with Files and the Operating System

In many data analysis situations, it will be necessary to interact with files in the computer, either by creating new folders, decompressing and compressing files, list-

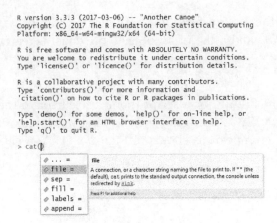

Figure 2.12: Usage of autocomplete for function arguments

ing and removing files from the hard drive of the computer or any other type of operation. In most cases, R will interact with files containing data.

2.21.1   Listing Files and Folders

To list files from your computer, use function `list.files`, where the `path` argument sets the directory to list the files from. For the compilation of the book, I've created a directory called *data*. This folder contains all the data needed to recreate the book's examples. You can check the files in the subfolder `data` with the following code:

```
# list files in data folder
my.f <- list.files(path = "data", full.names = TRUE)
print(my.f)
```

```
##  [1] "data/AdjustedPrices-InternacionalIndices.RDATA"
##  [2] "data/BovStocks_2011-12-01_2016-11-29.csv"
##  [3] "data/BovStocks_2011-12-01_2016-11-29.RData"
##  [4] "data/example_gethfdata.RDATA"
##  [5] "data/FileWithLatinChar.txt"
##  [6] "data/grunfeld.csv"
##  [7] "data/HFData.csv"
##  [8] "data/HFData_6_Assets_15 min.RData"
##  [9] "data/MktIndices_and_Symbols.csv"
## [10] "data/MySQLiteDatabase.SQLITE"
## [11] "data/SP500-Excel.xlsx"
## [12] "data/SP500-Stocks-WithRet.RData"
```

```
## [13] "data/SP500-Stocks_long.csv"
## [14] "data/SP500-Stocks_wide.csv"
## [15] "data/SP500.csv"
## [16] "data/SP500_2011-11-13_2016-11-11.csv"
## [17] "data/TDData.csv"
## [18] "data/temp.csv"
## [19] "data/temp.RData"
## [20] "data/temp.txt"
## [21] "data/temp.xlsx"
## [22] "data/temp_xts.RData"
```

Note that in this directory, there are several files with different extensions. These files contain data that will be used in future chapters. When using `list.files`, it is recommended to set input `full.names` as `TRUE`. This option makes sure that the names returned by the function contains the full path of the found files. This facilitates further manipulation, such as reading and importing information from data files. It is worth noting that you can also list the files recursively, that is, list all files from all subfolders contained in the original address. To check it, try using the following code in your computer:

```
# list all files for all subfolders (IT MAY TAKE SOME TIME...)
list.files(path = getwd(), recursive = T, full.names = TRUE)
```

The previous command will list all files in the current folder and subfolders. Depending on the current working directory, it may take some time to run it all. If you executed it, be patient or just cancel it pressing `esc`.

To list folders (directories) on your computer, use the command `list.dirs`. See below.

```
# store names of directories
my.dirs <- list.dirs(recursive = F)

# print it
print(my.dirs)
```

```
## [1] "./.Rproj.user"
## [2] "./_bookdown_files"
## [3] "./data"
## [4] "./docs"
## [5] "./eqs"
## [6] "./fig_ggplot"
## [7] "./figs"
## [8] "./ftp files"
## [9] "./latex_files"
```

```
## [10] "./many_datafiles"
## [11] "./ProcAnFinDataR_ed_1_cache"
## [12] "./ProcAnFinDataR_ed_1_files"
## [13] "./Removed chapters"
## [14] "./Scripts"
## [15] "./tabs"
```

The command list.dirs(recursive = F) listed all directories of the current path without recursion. The output shows the directories that I have used to write this book. It includes the output directory of the book (./_book), the directory with the data (./data), among others. In this same directory, you can find the chapters of the book, organized by files and based on the *RMarkdown* language (.Rmd file extension). To list only files with the extension .Rmd, we can use the **pattern** input in function list.files as follows:

```
# list all files with extension .Rmd
list.files(pattern = "*.Rmd")
```

```
##  [1] "_Welcome.Rmd"
##  [2] "00-Preface.Rmd"
##  [3] "01-Introduction.Rmd"
##  [4] "02-BasicOperations.Rmd"
##  [5] "03-BasicObjects.Rmd"
##  [6] "04-DataStructureObjects.Rmd"
##  [7] "05-Financial-data-and-common-operations.Rmd"
##  [8] "06-ImportingExportingLocal.Rmd"
##  [9] "07-ImportingInternet.Rmd"
## [10] "08-Figures.Rmd"
## [11] "09-Programming.Rmd"
## [12] "10-Models.Rmd"
## [13] "11-ResearchScripts.Rmd"
## [14] "12-references.Rmd"
## [15] "index.Rmd"
## [16] "ProcAnFinDataR_ed_1.Rmd"
```

The files presented above contain all the contents of this book, including this specific paragraph, located in file 02-BasicOperations.Rmd!

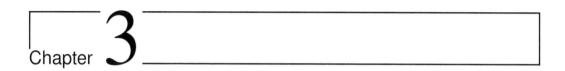

Chapter 3

Basic Object Classes

In R, everything is an object. Previously, we executed commands in the prompt, and it resulted in creating objects in our environment. Each type of object will have several different properties. A `numeric` object may interact with other `numeric` objects in operations such as multiplication, division, and addition. This is not true for objects belonging to the class `character`, where mathematical properties are not valid or intuitive - it does not make sense to add a numeric value to a text or to divide a text for other text.

But, the `character` class has other properties, such as allowing the user to look for a specific text within a larger text, splitting parts of a text, and replacing specific characters, among many other possibilities. **One of the most important aspects of working with R is learning the functionalities of the object classes**.

An important distinction here is the difference between basic and data structure type of classes. The basic classes are the primary elements in data representation. It includes numerical values, logical objects, characters (text), factors, dates, among many other cases. The basic classes are stored in more complex data structures that aggregate the information and facilitate the work. Imagine conducting a study based on closing prices of 500 stocks that belong to the SP500 market index. If we create a numeric vector of prices for each stock, we would have several *500* objects to handle in our environment! Although you can work this way, the resulting code would be disorganized, difficult to understand, and subject to several errors.

A simpler way to organize our data is to create an object with the name `SP500.data` and allocate the prices of all stocks there. All necessary information to perform our research would be available in that object, making it easier to import and export data. These objects that store other basic class objects are the data structure type. This classification includes lists, matrices, and data frames. In this section, we will address the most basic types of objects in R. The data structure types will be presented in the next chapter.

3.1 Numeric Objects

Objects of type numeric represent one or more quantities and are one of the most used objects in data research, for example, the price of a stock at a given date, the trading volume of a financial contract on any given day, the net profit of a company at the end of the year, among many other possibilities. Generally, numerical vectors are imported from an existing database. However, you can also register them from the editor.

3.1.1 Creating and Manipulating numeric Objects

The creation and manipulation of numeric objects is easy. As expected, we can use the common symbols of mathematical operations, such as sum (+), difference (−), division (/) and multiplication (*). When working with numeric vectors, all mathematical operations are carried out using an **element by element** orientation. See the next example, where we create two vectors and perform various operations.

```
# create numeric vectors
x <- 1:5
y <- 2:6

# print sum
print(x+y)
```

```
## [1]  3  5  7  9 11
```

```
# print multiplication
print(x*y)
```

```
## [1]  2  6 12 20 30
```

```
# print division
print(x/y)
```

```
## [1] 0.5000000 0.6666667 0.7500000 0.8000000 0.8333333
```

```
# print exponentiation
print(x^y)
```

```
## [1]     1     8    81  1024 15625
```

A difference between R and other programming languages is that operations between vectors of different sizes are accepted. We can add a `numeric` vector with four elements with the other containing only two elements. Whenever that happens, R calls for the **recycling rule**. It states, if two different sized vectors are interacting, the smaller vector is repeated as often as necessary to obtain the same number of elements as the larger vector. See the following example:

```
# set x with 4 elements and y with 2
x <- 1:4
y <- 2:1

# print multiplication
print(x + y)
```

```
## [1] 3 3 5 5
```

Here, the result of x + y is equivalent to 1:4 + c(2, 1, 2, 1). If you try to operate with vectors in which the length of the largest vector is not a multiple of the length of the smaller, R performs the same recycling procedure, but also sends a `warning` message to inform the user that the recycling procedure was not perfectly executed. See next.

```
# set x = 4 elements and y with 3
x <- c(1, 2, 3, 4)
y <- c(1, 2, 3)

# print sum (recycling rule)
print(x +y)
```

```
## Warning in x + y: longer object length is not a multiple of
## shorter object length
```

```
## [1] 2 4 6 5
```

The first three elements of x were summed to the first three elements of y. The fourth element of x was summed to the first element of y. Since there was no fourth element in y, R cycled through the values of the vector, restarting with the first element.

One great thing about R is that elements of a `numeric` vector can be named. See an example next, where we create a vector with several named items.

```
# create named vector
x <- c(item1 = 10, item2 = 14, item3 = 9, item4 = 2)

# print it
```

```
print(x)
```

```
## item1 item2 item3 item4
##    10    14    9    2
```

Notice how we used symbol = to set the names of the elements inside of function c (combine). As mentioned, the equality symbol is usually used to define arguments of a function call. To name elements of a **numeric** vector after creating it, we can use the **names** function. See below:

```
# create unnamed vector
x <- c(10, 14, 9, 2)

# set names of elements
names(x) <- c('item1', 'item2', 'item3', 'item4')

# print it
print(x)
```

```
## item1 item2 item3 item4
##    10    14    9    2
```

Notice how the use of function **names** works differently from the previous examples. Here, we use the function on the left side of <- and not on the right. The intuition of assigning a value using <- still holds as we are registering an attribute of the object, the name of its elements. This notation may seem strange, at first, but it gets familiar with time and use.

Empty **numeric** vectors can also be created. Sometimes, you need to set an empty vector to be filled with values later. For that, use the **numeric** function:

```
# create empty numeric vector of length 10
my.x <- numeric(length = 10)

# print it
print(my.x)
```

```
##  [1] 0 0 0 0 0 0 0 0 0 0
```

As you can see, when using numeric(length = 10), all values are set to zero.

3.1.2   Creating a numeric Sequence

In R, you have two ways to create a sequence of numerical values. The first, used extensively in the previous examples, is with operator :, as in my.seq <- 1:10.

This method is practical, because the notation is clear and direct.

However, using operator : limits the possibilities of the sequences we can create. It only creates sequences where the difference between adjacent elements is +1 or -1. A more powerful version for the creation of sequences is the use of function seq. With it, you can set the intervals between each value with argument by. See an example next:

```
# create sequence with seq
my.seq <- seq(from = -10, to = 10, by = 2)

# print it
print(my.seq)
```

```
##  [1] -10  -8  -6  -4  -2   0   2   4   6   8  10
```

Another interesting feature of function seq is the possibility of creating equally spaced vectors with an initial value, a final value, and the desired number of elements. This is accomplished using option length.out. In the following code, we create an array from 0 to 10 with exactly 20 elements:

```
# create sequence with defined number of elements
my.seq <- seq(from = 0, to = 10, length.out = 20)

# print it
print(my.seq)
```

```
##  [1]  0.0000000  0.5263158  1.0526316  1.5789474  2.1052632
##  [6]  2.6315789  3.1578947  3.6842105  4.2105263  4.7368421
## [11]  5.2631579  5.7894737  6.3157895  6.8421053  7.3684211
## [16]  7.8947368  8.4210526  8.9473684  9.4736842 10.0000000
```

Observe how the final size of my.seq is exactly 20, where R automatically calculates and sets the difference of 0.5263158 between the adjacent elements.

3.1.3 Creating Vectors with Repeated Elements

Another way to create numeric vectors is using repetition. Imagine a vector with the values c(1.2), where we want to create a larger vector with elements c(1, 2, 1, 2, 1, 2), repeating the smaller vector three times. For that, we use function rep:

```
# created a vector with repeated elements
my.x <- rep(x = c(1, 2), times = 3)
```

```
# print it
print(my.x)
```

```
## [1] 1 2 1 2 1 2
```

3.1.4 Creating Vectors with Random Numbers

Some applications in finance and economics require the use of random numbers. The simulation method of Monte Carlo can generate asset prices based on random numbers from a particular distribution. In R, several functions create random numbers for different statistical distributions. The most commonly used, however, are functions `rnorm`, `runif`, and `sample`.

Function `rnorm` generates random numbers from the Normal distribution, with options for the mean and standard deviation. An example of usage is given next.

```
# generate 10 random numbers from a Normal distribution
my.rnd.vec <- rnorm(n = 10, mean = 0, sd = 1)
```

```
# print it
print(my.rnd.vec)
```

```
##   [1] -0.39415168 -0.05119352 -0.21868209 -0.72085936
##   [5]  1.10516287  0.01805933 -1.35187931 -0.86121715
##   [9] -1.07540084 -1.37640193
```

In the previous code, we generated ten random numbers from a normal distribution, with mean zero and standard deviation equal to one.

Function `runif` generates random values uniformly distributed between a maximum and a minimum value. It is commonly used to simulate probabilities with values between zero and one. Function `runif` has three input parameters: the desired number of random values, the minimum value, and maximum value. See the following example:

```
# create a random vector with minimum and maximum
my.rnd.vec <- runif(n = 10, min = -5, max = 5)
```

```
# print it
print(my.rnd.vec)
```

```
##   [1]  4.2734767 -2.2309512  0.3704094 -2.4823967  4.2784927
##   [6]  0.1924810 -0.8472498  0.7042774 -4.9758363 -4.0238340
```

Note that both functions, **rnorm** and **runif**, are limited to their respective distribution. An alternative and flexible way to generate random values is to use the **sample** function. It accepts any vector as input and returns a scrambled version of its elements. Its flexibility lies in the fact that the input vector can be anything. For example, if we wanted to create a random vector with elements taken from vector c(0, 5, 15, 20, 25), we could do it as follows:

```
# create sequence
my.vec <- seq(from = 0, to = 25, by=5)
```

```
# sample sequence
my.rnd.vec <- sample(my.vec)
```

```
# print it
print(my.rnd.vec)
```

```
## [1] 10  5 25 20  0 15
```

Function **sample** also allows the random selection of several elements. If we wanted to select randomly only one element of **my.vec**, we could write the code as:

```
# sample one element of my.vec
my.rnd.vec <- sample(my.vec, size = 1)
```

```
# print it
print(my.rnd.vec)
```

```
## [1] 5
```

If we wanted two random elements from **my.rnd.vec**:

```
# sample one element of my.vec
my.rnd.vec <- sample(my.vec, size = 2)
```

```
# print it
print(my.rnd.vec)
```

```
## [1] 25  0
```

It is also possible to select values from a smaller vector to create a larger vector. Consider the case where you have a vector with numbers c(5, 10, 15) and want to create a random vector with ten elements removed from that smaller vector. For that, we use option **replace = TRUE**.

```
# create vector
my.vec <- c(5, 10, 15)
```

```
# sample
my.rnd.vec <- sample(x = my.vec, size = 10, replace = TRUE)
print(my.rnd.vec)
```

```
## [1] 10  5 10 15 10 15 15  5  5 10
```

Another important feature of `sample` is it works for any type of vector, not only for those of the `numeric` class. This means we can randomize any sort of object. Have a look:

```
# example of sample with characters
print(sample(c('elem 1','elem 2','elem 3'), 1))
```

```
## [1] "elem 3"
```

At this point, it is important to acknowledge that **the generation of random values in R is not entirely random!** Internally, the computer chooses values from a queue. Each time functions, such as `rnorm`, `runif`, and `sample`, are called in the code, the computer chooses a different place in this queue according to various parameters, such as time itself. The practical effect is that the chosen values from the queue are unpredictable from the user point of view.

However, you can select set the place in the queue of random values using function `set.seed`. In practical terms, the result is that all numbers and random selections will be the same in every code execution. Using `set.seed` is strongly recommended for the reproducibility of codes involving randomness. We will use this function throughout the book, so anyone can replicate the results from the code. See the following example.

```
# set seed with integer 10
set.seed(seed = 10)
```

```
# create and print "random" vectors
my.rnd.vec.1 <- runif(5)
print(my.rnd.vec.1)
```

```
## [1] 0.50747820 0.30676851 0.42690767 0.69310208 0.08513597
```

```
my.rnd.vec.2 <- runif(5)
print(my.rnd.vec.2)
```

```
## [1] 0.2254366 0.2745305 0.2723051 0.6158293 0.4296715
```

In the previous code, the value of `set.seed` is an integer chosen by the user. After the call to `set.seed(10)`, all selections and random numbers will start from the same point in the queue; therefore, the random vectors are the same. By running that previous chunk of code in your computer, you'll see that the values of `my.rnd.vec.1` and `my.rnd.vec.2` will be exactly the same as the ones printed in this book.

3.1.5 Accessing the Elements of a `numeric` Vector

As mentioned in the previous chapter, all elements of a numerical vector can be accessed with brackets (`[]`). For example, if we wanted only the first element of `x`, we can use `x[1]`:

```
# set vector
x <- c(-1, 4, -9, 2)

# get first element
first.elem.x <- x[1]

# print it
print(first.elem.x)
```

```
## [1] -1
```

The same notation is used to extract parts of a vector. If we wanted to create a sub-vector with the first and second element of `x`, we could achieve this goal with the code presented next:

```
# sub-vector of x
sub.x <- x[1:2]

# print it
print(sub.x)
```

```
## [1] -1  4
```

To access named elements of a numeric array, simply use its name as a `character` value or vector inside the brackets.

```
# set named vector
x <- c(item1 = 10, item2 = 14, item3 = -9, item4 = -2)

# access elements by name
print(x['item2'])
```

```
## item2
##    14
```

```
print(x[c('item2','item4')])
```

```
## item2 item4
##    14    -2
```

We can also access the elements of a numerical vector using logical tests. For example, if we were interested in knowing which values of x are larger than *0*, we could use the following code:

```
# find all values of x higher than zero
print(x[x > 0])
```

```
## item1 item2
##    10    14
```

The selection of elements from a vector, according to some criteria, is called logical indexing. Objects of type `logical` will be treated later in this same chapter.

3.1.6   Modifying and Removing Elements of a `numeric` Vector

The modification of a vector is very simple. Just indicate the changes with the *assign* symbol (<-):

```
# set vector
my.x <- 1:4

# modify first element to 5
my.x[1] <- 5

# print result
print(my.x)
```

```
## [1] 5 2 3 4
```

This modification can also be performed block-wise:

```
# set vector
my.x <- 0:5

# set the first three elements to 5
my.x[1:3] <- 5

# print result
print(my.x)
```

```
## [1] 5 5 5 3 4 5
```

Using conditions to change values in a vector is also possible:

```
# set vector
my.x <- -5:5

# set any value lower than 2 to 0
my.x[my.x<2] <- 0

# print result
print(my.x)
```

```
##  [1] 0 0 0 0 0 0 0 2 3 4 5
```

The removal of elements of a vector is carried out using a negative index. See the following example:

```
# create vector
my.x <- -5:5

# remove first and second element of my.x
my.x <- my.x[-(1:2)]

# show result
print(my.x)
```

```
## [1] -3 -2 -1  0  1  2  3  4  5
```

Notice how using negative index simply returns the original vector, without the elements in the brackets.

3.1.7 Creating Groups from a numeric Vector

In some situations in data analysis, you'll need to understand how many cases in the sample are located within a certain range. Imagine a vector of daily returns of a stock, the percentage change in prices from one day to another. A possible risk analysis that can be performed is to divide the return interval into five parts and verify the percentage of occurrences of returns at each range. We can do that by "labelling" each stock return to a particular group.

In R, the function used to create intervals from numerical vector is cut. See the following example, where we create a random vector from the Normal distribution and five groups from intervals defined by the data.

```
# set random vector
my.x <- rnorm(10)

# create groups with 5 breaks
my.cut <- cut(x = my.x, breaks = 5)

# print it!
print(my.cut)
```

```
##   [1] (0.0104,0.556]   (-1.63,-1.08]    (-0.535,0.0104]
##   [4] (-1.63,-1.08]    (-0.535,0.0104]  (0.556,1.1]
##   [7] (0.556,1.1]      (-0.535,0.0104]  (0.556,1.1]
##  [10] (0.556,1.1]
## 5 Levels: (-1.63,-1.08] (-1.08,-0.535] ... (0.556,1.1]
```

Note that the names in `my.cut` are defined by the ranges, and the result is an object of type `factor`. We will cover this type of object in a future section. For now, it is worthwhile to say `factors` are simply groups within our data.

With the `cut` function, you can also define custom breaks in data and group names. See next:

```
# create random vector
my.x <- rnorm(10)

# define breaks manually
my.breaks <- c(min(my.x)-1, -1, 1, max(my.x)+1)

# define labels manually
my.labels <- c('Low','Normal', 'High')

# create group from numerical vector
my.cut <- cut(x = my.x, breaks = my.breaks, labels = my.labels)

# print both!
print(my.x)
```

```
##   [1]   0.08934727 -0.95494386 -0.19515038   0.92552126
##   [5]   0.48297852 -0.59631064 -2.18528684 -0.67486594
##   [9]  -2.11906119 -1.26519802
```

```
print(my.cut)
```

```
##   [1] Normal Normal Normal Normal Normal Normal Low     Normal
##   [9] Low     Low
```

```
## Levels: Low Normal High
```

Notice that, in this example of creating a group from a numerical vector, the breaks were defined in `my.breaks` and the names in `my.labels`.

3.1.8 Other Functions for Manipulating Numerical Vectors

- **as.numeric** - Converts an object to the `numeric` class.

```
# create character object
my.text <- c('1', '2', '3')

# convert to numeric
my.x <- as.numeric(my.text)
print(my.x)
```

```
## [1] 1 2 3
```

```
class(my.x)
```

```
## [1] "numeric"
```

- **sum** - Sums all elements of a `numeric` vector.

```
# set vector
my.x <- 1:50

# print its sum
print(sum(my.x))
```

```
## [1] 1275
```

- **prod** - Returns the product (multiplication) of all the elements of a `numerical` vector.

```
# set vector
my.x <- 1:10

# print prod
print(prod(my.x))
```

```
## [1] 3628800
```

- **max** - Returns the maximum value of a `numeric` vector.

```
# set vector
x <- c(10, 14, 9, 2)
```

```
# print max value
print(max(x))
```

[1] 14

- **min** - Returns the minimum value of a **numeric** vector.

```
# set vector
x <- c(12, 15, 9, 2)
```

```
# print min value
print(min(x))
```

[1] 2

- **which.max** - Returns the position of the maximum value of a **numeric** object.

```
# set vector
x <- c(100, 141, 9, 2)
```

```
# find position of maximum value
which.max.x <- which.max(x)
```

```
# show text output
cat(paste('The position of the maximum value of x is',
          which.max.x))
```

The position of the maximum value of x is 2

```
cat(' Its value is ', x[which.max.x])
```

Its value is   141

- **which.min** - Returns the position of the minimum value of a **numeric** object.

```
# set vector
x <- c(10, 14, 9, 2)
```

```
# find min value of x
which.min.x <- which.min(x)
cat(paste('The position of the minimum value of x is ',
          which.min.x))
```

The position of the minimum value of x is   4

- **sort** - Returns a sorted (ascending or descending) version of a `numeric` vector.

```
# set random numbers
x <- runif(5)

# sort ascending and print
print(sort(x, decreasing = FALSE))
```

```
## [1] 0.1915609 0.2458664 0.3543281 0.4731415 0.9364325
```

```
# sort descending and print
print(sort(x, decreasing = TRUE))
```

```
## [1] 0.9364325 0.4731415 0.3543281 0.2458664 0.1915609
```

- **cumsum** - Returns the cumulative sum of the elements of a `numerical` vector.

```
# set vector
my.x <- 1:25

# print cumsum
print(cumsum(my.x))
```

```
##  [1]   1   3   6  10  15  21  28  36  45  55  66  78  91 105
## [15] 120 136 153 171 190 210 231 253 276 300 325
```

- **cumprod** - Returns the cumulative product of the elements of a `numeric` vector.

```
# set vector
my.x <- 1:10

# print cumprod
print(cumprod(my.x))
```

```
##  [1]       1       2       6      24     120     720    5040
##  [8]   40320  362880 3628800
```

- **unique** - Returns all unique values of a numeric vector.

```
# set vector
my.x <- c(1,1,2,3,3,5)

# print unique values
print(unique(my.x))
```

```
## [1] 1 2 3 5
```

3.2 Character Objects

The `character` class, or simply text class, is used to store textual information. With the recent publication of several access points for social media data, such as Facebook and Twitter posts, analyzing textual information is an upward trend. As an example, you can extract a measure of sentiment from a text and use this information for further analysis. Usually however, the manipulation of a `character` vector is related to cleaning up the data and extracting specific information in the text.

R has several features that facilitate the creation and manipulation of text type objects. The base functions shipped with the installation of R are comprehensive and suited for most cases. However, package `stringr` (Wickham, 2015) provides many functions that expand the basic functionality of string manipulation in R, and a positive aspect of `stringr` is that string procedures start with the name `str_` and are informative. So, using the auto completion feature described in the previous chapter, it is easy to find the names of functions in this package. In this chapter, we will provide both ways of manipulating strings, using the base code of R and `stringr`. This way, the user can read code written with both packages. First, let's load the package for use in the following code.

```
library(stringr)
```

3.2.1 Creating a Simple `character` Object

In R, every `character` object is created by encapsulating a text with double quotation marks (" ") or single ('). To create an array of characters with stock *tickers*, we can do it with the following code:

```
my.tickers <- c('MMM', 'FB', 'ICE')
print(my.tickers)
```

```
## [1] "MMM" "FB"  "ICE"
```

We can confirm the class of the created object with function `class`:

```
class(my.tickers)
```

```
## [1] "character"
```

3.2.2 Creating Structured `character` Objects

In some data analysis situations, it will be required to create a text vector with some sort of structure. For example, vector c('ticker 1', 'ticker 2', ..., 'ticker 19', 'ticker 20') has a clear logic. It combines a text `ticker` with values from a vector that starts in 1 and ends in 20.

To create a text vector with the junction of text and numbers, use the `paste` or `paste0` function. The difference between the functions is the symbol that separates the pasted text. Function `paste` adds a space automatically, while `paste0` does not. See the following example, which replicates the previous structured text.

```r
# create sequence
my.seq <- 1:20

# create character
my.text <- 'ticker'

# paste objects together (with space)
my.char <- paste(my.text, my.seq)
print(my.char)
```

```
##  [1] "ticker 1"  "ticker 2"  "ticker 3"  "ticker 4"
##  [5] "ticker 5"  "ticker 6"  "ticker 7"  "ticker 8"
##  [9] "ticker 9"  "ticker 10" "ticker 11" "ticker 12"
## [13] "ticker 13" "ticker 14" "ticker 15" "ticker 16"
## [17] "ticker 17" "ticker 18" "ticker 19" "ticker 20"
```

```r
# paste objects together (without space)
my.char <- paste0(my.text, my.seq)
print(my.char)
```

```
##  [1] "ticker1"  "ticker2"  "ticker3"  "ticker4"  "ticker5"
##  [6] "ticker6"  "ticker7"  "ticker8"  "ticker9"  "ticker10"
## [11] "ticker11" "ticker12" "ticker13" "ticker14" "ticker15"
## [16] "ticker16" "ticker17" "ticker18" "ticker19" "ticker20"
```

We can do the same procedure with text vectors:

```r
# set character value
my.x <- 'My name is'

# set character vector
my.names <- c('Marcelo', 'Ricardo', 'Tarcizio')
```

```
# paste and print
print(paste(my.x, my.names))
```

```
## [1] "My name is Marcelo"   "My name is Ricardo"
## [3] "My name is Tarcizio"
```

In `stringr`, the equivalent function for pasting strings together is `str_c`, which works similarly to `paste0`.

```
# paste and print
print(str_c(my.x, my.names))
```

```
## [1] "My name isMarcelo"   "My name isRicardo"
## [3] "My name isTarcizio"
```

Another possibility of building structured text is the repetition of the content of another object. With `character` objects, use function `strrep` or `stringr!str_dup` for this purpose. Consider the following example:

```
# replicate with strrep
my.char <- strrep(x = 'abc', times = 5)
print(my.char)
```

```
## [1] "abcabcabcabcabc"
```

```
# replicate with stringr::str_dup
print(str_dup(my.char, 2))
```

```
## [1] "abcabcabcabcabcabcabcabcabcabc"
```

3.2.3 character Constants

R also allows direct access to all letters of the Roman alphabet. They are stored in the reserved (constant) objects, called `letters` and `LETTERS`. See an example next.

```
# print all letters in alphabet (no cap)
print(letters)
```

```
##  [1] "a" "b" "c" "d" "e" "f" "g" "h" "i" "j" "k" "l" "m" "n"
## [15] "o" "p" "q" "r" "s" "t" "u" "v" "w" "x" "y" "z"
```

```
# print all letters in alphabet (WITH CAP)
print(LETTERS)
```

```
##  [1] "A" "B" "C" "D" "E" "F" "G" "H" "I" "J" "K" "L" "M" "N"
```

```
## [15] "O" "P" "Q" "R" "S" "T" "U" "V" "W" "X" "Y" "Z"
```

Note that, in both cases, `letters` and `LETTERS` are not functions. They are `character` objects automatically embedded as constants in R. Even though they do not appear in the environment, they are available for use. You can overwrite their names, but this is not advised. Other constant `character` objects in R are `month.abb`, which shows an abbreviation of months and `month.name`. Their content is presented next.

```
# print abreviation and full names of months
print(month.abb)
```

```
##  [1] "Jan" "Feb" "Mar" "Apr" "May" "Jun" "Jul" "Aug" "Sep"
## [10] "Oct" "Nov" "Dec"
```

```
print(month.name)
```

```
##  [1] "January"   "February"  "March"     "April"
##  [5] "May"       "June"      "July"      "August"
##  [9] "September" "October"   "November"  "December"
```

3.2.4 Selecting Characters of a Text Object

A common beginner's mistake is to select characters of a text using brackets, as it is done for selecting elements of a vector. Consider the following code:

```
# set char object
my.char <- 'ABCDE'
```

```
# print its second element (WRONG - RESULT is NA)
print(my.char[2])
```

```
## [1] NA
```

The return value `NA` indicates the second element of `my.char` does not exist. This happens because the use of square brackets is reserved for accessing the element of an atomic vector, not characters within a larger text. Watch what happens when we use `my.char[1]`:

```
print(my.char[1])
```

```
## [1] "ABCDE"
```

The result is simply the *ABCDE* text, located on the first item of `my.char`, available with command `my.char[1]`. To select pieces of text, we need to use function `substr` from the base code or `str_sub` from `stringr`.

```
# print third and fourth characters with base function
my.substr <- substr(x = my.char, start = 3, stop = 4)
print(my.substr)
```

```
## [1] "CD"
```

```
# print third and fourth characters with stringr function
my.substr <- str_sub(string = my.char, start = 3, end = 4)
print(my.substr)
```

```
## [1] "CD"
```

These functions also work for atomic vectors. Let's assume you imported text data, and the raw dataset contains a 3-digit identifier of a company, always in the same location of the string. Let's simulate the situation in R:

```
# build char vec
my.char.vec <- paste0(c('123','231','321'),
                      ' - other ignorable text')
print(my.char.vec)
```

```
## [1] "123 - other ignorable text"
## [2] "231 - other ignorable text"
## [3] "321 - other ignorable text"
```

Here, we only want the information in the first three characters of each element in `my.char.vec`. To select them, we can use the same functions as before.

```
# get ids with substr
ids.vec <- substr(my.char.vec, 1, 3)
print(ids.vec)
```

```
## [1] "123" "231" "321"
```

```
# get ids with stringr::str_sub
ids.vec <- str_sub(my.char.vec, 1, 3)
```

Vector operations are common in R. Almost anything you can do to a single element can be expanded to vectors . This facilitates the development of research scripts as you can easily perform complicated tasks to a series of elements in a single line of code.

3.2.5   Finding and Replacing Characters of a Text

A useful operation in handling texts is to locate specific patterns of text within a `character` object. From the base functions in R, you can use `regexpr` and `gregexpr`.

The equivalent functions in `stringr` are `str_locate` and `str_locate_all`.

Before moving to the examples, it is important to point out, by default, these functions use expressions of the type `regex` - regular expressions (Thompson, 1968). This is a specific language for the identification of patterns in text. When used correctly, it is a useful and valuable format. Usually, the most common case in research is to verify the position or the existence of a smaller text within a larger text. For these cases, however, using language `regex` is unnecessary. Therefore, the location and replacement of characters in the next example is of the fixed type, i.e., without using `regex`. Such information should be passed to functions with argument `fixed` or using function `fixed` from `stringr`.

The following example shows how to find the *D* character from a range of characters.

```
# set character object
my.char <- 'ABCDEF-ABCDEF-ABC'

# find position of FIRST 'D' using regexpr
pos <- regexpr(pattern = 'D', text = my.char, fixed = TRUE)
print(pos)
```

```
## [1] 4
## attr(,"match.length")
## [1] 1
## attr(,"useBytes")
## [1] TRUE
```

```
# find position of 'D' using str_locate
pos <- str_locate(my.char, fixed('D'))
print(pos)
```

```
##      start end
## [1,]     4   4
```

Note the `regexp` and `str_locate` function return only the first occurrence of *D*. To locate all instances, we use function `gregexpr`, where *g* indicates a *global* search, and `str_locate_all`.

```
# set object
my.char <- 'ABCDEF-ABCDEF-ABC'

# find position of ALL 'D' using regexpr
pos <- gregexpr(pattern = 'D', text = my.char, fixed = TRUE)
print(pos)
```

```
## [[1]]
```

```
## [1]   4 11
## attr(,"match.length")
## [1] 1 1
## attr(,"useBytes")
## [1] TRUE
# find position of ALL 'D' using str_locate_all
pos <- str_locate_all(my.char, fixed('D'))
print(pos)
```

```
## [[1]]
##        start end
## [1,]      4   4
## [2,]     11  11
```

To replace characters in a text, use functions **sub** and **gsub** from the base package or **str_replace** and **str_replace_all** from **stringr**. As with previous example, **sub** replaces the first occurrence of the character to be replaced, while **gsub** performs a global substitution; applies to all matches. Here are the differences:

```
# set char object
my.char <- 'ABCDEF-ABCDEF-ABC'

# substitute the FIRST 'ABC' for 'XXX' with sub
my.char <- sub(x = my.char,
               pattern = 'ABC',
               replacement = 'XXX')
print(my.char)
```

```
## [1] "XXXDEF-ABCDEF-ABC"
```

```
# substitute the FIRST 'ABC' for 'XXX' with str_replace
my.char <- str_replace(string = my.char,
                       pattern = 'ABC',
                       replacement = 'XXX')
print(my.char)
```

```
## [1] "XXXDEF-XXXDEF-ABC"
```

And now we do a global substitution of characters.

```
# set char object
my.char <- 'ABCDEF-ABCDEF-ABC'

# substitute all 'ABC' for 'XXX'  with gsub
my.char <- gsub(x = my.char,
```

```
                      pattern = 'ABC',
                      replacement = 'XXX')

print(my.char)
```

```
## [1] "XXXDEF-XXXDEF-XXX"
```

```
# substitute ALL 'ABC' for 'XXX' with str_replace_all
my.char <- str_replace_all(string = my.char,
                           pattern = 'ABC',
                           replacement = 'XXX')
print(my.char)
```

```
## [1] "XXXDEF-XXXDEF-XXX"
```

Again, it is worth pointing out that the operations of replacements of strings also works in vectors. Have a look at the next example.

```
# set char object
my.char <- c('ABCDEF','DBCFE','ABC')

# create an example of vector
my.char.vec <- paste(sample(my.char, 5, replace = T),
                      sample(my.char, 5, replace = T),
                      sep = ' - ')

# show it
print(my.char.vec)
```

```
## [1] "DBCFE - ABCDEF" "DBCFE - ABCDEF" "DBCFE - DBCFE"
## [4] "DBCFE - DBCFE"  "DBCFE - ABC"
```

```
# substitute all occurrences of 'ABC'
my.char.vec <- str_replace_all(string = my.char.vec,
                               pattern = 'ABC',
                               replacement = 'XXX')

# print result
print(my.char.vec)
```

```
## [1] "DBCFE - XXXDEF" "DBCFE - XXXDEF" "DBCFE - DBCFE"
## [4] "DBCFE - DBCFE"  "DBCFE - XXX"
```

3.2.6   Splitting Text

In some situations of analyzing text data, it will be necessary to break a text into different parts. Most of the time, you want to isolate a particular information in the full string by using a delimiter in the text. For example, the text `'ABC;DEF;GHI'` has three subcharacters divided by symbol `;`. To separate a text into several parts, use `strsplit` from the base functions or `str_split` from `stringr`. Both functions break the original text into several fractions, according to a chosen delimiter character. See an example next.

```
# set char
my.char <- 'ABCXABCXBCD'

# split it based on 'X' and using strsplit
split.char <- strsplit(my.char, 'X')

# print result
print(split.char)
```

```
## [[1]]
## [1] "ABC" "ABC" "BCD"
```

```
# split it based on 'X' and using stringr::str_split
split.char <- str_split(my.char, 'X')

# print result
print(split.char)
```

```
## [[1]]
## [1] "ABC" "ABC" "BCD"
```

The output of this function is an object of type `list`. Since each split operation results in more than one element, and it is impossible to store multidimensional outputs in a single vector, the use of a `list`is justified. But, to access its results, you can use a `list` operator `[[ ]]`, which will be discussed later. For example, to access the text `BCD` in object `split.char`, we can use the following code:

```
print(split.char[[1]][3])
```

```
## [1] "BCD"
```

To visualize an example of split in character vectors, see the next code.

```
# set char
my.char.vec <- c('ABCDEF','DBCFE','ABFC','ACD')
```

```r
# split it based on 'B' and using stringr::strsplit
split.char <- strsplit(my.char.vec, 'B')

# print result
print(split.char)
```

```
## [[1]]
## [1] "A"     "CDEF"
##
## [[2]]
## [1] "D"     "CFE"
##
## [[3]]
## [1] "A"    "FC"
##
## [[4]]
## [1] "ACD"
```

Notice how, again, an object of type `list` is returned.

3.2.7   Finding the Number of Characters in a Text

To find out the number of characters in a `character` object, you can use function `nchar` from the base package or `str_length` from `stringr`. Both functions also work for atomic vectors. See the examples below:

```r
# set char
my.char <- 'abcdef'

# print number of characters using nchar
print(nchar(my.char))
```

```
## [1] 6
```

```r
# print number of characters using stringr::str_length
print(str_length(my.char))
```

```
## [1] 6
```

And now an example with vectors.

```r
#set char
my.char <- c('a', 'ab', 'abc')
```

```r
# print number of characters using nchar
print(nchar(my.char))
```

```
## [1] 1 2 3
```

```r
# print number of characters using stringr::str_length
print(str_length(my.char))
```

```
## [1] 1 2 3
```

3.2.8   Generating Combinations of Text

One useful trick in R is to use functions `outer` and `expand.grid` to create all possible combinations of elements in different objects. This is useful when you want to create a `character` vector by combining all possible elements from different vectors. For example, if we wanted to create a vector with all combinations between c('a', 'b') and 'c('A','A') as c('a-A', 'a-B',...), we could write:

```r
# set char vecs
my.vec.1 <- c('a','b')
my.vec.2 <- c('A','B')

# combine in matrix
comb.mat <- outer(my.vec.1, my.vec.2, paste,sep='-')

# print it!
print(comb.mat)
```

```
##       [,1]  [,2]
## [1,] "a-A" "a-B"
## [2,] "b-A" "b-B"
```

The output of `outer` is a `matrix` type of object, a specific class for storing two dimensional data. Its properties will be better explained in chapter 4. If we wanted to change `comb.mat` to an atomic vector, we can use function `as.character`:

```r
print(as.character(comb.mat))
```

```
## [1] "a-A" "b-A" "a-B" "b-B"
```

Another way to reach the same objective is using function `expand.grid`. Look at the next example.

```r
# create df with all combinations
my.df <- expand.grid(my.vec.1, my.vec.2)
```

```
# print df
print(my.df)
```

```
##   Var1 Var2
## 1    a    A
## 2    b    A
## 3    a    B
## 4    b    B
```

```
# paste columns together
my.comb.vec <- paste(my.df$Var1, my.df$Var2, sep='-')
```

```
# print result
print(my.comb.vec)
```

```
## [1] "a-A" "b-A" "a-B" "b-B"
```

Here, we used function `expand.grid` to create a `dataframe` containing all possible combinations of `my.vec.1` and `my.vec.2`. We pasted the contents of these columns using `paste`. For now, do not worry about the commands for handling `dataframes`. These will be discussed in the next chapter.

3.2.9 Encoding of `character` Objects

Every `character` object in R is encoded in a particular format. In R's memory, a string is just a sequence of bytes. We can define how these bytes are read as characters by encoding it in a particular format. For most cases of using R, especially in English speaking countries, the codification of strings should not be a problem. When dealing with text data in different languages, however, the encoding of strings is something you must understand, especially if you are importing text data from external sources.

Let's explore an example. Here, we will import data from a text file with the `UTF-8` encoding and check the result.

```
# read text file
my.char <- readLines('data/FileWithLatinChar.txt')
```

```
# print it
print(my.char)
```

```
## [1] "A casa Ã© bonita e tem muito espaÃ§o"
```

The original content of the file is a text in Portuguese. As you can see, the output of **readLines** shows all Latin characters as ugly, unreadable symbols. The problem is the function did not recognize the characters because the default encoding differs from the one in the file. The easiest solution is to set the encoding manually using input **encoding**, as in:

```
# read text file with utf-8
my.char <- readLines('data/FileWithLatinChar.txt',
                      encoding = 'UTF-8')
```

The output in **my.char** should now be properly displayed, as R could interpret and correctly display the Latin symbols. A good policy in this topic is always to check the encoding of imported text files and match it in R. Most of the import functions have an option for doing so.

As for objects available in the environment, you can use function **Encoding** for checking and setting its encoding. Look at the next example:

```
# read text file
my.char <- readLines('data/FileWithLatinChar.txt')

# show its encoding
print(Encoding(my.char))
```

```
## [1] "unknown"
```

```
# change encoding
Encoding(my.char) <- 'UTF-8'

# show its encoding
print(Encoding(my.char))
```

```
## [1] "UTF-8"
```

After reading the contents of **"data/FileWithLatinChar.txt"**, we changed the encoding of the output by using function **Encoding**. This function also works on vectors, making it easy to change the encoding of large **character** objects.

3.2.10   Other Functions for Manipulating character

- **tolower** and **stringr::str_to_lower** - Converts a string to small caps.

```
print(tolower('ABC'))
```

```
## [1] "abc"
```

```
print(stringr::str_to_lower('ABC'))
```

```
## [1] "abc"
```

- **toupper** and **stringr::str_to_upper** - Converts a string to upper caps.

```
print(toupper('abc'))
```

```
## [1] "ABC"
```

```
print(stringr::str_to_upper('abc'))
```

```
## [1] "ABC"
```

3.3   Factor Objects

Object class `factor` is used to represent groups in a database. Imagine a dataset containing financial expenses of different people over a year. In this database, you find a column that defines gender (male or female). This information can be imported in R as a `character` object; however, the best way to represent it is by mutating it to class `factor`.

The object class `factor` offers a special object to denote groups within the data. This integrates nicely with statistical procedures and packages, so the work of dealing with groups becomes easier. For example, if we wanted to create a chart for each group within our database, we could do it by simply telling the graphing function we have a grouping variable of type `factor`. If we wanted to check whether the medians of different groups are statistically different from each other, all we need to do is to pass the numerical values and the grouping factor to the function that performs the statistical test. When the categories of data are appropriately represented in R, working with them becomes easier and more efficient.

3.3.1   Creating `factors`

The creation of factors is accomplished with function `factor`:

```
# create factor
my.factor <- factor(c('M','F','M','M','F'))

# print it
print(my.factor)
```

```
## [1] M F M M F
```

```
## Levels: F M
```

Notice that, in the previous example, the presentation of factors with function **print** shows its content and an extra item called **Levels**, which identifies the possible groups in the object, in this case, only M and F. If we had a larger number of groups, the item **Levels** increases. See next:

```
# create factor with 3 levels
my.factor <- factor(c('M','F','M','M','F','ND'))

# print factor
print(my.factor)
```

```
## [1] M  F  M  M  F  ND
## Levels: F M ND
```

Here, we also have the ND (not defined) group.

An important point about creating factors is that the **Levels** are inferred from the data, and that may not correspond to reality. Consider the following example:

```
# set factors with 1 level
my.status <- factor(c('Single', 'Single', 'Single'))

# print it
print(my.status)
```

```
## [1] Single Single Single
## Levels: Single
```

On occasion, the data in **my.status** only shows one category: **Single**. However, it is well-known that another category, **Married**, is expected. If we used **my.status** as it is, we may omit information, and that may cause problems. The correct procedure is to manually define the **Levels**, as follows:

```
my.status <- factor(c('Single', 'Single', 'Single'),
                    levels = c('Single', 'Married'))
print(my.status)
```

```
## [1] Single Single Single
## Levels: Single Married
```

3.3.2 Modifying factors

An important point about **factor** type of objects is their **Levels** are immutable and will not update with the input of new data. You cannot modify the **Levels** after the creation of a `factor`. All new groups not in the `Levels` will be transformed into `NA` (*not available*) and a `warning` message will appear on the screen. This behavior may seem strange, at first, but it avoids possible errors in the code. See the following example:

```
# set factor
my.factor <- factor(c('a', 'b', 'a', 'b'))

# change first element of a factor to 'c'
my.factor[1] <- 'c'
```

```
## Warning in `[<-.factor`(`*tmp*`, 1, value = "c"): invalid
## factor level, NA generated
```

```
# print result
print(my.factor)
```

```
## [1] <NA> b    a    b
## Levels: a b
```

As we expected, the first element of `my.factor` becomes an `NA`. Here, the proper way to add a new factor is to first transform the `factor` object to a `character` object, change the content and, finally, change the class back from `character` to `factor`. See an example next.

```
# set factor
my.factor <- factor(c('a', 'b', 'a', 'b'))

# change factor to character
my.char <- as.character(my.factor)

# change first element
my.char[1] <- 'c'

# mutate it back to class factor
my.factor <- factor(my.char)

# show result
print(my.factor)
```

```
## [1] c b a b
## Levels: a b c
```

Using these steps, we have the desired result in vector `my.factor`, with three `Levels`: a, b and c.

3.3.3   Converting factors to Other Classes

Attention is required when converting a `factor` to another class. When converting a `factor` to the `character` class, the result is as expected:

```
# create factor
my.char <-factor(c('a', 'b', 'c'))

# convert and print
print(as.character(my.char))
```

```
## [1] "a" "b" "c"
```

However, when the same procedure is performed for a conversion from `factor` to the `numeric` class, the result is far from expected:

```
# set factor
my.values <- factor(5:10)

# convert to numeric (WRONG)
print(as.numeric(my.values))
```

```
## [1] 1 2 3 4 5 6
```

As you can see, all elements in `my.values` were converted to `c(1, 2, 3, 4, 5)`. This happens because, internally, `factors` are stored as numerical counters, ranging from 1 to the total number of `Levels`. This simplification minimizes the use of computer memory. When we asked R to transform the `factor` object into numbers, it returns the values of the counters, not the actual numbers stored as `factors`. Solving this problem and getting what we wanted is easy; just turn the `factor` object into a `character` and then to `numeric`, as shown next:

```
# converting factors to character and then to numeric
print(as.numeric(as.character(my.values)))
```

```
## [1]  5  6  7  8  9 10
```

As we can see, now we got the result we wanted.

3.3.4   Creating Contingency Tables

After creating a factor, we can find the number of times that each group, or combination of groups, is found with function `table`. This is also called a contingency table. In a simple case, with only one factor, function `table` counts the number of occurrences of each category:

```
# create factor
my.factor <- factor(sample(c('Pref', 'Ord'),
                           size = 20,
                           replace = TRUE))

# print it
print(my.factor)
```

```
##  [1] Ord  Ord  Pref Pref Pref Pref Ord  Ord  Ord  Pref Ord
## [12] Pref Ord  Pref Pref Ord  Pref Pref Ord  Pref
## Levels: Ord Pref
```

```
# print contingency table
print(table(my.factor))
```

```
## my.factor
##  Ord Pref
##    9   11
```

A more advanced usage of function `table` is to consider more than one `factor`.
Look at the following example.

```
# set factors
my.factor.1 <- factor(sample(c('Pref', 'Ord'),
                             size = 20,
                             replace = TRUE))

my.factor.2 <- factor(sample(paste('Grupo', 1:3),
                             size = 20,
                             replace = TRUE))

# print contingency table with two factors
print(table(my.factor.1, my.factor.2))
```

```
##             my.factor.2
## my.factor.1 Grupo 1 Grupo 2 Grupo 3
##        Ord        2       2       4
##        Pref       3       4       5
```

The previously created table shows the number of occurrences for each combination
of groups. You can also use it with more than two factors.

3.3.5   Other Functions for Manipulating `factors`

- **levels** - Returns the Levels an object of class `factor`.

```
# set factor
my.factor <- factor(c('A', 'A', 'B', 'C', 'B'))

# print levels
print(levels(my.factor))
```

```
## [1] "A" "B" "C"
```

- **as.factor** - Transforms an object to the class `factor`.

```
# set char
my.y <- c('a','b', 'c', 'c', 'a')

# mutate to factor
my.factor <- as.factor(my.y)

# print it
print(my.factor)
```

```
## [1] a b c c a
## Levels: a b c
```

- **split** - Based on a grouping variable and another vector, creates a list with subsets of groups of the target object. This function is best used to separate different samples according to groups.

```
# set factor and numeric
my.factor <- factor(c('A','B','C','C','C','B'))
my.x <- 1:length(my.factor)

# split numeric vector into a list, based on factor
my.l <- split(x = my.x, f = my.factor)

print(my.l)
```

```
## $A
## [1] 1
##
## $B
## [1] 2 6
##
## $C
```

```
## [1] 3 4 5
```

3.4 Logical Objects

Logical tests are at the heart of R. In one line of code, we can test a condition for a large vector of data. This procedure is commonly used to find outliers in a dataset and to split the sample according to some condition, such as a particular time period.

3.4.1 Creating `logical` Objects

In a sequence from 1 to 10, we can check what elements are higher than five with the following code:

```
# set numerical
my.x <- 1:10

# print a logical test
print(my.x > 5)
```

```
##  [1] FALSE FALSE FALSE FALSE FALSE  TRUE  TRUE  TRUE  TRUE
## [10]  TRUE
```

```
# print position of elements from logical test
print(which(my.x > 5))
```

```
## [1]  6  7  8  9 10
```

In the previous example, function `which` returned the index (position) where the condition is true (`TRUE`).

To perform equality tests, simply use the equality symbol twice (`==`).

```
# create char
my.char <- rep(c('abc','bcd'),5)

# print its contents
print(my.char)
```

```
##  [1] "abc" "bcd" "abc" "bcd" "abc" "bcd" "abc" "bcd" "abc"
## [10] "bcd"
```

```
# print logical test
print(my.char=='abc')
```

```
##  [1]  TRUE FALSE  TRUE FALSE  TRUE FALSE  TRUE FALSE  TRUE
## [10] FALSE
```

For an inequality test, use symbol !=, as shown in the next code:

```
# print inequality test
print(my.char!='abc')
```

```
##  [1] FALSE  TRUE FALSE  TRUE FALSE  TRUE FALSE  TRUE FALSE
## [10]  TRUE
```

It is also possible to test multiple logical conditions. For simultaneous occurrences of events, use operator &. For example, if we wanted to check the values from a sequence between 1 and 10 that are larger than 4 **and** smaller than 7, we write:

```
my.x <- 1:10
```

```
# print logical for values higher than 4 and lower than 7
print((my.x > 4)&(my.x < 7) )
```

```
##  [1] FALSE FALSE FALSE FALSE  TRUE  TRUE FALSE FALSE FALSE
## [10] FALSE
```

```
# print the actual values
idx <- which( (my.x > 4)&(my.x < 7) )
print(my.x[idx])
```

```
## [1] 5 6
```

For non-simultaneous conditions, i.e., the occurrence of one event or other, use operator |. For instance, considering the previous sequence, we can find the values greater than 7 **or** lower than 4 by writing:

```
# location of elements higher than 7 or lower than 4
idx <- which( (my.x > 7)|(my.x < 4) )
```

```
# print elements from previous condition
print(my.x[idx])
```

```
## [1]  1  2  3  8  9 10
```

Be aware that, in both cases, we used parentheses to encapsulate the logical conditions. While not strictly necessary, it is good coding policy. We could have used idx <- which(my.x > 7 | my.x < 4) for the same result, but using parentheses makes the code cleaner by isolating the logical tests. Sometimes, however, it may be a requisite to set the parentheses correctly, as they indicate the hierarchy in the order of mathematical operations.

3.5 Date and Time Objects

The representation and manipulation of dates is an important aspect of research in finance. When you have dates in your dataset, you must represent them correctly in R. In this section, we will study the native functions and classes that represent time in R. There are, however, many packages that can also help the user in processing time information and perform advanced procedures with it. If the reader must perform a date operation not covered here, I suggest looking into packages `chron` (James and Hornik, 2017), `timeDate` (Team et al., 2015), `lubridate` (Grolemund and Wickham, 2011)and `bizdays` (Freitas, 2016).

3.5.1 Creating Simple Dates

In R, several classes can represent dates. The most basic class, indicating the day, month, and year, is `Date`. We can create a date through a character object with the command `as.Date`:

```
# set Date object
my.date <- as.Date('2016-06-24')

# check its class
class(my.date)
```

```
## [1] "Date"
```

```
# print it
print(my.date)
```

```
## [1] "2016-06-24"
```

Notice, in the previous example, dates are represented in R as `Year-Month-Day` (YYYY-MM-DD). This may not be the case for your country. In Brazil, we use the format `day/month/year` (DD/MM/YYYY). If we tried to create a character object from this format, the displayed result would be wrong. See an example with code next:

```
# set Date from dd/mm/yyyy
my.date <- as.Date('24/06/2016')

# print result (WRONG)
print(my.date)
```

```
## [1] "0024-06-20"
```

The date of 0024-06-20 is wrong! To fix this formatting issue, use input `format`, as shown below:

```
# set Date from dd/mm/yyyy with the definition of format
my.date <- as.Date('24/06/2016', format = '%d/%m/%Y')

# print result (CORRECT)
print(my.date)
```

```
## [1] "2016-06-24"
```

The symbols used in *input* `format`, such as `%d`, `%m` and `%y`, indicates how the character object should be converted and where day, month and year are located in the text. There are many other symbols that may be used for processing dates in specific formats. An overview of the main symbols is given next.

Symbol	Description	Example
%d	day of month (decimal)	0
%m	month (decimal)	12
%b	month (abbreviation)	Apr
%B	month (complete name)	April
%y	year (2 digits)	16
%Y	month (4 digits)	2016

By using the previous table, you'll be able to create and represent dates in a vast number of ways.

3.5.2 Creating a Sequence of `Dates`

An interesting aspect of objects `Date` is they interact with `numeric` objects and can be used for logical tests. If we wanted to add a day after a particular date, all we need to do is to add value 1 to the object, as shown next:

```
# create date
my.date <- as.Date('2016-06-24')

# find next day
my.date.2 <- my.date + 1

# print result
print(my.date.2)
```

```
## [1] "2016-06-25"
```

This property also works with vectors, facilitating the creation of `Date` sequences. See an example next.

```
# create a sequence of Dates
my.date.vec <- my.date + 0:15
```

```
# print it
print(my.date.vec)
```

```
##  [1] "2016-06-24" "2016-06-25" "2016-06-26" "2016-06-27"
##  [5] "2016-06-28" "2016-06-29" "2016-06-30" "2016-07-01"
##  [9] "2016-07-02" "2016-07-03" "2016-07-04" "2016-07-05"
## [13] "2016-07-06" "2016-07-07" "2016-07-08" "2016-07-09"
```

A more customizable way for creating `Date` sequences is using function `seq`. The same way it worked for numerical object, we can use function `seq` to create sequences of dates with custom time intervals or use it to create a `Date` sequence with fixed size. If we wanted a `Date` sequence, where the elements are set every two days, we can use the following code:

```
# set first and last Date
my.date.1 <- as.Date('2017-03-07')
my.date.2 <- as.Date('2017-03-20')
```

```
# set sequence
my.vec.date <- seq(from = my.date.1,
                   to = my.date.2,
                   by = '2 days')
```

```
# print result
print(my.vec.date)
```

```
## [1] "2017-03-07" "2017-03-09" "2017-03-11" "2017-03-13"
## [5] "2017-03-15" "2017-03-17" "2017-03-19"
```

Likewise, if we wanted a sequence of dates containing every one month, we can simply change input `by` to `'1 month'`:

```
# set first and last Date
my.date.1 <- as.Date('2017-03-07')
my.date.2 <- as.Date('2017-10-20')
```

```
# set sequence
my.vec.date <- seq(from = my.date.1,
                   to = my.date.2,
```

```
                          by = '1 month')

# print result
print(my.vec.date)
```

```
## [1] "2017-03-07" "2017-04-07" "2017-05-07" "2017-06-07"
## [5] "2017-07-07" "2017-08-07" "2017-09-07" "2017-10-07"
```

Another way to use function seq is by setting the desired length of the sequence of dates. For example, if we wanted an array of dates with 10 elements, we would use:

```
# set dates
my.date.1 <- as.Date('2016-06-27')
my.date.2 <- as.Date('2016-07-27')

# set sequence with 10 elements
my.vec.date <- seq(from = my.date.1,
                   to = my.date.2,
                   length.out = 10)

# print result
print(my.vec.date)
```

```
##   [1] "2016-06-27" "2016-06-30" "2016-07-03" "2016-07-07"
##   [5] "2016-07-10" "2016-07-13" "2016-07-17" "2016-07-20"
##   [9] "2016-07-23" "2016-07-27"
```

3.5.3 Operations with Dates

We can calculate difference of days between two dates by simply subtracting one from the other. Have a look:

```
# set dates
my.date.1 <- as.Date('2015-06-24')
my.date.2 <- as.Date('2016-06-24')

# calculate difference
diff.date <- my.date.2 - my.date.1

# print result
print(diff.date)
```

```
## Time difference of 366 days
```

The output of the subtraction operation is an object of class `diffdate`, based on the `list` class. As mentioned, we can access the elements of a `list` using double brackets. The numerical value of the difference of days is contained in the first element of `diff.date`:

```
# print difference of days as numerical value
print(diff.date[[1]])
```

```
## [1] 366
```

Going further, we can test whether a date is more recent or not than another with comparison operations:

```
# set date and vector
my.date.1 <- as.Date('2016-06-20')
my.date.vec <- as.Date('2016-06-20') + seq(-5,5)

# test which elements of my.date.vec are older than my.date.1
my.test <- my.date.vec > my.date.1

# print result
print(my.test)
```

```
##  [1] FALSE FALSE FALSE FALSE FALSE FALSE  TRUE  TRUE  TRUE
## [10]  TRUE  TRUE
```

The previous operation is useful when trying to select a certain period of time in your dataset. This is a common practice in research. Here, set the first and last dates of the time you are interested in and use a logical test to find all dates between. Look at the following code:

```
# set first and last dates
first.date <- as.Date('2016-06-01')
last.date <- as.Date('2016-06-15')

# create a vector of dates and a vector of "fake" prices
my.date.vec <- as.Date('2016-05-25') + seq(0,30)
my.prices <- seq(1,10, length.out = length(my.date.vec))

# print vectors
print(my.prices)
```

```
##  [1]  1.0  1.3  1.6  1.9  2.2  2.5  2.8  3.1  3.4  3.7  4.0
## [12]  4.3  4.6  4.9  5.2  5.5  5.8  6.1  6.4  6.7  7.0  7.3
## [23]  7.6  7.9  8.2  8.5  8.8  9.1  9.4  9.7 10.0
```

```
print(my.date.vec)
```

```
##  [1] "2016-05-25" "2016-05-26" "2016-05-27" "2016-05-28"
##  [5] "2016-05-29" "2016-05-30" "2016-05-31" "2016-06-01"
##  [9] "2016-06-02" "2016-06-03" "2016-06-04" "2016-06-05"
## [13] "2016-06-06" "2016-06-07" "2016-06-08" "2016-06-09"
## [17] "2016-06-10" "2016-06-11" "2016-06-12" "2016-06-13"
## [21] "2016-06-14" "2016-06-15" "2016-06-16" "2016-06-17"
## [25] "2016-06-18" "2016-06-19" "2016-06-20" "2016-06-21"
## [29] "2016-06-22" "2016-06-23" "2016-06-24"
```

```
# find dates that are between the first and last date
my.idx <- (my.date.vec >= first.date) & (my.date.vec <= last.date)
```

```
# use index to select prices
my.prices <- my.prices[my.idx]
```

```
# print result
print(my.prices)
```

```
##  [1] 3.1 3.4 3.7 4.0 4.3 4.6 4.9 5.2 5.5 5.8 6.1 6.4 6.7 7.0
## [15] 7.3
```

In the previous code, object `my.prices` will only contain values for the time between 2016-06-01 and 2016-06-15.

3.5.4   Dealing with Time

Using the `Date` class is sufficient when dealing only with dates and the hours of the day are irrelevant. When it is necessary to consider time, we have to use an object of type `datetime`.

In R, one of the classes used for this purpose is `POSIXlt`, which stores the content of a date in the form of a list. Another class you can use is `POSIXct`, which stores dates as seconds counted from 1970-01-01. Class `POSIXct` takes less space of computer memory because of its storage format and should be prioritized when working with large datasets. However, using the `POSIXlt` class has benefits. It internally stores information about the time object. We can show it in R by looking at the result of calling function `attribute` in a `POSIXlt` object. Have a look:

```
my.timedate <- as.POSIXlt('2016-01-01 16:00:00')
print(attributes(my.timedate))
```

```
## $names
```

```
##   [1] "sec"     "min"     "hour"    "mday"    "mon"     "year"
##   [7] "wday"    "yday"    "isdst"   "zone"    "gmtoff"
##
## $class
## [1] "POSIXlt" "POSIXt"
```

As you can see, it stores the hour, minutes, weekday, among other information. To access it, use the list notation for names values:

```
print(my.timedate[['hour']])
```

```
## [1] 16
```

Since computer memory is not limited these days, we will give preference to the `datetime` object of type `POSIXlt` for the rest of this section. All examples presented here can also be replicated for `POSIXct` objects.

For both `datetime` objects, `POSIXct` and `POSIXlt`, the format is *year-month-day hours:minutes:seconds timezone* (YYYY-MM-DD HH:MM:SS TMZ). See the following example:

```
# creating a POSIXlt object
my.timedate <- as.POSIXlt('2016-01-01 16:00:00')

# print result
print(my.timedate)
```

```
## [1] "2016-01-01 16:00:00 BRST"
```

When creating a `POSIXlt` object, the time zone is added automatically with the information from the operating system. If you need to represent a time zone different from the one in your computer, use input `tz`:

```
# creating a POSIXlt object with custom timezone
my.timedate.tz <- as.POSIXlt('2016-01-01 16:00:00', tz = 'GMT')

# print it
print(my.timedate.tz)
```

```
## [1] "2016-01-01 16:00:00 GMT"
```

An important note in the case of `POSIXlt` and `POSIXct` objects, the operations of sum and subtraction refer to seconds, not days, as with objects from the `Date` class. Have a look in the next example:

```
# Adding values (seconds) to a POSIXlt object and printing it
print(my.timedate.tz + 30)
```

```
## [1] "2016-01-01 16:00:30 GMT"
```

In the same way as objects of class Date, there are specific symbols for dealing with components of a POSIXlt object. These symbols allow for custom formatting. We present next a table with the main symbols and their meanings.

Symbol	Description	Example
%H	Hour (decimal, 24 hours)	23
%I	Hour (decimal, 12 hours)	11
%M	Minutes (decimal, 0-59)	12
%p	AM/PM indicator	AM
%S	Seconds (decimal, 0-59)	50

3.5.5   Customizing the Output Format of Dates and Times

The basic notation for representing dates and datetime object in R may not be optimal sometimes. When writing reports, using a date-time format different than the local one can generate confusion. The recommendation here is to modify the representation of dates for the expected format, so the output is locally accepted.

To format a date, use the format function. Its use is based on the symbols presented in previous tables. Using these symbols, the user can create any desired customization. See the following example, where we change a date vector to the Brazilian format:

```
# create vector of dates
my.dates <- seq(from = as.Date('2016-01-01'),
                to = as.Date('2016-01-15'),
                by = '1 day')

# change format
my.dates.brformat <- format(my.dates, '%d/%m/%Y')

# print result
print(my.dates.brformat)
```

```
##  [1] "01/01/2016" "02/01/2016" "03/01/2016" "04/01/2016"
##  [5] "05/01/2016" "06/01/2016" "07/01/2016" "08/01/2016"
##  [9] "09/01/2016" "10/01/2016" "11/01/2016" "12/01/2016"
## [13] "13/01/2016" "14/01/2016" "15/01/2016"
```

The same procedure can be performed for POSIXlt objects:

```
# create vector of date-time
my.datetime <- as.POSIXlt('2016-01-01 12:00:00') + seq(0,560,60)

# change to Brazilian format
my.dates.brformat <- format(my.datetime, '%d/%m/%Y %H:%M:%S')

# print result
print(my.dates.brformat)
```

```
##   [1] "01/01/2016 12:00:00" "01/01/2016 12:01:00"
##   [3] "01/01/2016 12:02:00" "01/01/2016 12:03:00"
##   [5] "01/01/2016 12:04:00" "01/01/2016 12:05:00"
##   [7] "01/01/2016 12:06:00" "01/01/2016 12:07:00"
##   [9] "01/01/2016 12:08:00" "01/01/2016 12:09:00"
```

One can also customize for very specific formats. See next:

```
# set custom format
my.dates.myformat <- format(my.dates,
                            'Year=%Y | Month=%m | Day=%d')

# print result
print(my.dates.myformat)
```

```
##   [1] "Year=2016 | Month=01 | Day=01"
##   [2] "Year=2016 | Month=01 | Day=02"
##   [3] "Year=2016 | Month=01 | Day=03"
##   [4] "Year=2016 | Month=01 | Day=04"
##   [5] "Year=2016 | Month=01 | Day=05"
##   [6] "Year=2016 | Month=01 | Day=06"
##   [7] "Year=2016 | Month=01 | Day=07"
##   [8] "Year=2016 | Month=01 | Day=08"
##   [9] "Year=2016 | Month=01 | Day=09"
##  [10] "Year=2016 | Month=01 | Day=10"
##  [11] "Year=2016 | Month=01 | Day=11"
##  [12] "Year=2016 | Month=01 | Day=12"
##  [13] "Year=2016 | Month=01 | Day=13"
##  [14] "Year=2016 | Month=01 | Day=14"
##  [15] "Year=2016 | Month=01 | Day=15"
```

Using function `format` is also very helpful when you want only particular information from the date-time object. Look at the next example, where we retrieve only the hours from a `POSIXlt` object.

```
# create vector of date-time
my.datetime <- seq(from = as.POSIXlt('2016-01-01 12:00:00'),
                   to = as.POSIXlt('2016-01-01 18:00:00'),
                   by = '1 hour')

# get hours from POSIXlt
my.hours <- format(my.datetime, '%H')

# print result
print(my.hours)
```

```
## [1] "12" "13" "14" "15" "16" "17" "18"
```

Likewise, by using symbols %Y% and $m, we could easill retrieve years and months from a vector of POSIXlt or Date objects.

3.5.6   Find the Current Date and Time

R has specific functions that allow the user to find the current date and time from the operating system. This is useful when creating log records.

To find the the present day, use function Sys.Date:

```
# get today
my.day <- Sys.Date()

# print it
print(my.day)
```

```
## [1] "2017-05-05"
```

To find the current date and time, we use function Sys.time:

```
# get time!
print(Sys.time())
```

```
## [1] "2017-05-05 14:15:01 BRT"
```

Going further, based on these functions, we can write:

```
# example of log message
my.str <- paste0('This code was executed in ', Sys.time())

# print it
print(my.str)
```

```
## [1] "This code was executed in 2017-05-05 14:15:01"
```

3.5.7   Other Functions for Manipulating Dates and Time

- **weekdays** - Returns the day of the week from one or more dates.

```
# set date vector
my.dates <- seq(from = as.Date('2016-01-01'),
                to = as.Date('2016-01-5'),
                by = '1 day')

# find corresponding weekdays
my.weekdays <- weekdays(my.dates)

# print it
print(my.weekdays)
```

```
## [1] "Friday"   "Saturday" "Sunday"   "Monday"   "Tuesday"
```

- **months** - Returns the month of one or more dates.

```
# create date vector
my.dates <- seq(from = as.Date('2016-01-01'),
                to = as.Date('2016-12-31'),
                by = '1 month')

# find months
my.months <- months(my.dates)

# print result
print(my.months)
```

```
##  [1] "January"   "February" "March"    "April"
##  [5] "May"       "June"     "July"     "August"
##  [9] "September" "October"  "November" "December"
```

- **quarters** - Returns the location of one or more dates within the year quartiles.

```
# get quartiles of the year
my.quarters <- quarters(my.dates)
print(my.quarters)
```

```
##  [1] "Q1" "Q1" "Q1" "Q2" "Q2" "Q2" "Q3" "Q3" "Q3" "Q4" "Q4"
## [12] "Q4"
```

- **OlsonNames** - Returns an array with the time zones available in R. In total, there are over 500 items. Here, we present only the first five elements.

```
# get possible timezones
possible.tz <- OlsonNames()

# print it
print(possible.tz[1:5])
```

```
## [1] "Africa/Abidjan"     "Africa/Accra"
## [3] "Africa/Addis_Ababa" "Africa/Algiers"
## [5] "Africa/Asmara"
```

- **Sys.timezone** - Returns the current timezone of the operating system.

```
# get current timezone
print(Sys.timezone())
```

```
## [1] "America/Sao_Paulo"
```

- **cut** - Returns a factor by grouping dates and time.

```
# set example date vector
my.dates <- seq(from = as.Date('2016-01-01'),
                to = as.Date('2016-03-01'),
                by = '5 days')

# group vector based on monthly breaks
my.month.cut <- cut(x = my.dates,
                    breaks = 'month',
                    labels = c('Jan', 'Fev', 'Mar'))

# print result
print(my.month.cut)
```

```
##  [1] Jan Jan Jan Jan Jan Jan Jan Fev Fev Fev Fev Fev Mar
## Levels: Jan Fev Mar
```

```
# set example datetime vector
my.datetime <- as.POSIXlt('2016-01-01 12:00:00') + seq(0,250,15)

# set groups for each 30 seconds
my.cut <- cut(x = my.datetime, breaks = '30 secs')

# print result
print(my.cut)
```

```
##  [1] 2016-01-01 12:00:00 2016-01-01 12:00:00
##  [3] 2016-01-01 12:00:30 2016-01-01 12:00:30
##  [5] 2016-01-01 12:01:00 2016-01-01 12:01:00
##  [7] 2016-01-01 12:01:30 2016-01-01 12:01:30
##  [9] 2016-01-01 12:02:00 2016-01-01 12:02:00
## [11] 2016-01-01 12:02:30 2016-01-01 12:02:30
## [13] 2016-01-01 12:03:00 2016-01-01 12:03:00
## [15] 2016-01-01 12:03:30 2016-01-01 12:03:30
## [17] 2016-01-01 12:04:00
## 9 Levels: 2016-01-01 12:00:00 ... 2016-01-01 12:04:00
```

3.6 Missing Data - `NA` (*Not available*)

One of the main innovations of R, with respect to other programming languages, is the representation of missing data with objects of class `NA` (*Not Available*). The lack of data can have many reasons, such as failure to collect information or simply the absence of it. These cases are generally treated by removing or replacing the missing data prior to analyzing the data. The identification of these cases, therefore, is imperative.

3.6.1 Defining `NA` Values

To define omissions in the dataset, use symbol `NA` without quotes:

```
# a vector with NA
my.x <- c(1,2,NA, 4, 5)

# print it
print(my.x)
```

```
## [1]  1  2 NA  4  5
```

An important property, at this point, is that a `NA` object is contagious. Any other object that interacts with a `NA` will turn into the same class of missing data. Look at the next example.

```
# example of NA interacting with other objects
print(my.x + 1)
```

```
## [1]  2  3 NA  5  6
```

This property demands special attention if you are calculating a value recursively, such as in using `cumsum` and `cumprod`. In these cases, any value after `NA` will turn into NA. Here is an example with code:

```
# set vector with NA
my.x <- c(1:5, NA, 5:10)

# print cumsum (NA after sixth element)
print(cumsum(my.x))
```

```
##  [1]  1  3  6 10 15 NA NA NA NA NA NA NA
# print cumprod (NA after sixth element)
print(cumprod(my.x))
```

```
##  [1]   1   2   6  24 120  NA  NA  NA  NA  NA  NA  NA
```

Therefore, when using functions cumsum and cumprod, make sure no NA value is found in the input vector.

3.6.2   Finding and Replacing NA

To find NA values, use function is.na:

```
# set vector with NA
my.x <- c(1:2, NA, 4:10)

# find location of NA
idx.na <- is.na(my.x)
print(idx.na)
```

```
##  [1] FALSE FALSE  TRUE FALSE FALSE FALSE FALSE FALSE FALSE
## [10] FALSE
```

To replace it, use indexing with the output of is.na. See next:

```
# set vector
my.x <- c(1, NA, 3:4, NA)

# replace NA for 2
my.x[is.na(my.x)] <- 2

# print result
print(my.x)
```

```
## [1] 1 2 3 4 2
```

Another way to remove NA values is to use function na.omit, which returns the same object, but without the `NA` values. Note, however, the vector size will change and the output will be an object of class `omit`. Have a look:

```
# set vector
my.char <- c(letters[1:3], NA, letters[5:8])

# print it
print(my.char)
```

```
## [1] "a" "b" "c" NA  "e" "f" "g" "h"
```

```
# use na.omit to remove NA
my.char <- na.omit(my.char)

# print result
print(my.char)
```

```
## [1] "a" "b" "c" "e" "f" "g" "h"
## attr(,"na.action")
## [1] 4
## attr(,"class")
## [1] "omit"
```

Although the type of object has been changed due to the use of `na.omit`, the basic properties of the initial vector remain. For example, the use of function `nchar` in the resulting object is still possible.

```
# trying nchar on a na.omit object
print(nchar(my.char))
```

```
## [1] 1 1 1 1 1 1 1
```

For other objects, however, this property may not hold. Some caution is advised.

3.6.3 Other Useful Functions for Treating `NA`

- **complete.cases** - Returns a logical vector indicating whether the lines of a bi-dimensional object only have non `NA` values that are complete rows. This function is used exclusively for data frames and matrices.

```
# create matrix
my.mat <- matrix(1:15, nrow = 5)

# set an NA value
my.mat[2,2] <- NA
```

```
# print index with rows without NA
print(complete.cases(my.mat))
```

```
## [1]  TRUE FALSE  TRUE  TRUE  TRUE
```

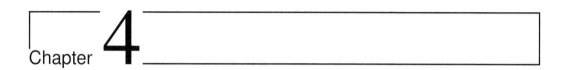

Chapter 4

Data Structure Objects

In chapter 3 we learned about the basic classes of objects in R. Together, the basic classes can represent a wide variety of data. When dealing with rich datasets, the number of created objects increases significantly. While you can work storing each information in each object, the code becomes messy. In practice, we organize our information in table like structures, with rows and columns, containing numeric or textual data. When we represent our dataset in a tabular format, the code using this data becomes simpler and more efficient. This is the main format of how raw data is imported into R.

In this section, we will present details about the classes that can store and organize our datasets, `lists`, `dataframes`, and `matrix`.

4.1 Lists

A `list` is a flexible object that can hold different types of objects. Unlike atomic vectors, a `list` has no restriction on the classes or types of elements. In the same `list` object, we can group `numeric` objects with `character` objects, `factor` with `Dates`, and even `lists` within `lists`. Each element of a list need not have the same length as the others. These properties make the `list` class the most flexible object in R. It is not by accident that most functions in R return an object of type `list`.

4.1.1 Creating lists

A list can be created with the `list` command, followed by their comma-separated elements:

119

```
# create a list with three elements
my.l <- list(1, c(1,2,3), c('a', 'b'))

# print result
print(my.l)
```

```
## [[1]]
## [1] 1
##
## [[2]]
## [1] 1 2 3
##
## [[3]]
## [1] "a" "b"
```

Notice how a `list` type object is printed differently than atomic vectors. The elements of the `list` are separated vertically and the content appears within double brackets (`[[ ]]`).

The elements of a `list` can also be named. This greatly facilitates working with `lists` because the names can give the user a hint about its content. An example:

```
# create named list
my.named.l <- list(ticker = 'ABC',
                   name.company = 'Company ABC',
                   price = c(1,1.5,2,2.3),
                   market = 'NYSE',
                   date.price = as.Date('2016-01-01')+0:3)

# print list
print(my.named.l)
```

```
## $ticker
## [1] "ABC"
##
## $name.company
## [1] "Company ABC"
##
## $price
## [1] 1.0 1.5 2.0 2.3
##
## $market
## [1] "NYSE"
##
```

```
## $date.price
## [1] "2016-01-01" "2016-01-02" "2016-01-03" "2016-01-04"
```

In this example, we have a named list with several elements with different classes and lengths. Each element provides different information about a company. We could use the same data structure for storing information in a large number of companies.

4.1.2 Accessing the Elements of a `list`

As mentioned, the individual elements of a `list` can be accessed with double brackets (`[[ ]]`), as in:

```
# set list
my.l <- list(2, 1:5, c('a', 'b'))

# print second element of my.l
print(my.l[[2]])
```

```
## [1] 1 2 3 4 5
```

```
# print third element of my.l
print(my.l[[3]])
```

```
## [1] "a" "b"
```

You can also access the elements of a `list` with simple brackets (`[]`), but be careful with this operation as the result will not be the element itself, but another `list`. This is an easy and common mistake to go unnoticed, resulting in errors in the code. See below:

```
# accessing list with [[ ]]
class(my.l[[2]])
```

```
## [1] "integer"
```

```
# accessing list with [ ]
class(my.l[2])
```

```
## [1] "list"
```

If we try to add an element to `my.l[2]`, we will receive an error message.

```
# adding an element to a list (WRONG)
my.l[2] + 1
```

```
## Error in my.l[2] + 1: non-numeric argument to binary operator
```

An error is returned because a `list` object cannot be summed with a `numeric` object. To fix it, simply use double brackets, as in `my.1[[2]] + 1`. Accessing elements of a list with simple brackets is only useful when looking for a sublist within a larger list. As an example, if we wanted to obtain the first and second elements of `my.1`, we would write:

```
# set new list with first and second element of my.l
my.new.l <- my.l[c(1,2)]

# print result
print(my.new.l)
```

```
## [[1]]
## [1] 2
##
## [[2]]
## [1] 1 2 3 4 5
```

Using its position to access elements of a `list` is not advised. The problem is, if you are working interactively with a `list`, the position of the elements may change as new data arrives. The best way of working with this object is to name each element. Here, the named elements can be accessed with the symbol `$` or `[['name']]`. This prevents errors because, by modifying the `list` and adding elements, you can change the order of elements, but not the names.

Next, we provide several examples of how to access the elements of a `list` using `$` and double brackets.

```
# accessing elements of a list using $
print(my.named.l$ticker)
```

```
## [1] "ABC"
```

```
print(my.named.l$price)
```

```
## [1] 1.0 1.5 2.0 2.3
```

```
# accessing elements of a list using [['name']]
print(my.named.l[['ticker']])
```

```
## [1] "ABC"
```

```
print(my.named.l[['price']])
```

```
## [1] 1.0 1.5 2.0 2.3
```

Another useful trick for working with lists is you can access all inner elements directly, in one line of code, by simply using consecutive brackets or names. See below:

```
my.l <- list(slot1 = c(num1 = 1, num2 = 2, num3 = 3),
             slot2 = c('a', 'b'))

# access the second value of the first element of my.l
print(my.l[[1]][2])

## num2
##    2
# access the first value of the second element of my.l
print(my.l[[2]][1])

## [1] "a"
# access the value 'num3' in 'slot1'
print(my.l[['slot1']]['num3'])

## num3
##    3
```

This operation is very useful when interested in a few elements within a larger object. It avoids the need for creating intermediate objects.

4.1.3   Adding and Removing Elements from a `list`

To add or replace elements in a `list`, just set the new object in the desired position:

```
# set list
my.l <- list('a',1,3)

# show it
print(my.l)

## [[1]]
## [1] "a"
##
## [[2]]
## [1] 1
##
## [[3]]
## [1] 3
# change value at position 4
my.l[[4]] <- c(1:5)
```

```
# change value at position 2
my.l[[2]] <- c('b')
```

```
# print result
print(my.l)
```

```
## [[1]]
## [1] "a"
##
## [[2]]
## [1] "b"
##
## [[3]]
## [1] 3
##
## [[4]]
## [1] 1 2 3 4 5
```

This operation is also possible with the use of names and $:

```
# set named list
my.l <- list(slot1 = 'a', slot2 = 5)
```

```
# print it
print(my.l)
```

```
## $slot1
## [1] "a"
##
## $slot2
## [1] 5
```

```
# add a new slot
my.l$slot3 <- 10
```

```
# print result
print(my.l)
```

```
## $slot1
## [1] "a"
##
## $slot2
## [1] 5
##
```

```
## $slot3
## [1] 10
```

To remove elements from a `list`, set the element to the reserved symbol `NULL`, as in:

```
# set list
my.l <- list(text = 'b', num1 = 2, num2 = 4)

# remove third element
my.l[[3]] <- NULL

# show result
print(my.l)
```

```
## $text
## [1] "b"
##
## $num1
## [1] 2
```

```
# remove element 'num1'
my.l$num1 <- NULL

# print result
print(my.l)
```

```
## $text
## [1] "b"
```

Another way of removing elements from a `list` is to use a negative index, which will exclude it from the returned object. See the next example, where we remove the second element of a `list` using a negative index.

```
# set list
my.l <- list(a=c(1,2), b='text')

# print my.l without second element
print(my.l[[-2]])
```

```
## [1] 1 2
```

As with atomic vectors, removing elements of a `list` can also be accomplished with logical conditions. See next:

```
# set list
my.l <- list(1, 2, 3, 4)
```

```
# remove all elements higher than 2
my.l[my.l > 2] <- NULL

# print result
print(my.l)
```

```
## [[1]]
## [1] 1
##
## [[2]]
## [1] 2
```

However, note this operation only works because all elements of my.l are numeric, and a logical test can be applied to all cases. If that is not possible for a particular element, R returns a NA value. See an example next:

```
# set list
my.l <- list(1, 2, 3, 4, 'a', 'b')

# print logical test (return NA value)
print(my.l > 2)
```

```
## [1] FALSE FALSE  TRUE  TRUE    NA    NA
```

4.1.4 Processing the Elements of a list

Important information about objects of the type list is that its elements can be processed and handled individually with specific functions. We will learn more about this topic in chapter 9. For now, it is important to give a summary of how that works.

As an example, consider a list of numeric vectors of different sizes, as follows:

```
# set list with different numerical vectors.
my.l.num <- list(c(1,2,3),
                 seq(1:50),
                 seq(-5,5, by=0.5))
```

Let's assume we wanted to calculate the average of each vector in my.l.num and store the result in an atomic vector. We could do this by calling the mean function to each element of the list, as in:

```
# calculate means
mean.1 <- mean(my.l.num[[1]])
```

```
mean.2 <- mean(my.l.num[[2]])
mean.3 <- mean(my.l.num[[3]])

# print result
print(c(mean.1, mean.2, mean.3))
```

```
## [1]  2.0 25.5  0.0
```

An easier, more elegant, and smarter way of doing that would be to use the `sapply` function. All you need is the name of the list and the name of the function used to process each element. See next:

```
# using sapply
my.mean <- sapply(my.l.num, mean)

# print result
print(my.mean)
```

```
## [1]  2.0 25.5  0.0
```

As expected, the result is identical to the previous example. Using function `sapply` is preferable, because it is more compact and efficient than the alternative - creating `mean.1`, and `mean.2` and `mean.3`. Notice the first example code only works for a `list` with three elements. If we had a fourth element and we wanted to keep this code structure, we would have to add a new line `mean.4 <- mean(my.l.num[[4]])` and modify the output command to `print <-c(mean.1, mean.2, mean.3, mean.4))`. Function `sapply` works the same way in `lists` of any size. If we had more elements in `my.l.num`, no modification is necessary in `my.mean <- sapply(my.l.num, mean)`, making it easier to extend the code for more information. By combining a flexible object, such as a `list`, and processing capabilities, performing extensive operations in many complex objects in R is easy.

This use of generic procedures is one of the premises of good and efficient programming practices. For the case of R, the rule is simple: always write code that is flexible to the size of your objects. The arrival of new data should never require modifications in the code. This is called the *DRY* rule (**don't repeat yourself**). If you are repeating codes, as in the previous example, certainly there is a more elegant and flexible solution that could be used. In R, there are several other functions for processing `lists`. These will be explained in greater detail in chapter 9.

4.1.5   Other Functions for Manipulating `lists`

- **unlist** - Returns the elements of a `list` in a single atomic vector.

```
# create list
my.named.l <- list(ticker = 'XXXX4',
                   price = c(1,1.5,2,3),
                   market = 'Bovespa')

# unlist its elements
my.unlisted <- unlist(my.named.l)

# print result
print(my.unlisted)
```

```
##    ticker    price1    price2    price3    price4    market
##    "XXXX4"       "1"     "1.5"       "2"       "3" "Bovespa"
```

```
class(my.unlisted)
```

```
## [1] "character"
```

- **as.list** - Converts an object to the `list` type.

```
# set atomic vector
my.x <- 10:13

# convert to list
my.x.as.list <- as.list(my.x)

# print result
print(my.x.as.list)
```

```
## [[1]]
## [1] 10
##
## [[2]]
## [1] 11
##
## [[3]]
## [1] 12
##
## [[4]]
## [1] 13
```

- **names** - Returns or defines the names of the elements of a `list`.

```
# set named list
my.l <- list(value1 = 1, value2 = 2, value3 = 3)
```

```r
# print its names
print(names(my.l))
```

```
## [1] "value1" "value2" "value3"
```

```r
# change its names
names(my.l) <- c('num1', 'num2', 'num3')
```

```r
# print result
print(my.l)
```

```
## $num1
## [1] 1
##
## $num2
## [1] 2
##
## $num3
## [1] 3
```

4.2 Matrices

As you may remember from your math classes, a matrix is a two-dimensional representation of numbers, arranged in rows and columns. Using matrices is a powerful way of representing numerical data in two dimensions, and in certain cases, matrix functions can simplify complex mathematical operations.

In R, matrix are objects with two dimensions, where all elements must have the same class. You can think of matrices as atomic vectors with one extra dimension. In matrices, lines and columns are named. When used correctly, `matrix` objects facilitate the storage and context of the data.

A simple example of using matrices in finance is the representation of stock prices over time. The row of the matrix represents the different dates, and the columns set each stock apart. An example is given next.

	AAP	COG	BLK	CAM
2010-01-04	40.38	46.23	238.58	43.43
2010-01-05	40.14	46.17	239.61	43.96
2010-01-06	40.49	45.97	234.67	44.26
2010-01-07	40.48	45.56	237.25	44.50
2010-01-08	40.64	45.46	238.92	44.86

AAP	COG	BLK	CAM

The above matrix could be created in R with the following code:

```
# set raw data with prices
raw.data <- c(40.38,   40.14,   40.49,   40.48,   40.64,
              46.23,   46.17,   45.97,   45.56,   45.46,
              238.58, 239.61, 234.67, 237.25, 238.92,
              43.43,   43.96,   44.26,   44.5,    44.86)

# create matrix
my.mat <- matrix(raw.data, nrow = 5, ncol = 4)
colnames(my.mat) <- c('AAP', 'COG', 'BLK', 'CAM')
rownames(my.mat) <- c("2010-01-04", "2010-01-05", "2010-01-06",
                      "2010-01-07", "2010-01-08")

# print result
print(my.mat)
```

```
##             AAP   COG    BLK   CAM
## 2010-01-04 40.38 46.23 238.58 43.43
## 2010-01-05 40.14 46.17 239.61 43.96
## 2010-01-06 40.49 45.97 234.67 44.26
## 2010-01-07 40.48 45.56 237.25 44.50
## 2010-01-08 40.64 45.46 238.92 44.86
```

That was a long code! But, do not worry. In practical situations, the financial data will be imported from an external source, a local file on your computer, or from the internet. Rare are the cases where actual data is typed in the editor.

In the previous example of creating a `matrix` object, we set the number of rows and columns explicitly with arguments `nrow = 4` and `ncol = 3`. The names of rows and columns are defined with functions `colnames` and `rownames`, using a left side notation as in `rownames(my.mat) <- c(...)`. Going further, we can also retrieve the names of rows and columns with the same functions:

```
# print the names of columns
print(colnames(my.mat))
```

```
## [1] "AAP" "COG" "BLK" "CAM"
```

```
# print the names of rows
print(rownames(my.mat))
```

```
## [1] "2010-01-04" "2010-01-05" "2010-01-06" "2010-01-07"
## [5] "2010-01-08"
```

After matrix `my.mat` is created, we have at our disposal all its numerical properties. A simple example of using matrix operations in finance is the calculation of the value of a portfolio. If an investor has 200 shares of AAP, 300 share of COG, 100 of BLK and 50 of CAM, the value of his portfolio over time can be calculated as follows:

$$V_t = \sum_{i=1}^{4} N_i P_{i,t}$$

In this formula, N_i is the number of shares purchased for each asset, and $P_{i,t}$ is the price of stock i at date t. This is a simple operation to be performed with a matrix multiplication. Translating the procedure to R code, we have:

```
# set vector with shares purchased
my.stocks <- as.matrix(c(200, 300, 100, 50), nrow = 4)

# get value of portfolio with matrix multiplication
my.port <- my.mat %*% my.stocks

# print result
print(my.port)
```

```
##                 [,1]
## 2010-01-04 47974.5
## 2010-01-05 48038.0
## 2010-01-06 47569.0
## 2010-01-07 47714.0
## 2010-01-08 47901.0
```

In this last example, we use symbol `%*%`, which does a matrix multiplication between two objects of the class `matrix`. The result shows the value of the portfolio over time, resulting in a small loss for the investor at the last date.

In R, a `matrix` type of object does not need to be composed of `numeric` values. You can also create matrices with `character` elements or other types. See the following examples:

```
# create matrix with character
my.mat.char <- matrix(rep(c('a','b','c'), 3),
                      nrow = 3,
                      ncol = 3)
```

```
# print it
print(my.mat.char)
```

```
##      [,1] [,2] [,3]
## [1,] "a"  "a"  "a"
## [2,] "b"  "b"  "b"
## [3,] "c"  "c"  "c"
```

Now with a `logic` type:

```
# create matrix with logical
my.mat.logical <- matrix(sample(c(TRUE,FALSE),
                                size = 3*3,
                                replace = TRUE),
                         nrow = 3,
                         ncol = 3)
```

```
# print it
print(my.mat.logical)
```

```
##       [,1]  [,2]  [,3]
## [1,]  TRUE FALSE  TRUE
## [2,] FALSE FALSE FALSE
## [3,]  TRUE FALSE  TRUE
```

This flexibility allows the user to expand the representation of two-dimensional data beyond numerical values.

4.2.1   Selecting Elements from a `matrix`

Following the same notation of atomic vector, you can select *pieces* of a `matrix` using indexing. A difference here is that matrices are two-dimensional objects, while atomic vectors are one-dimensional.[1] The extra dimension of matrices requires selecting elements not only by lines, but also by columns. The elements of an array can be accessed with notation [i, j] where i represents the row and j the column. See the following example:

```
# create matrix
my.mat <- matrix(1:9, nrow = 3)
```

---

[1]To avoid confusion, atomic vectors in R have no dimension attribute in the strict sense of the function. When using the `dim` function in an atomic vector, such as `dim(c(1,2,4))`, the result is `NULL`. Away from the computing environment, however, atomic vectors can be considered one-dimensional objects as it can only increases its size in one direction.

```
# display it
print(my.mat)
```

```
##      [,1] [,2] [,3]
## [1,]    1    4    7
## [2,]    2    5    8
## [3,]    3    6    9
```
```
# display element in [1,2]
print(my.mat[1,2])
```

```
## [1] 4
```

To select an entire row or column, simply leave a blank index, as in the following example:

```
# select all rows from column 2
print(my.mat[ , 2])
```

```
## [1] 4 5 6
```
```
# select all columns from row 1
print(my.mat[1, ])
```

```
## [1] 1 4 7
```

Notice the result of indexing is an atomic vector, not a `matrix`. If we wanted the extracted piece to maintain its `matrix` class, with vertical or horizontal orientation, we could force this conversion using functions `as.matrix` and `matrix`:

```
# force matrix conversion and print result
print(as.matrix(my.mat[ ,2]))
```

```
##      [,1]
## [1,]    4
## [2,]    5
## [3,]    6
```
```
# force matrix conversion for one row and print result
print(matrix(my.mat[1, ], nrow=1))
```

```
##      [,1] [,2] [,3]
## [1,]    1    4    7
```

Pieces of the `matrix` can also be selected using vectors. If we wanted a new `matrix` with all elements from the second row and first column to the third row and second column, we could use the following code:

```r
# select some elements and print it
print(my.mat[2:3,1:2])
```

```
##        [,1] [,2]
## [1,]    2    5
## [2,]    3    6
```

Finally, using logical tests to select elements of matrices is also possible. See next:

```r
# set matrix
my.mat <- matrix(1:9, nrow = 3)
```

```r
# print logical matrix where value is higher than 5
print(my.mat >5)
```

```
##        [,1]   [,2] [,3]
## [1,] FALSE FALSE TRUE
## [2,] FALSE FALSE TRUE
## [3,] FALSE  TRUE TRUE
```

```r
# print the result
print(my.mat[my.mat >5])
```

```
## [1] 6 7 8 9
```

4.2.2   Other Useful Functions for Manipulating Matrices

- **as.matrix** - Transforms raw data to a `matrix` object.

```r
# set matrix
my.mat <- as.matrix(1:5)
```

```r
# print it
print(my.mat)
```

```
##        [,1]
## [1,]    1
## [2,]    2
## [3,]    3
## [4,]    4
## [5,]    5
```

- **t** - Returns a transposed `matrix`.

```
# set matrix
my.mat <- matrix(seq(10,20, length.out = 6), nrow = 3)

# print it
print(my.mat)
```

```
##       [,1] [,2]
## [1,]   10   16
## [2,]   12   18
## [3,]   14   20
```

```
# transpose and print
print(t(my.mat))
```

```
##       [,1] [,2] [,3]
## [1,]   10   12   14
## [2,]   16   18   20
```

- **rbind** - Returns the merger (bind) of matrices, with row orientation.

```
# set matrices and print
my.mat.1 <- matrix(1:5, nrow = 1)
print(my.mat.1)
```

```
##       [,1] [,2] [,3] [,4] [,5]
## [1,]    1    2    3    4    5
```

```
my.mat.2 <- matrix(10:14, nrow = 1)
print(my.mat.2)
```

```
##       [,1] [,2] [,3] [,4] [,5]
## [1,]   10   11   12   13   14
```

```
# bind them together using the rows
my.rbind.mat <- rbind(my.mat.1, my.mat.2)

# print result
print(my.rbind.mat)
```

```
##       [,1] [,2] [,3] [,4] [,5]
## [1,]    1    2    3    4    5
## [2,]   10   11   12   13   14
```

- **cbind** - Returns the merger (bind) of matrices, with column orientation.

```
# set matrices and print
my.mat.1 <- matrix(1:4, nrow = 2)
```

```
print(my.mat.1)
```

```
##      [,1] [,2]
## [1,]    1    3
## [2,]    2    4
```

```
my.mat.2 <- matrix(10:13, nrow = 2)
print(my.mat.2)
```

```
##      [,1] [,2]
## [1,]   10   12
## [2,]   11   13
```

```
# bind them together using the columns
my.cbind.mat <- cbind(my.mat.1, my.mat.2)
```

```
# print the result
print(my.cbind.mat)
```

```
##      [,1] [,2] [,3] [,4]
## [1,]    1    3   10   12
## [2,]    2    4   11   13
```

- **rowMeans** - Returns the mean of a matrix, row wise.

```
# set matrix
my.mat <- matrix(1:9, nrow=3)
print(rowMeans(my.mat))
```

```
## [1] 4 5 6
```

- **colMeans** - Returns the mean of a matrix, column wise.

```
# set matrix
my.mat <- matrix(1:9, nrow=3)
print(colMeans(my.mat))
```

```
## [1] 2 5 8
```

4.3 Dataframes

In R, `dataframe` objects are the most used and most important to understand. In short, `dataframes` is a table with rows and columns. Its big difference from the `matrix` type is it allows for each column to have a different class. This flexibility makes the `dataframe` a better object to represent heterogeneous datasets. There is also a positive aspect of data organization. The tabular structure forces the data to be *paired*, where each row is a different data point and each data point has several pieces of information (columns). This simple data structure can accommodate an infinite variety of information. New data points increase the rows, and new information increases the columns.

Another positive aspect of using `dataframes` in R is that several functions expect a `dataframe` as input. For example, the data manipulation package `dplyr` and the graphical package `ggplot2` work from a `dataframe` only. Operations of importing and exporting information are mostly `dataframe` oriented. Without doubt, `dataframes` are at the centre of a series of functionalities in R, and they are one of the most important classes to learn. Most of the work in processing financial data will be related to this object.

4.3.1 Creating `dataframes`

As with other classes, the creation of a `dataframe` can be accomplished with a function with the same name, `data.frame`. In the next example, we use a `dataframe` to accommodate the financial data used before. Have a look:

```
# set ticker symbols as a vector
ticker <- c(rep('AAP',5), rep('COG', 5), rep('BLK', 5), rep('CAM',5))

# set a date vector
date <- as.Date(rep(c("2010-01-04", "2010-01-05", "2010-01-06",
                       "2010-01-07", "2010-01-08"), 4) )

# set prices
prices <- c(40.38,  40.14,  40.49,  40.48,  40.64,
            46.23,  46.17,  45.97,  45.56,  45.46,
            238.58, 239.61, 234.67, 237.25, 238.92,
            43.43,  43.96,  44.26,  44.5,   44.86)

# create dataframe
my.df <- data.frame(ticker = ticker,
                    date = date,
                    prices = prices)

# print result
print(my.df)

##    ticker       date prices
## 1     AAP 2010-01-04  40.38
```

```
## 2       AAP 2010-01-05   40.14
## 3       AAP 2010-01-06   40.49
## 4       AAP 2010-01-07   40.48
## 5       AAP 2010-01-08   40.64
## 6       COG 2010-01-04   46.23
## 7       COG 2010-01-05   46.17
## 8       COG 2010-01-06   45.97
## 9       COG 2010-01-07   45.56
## 10      COG 2010-01-08   45.46
## 11      BLK 2010-01-04  238.58
## 12      BLK 2010-01-05  239.61
## 13      BLK 2010-01-06  234.67
## 14      BLK 2010-01-07  237.25
## 15      BLK 2010-01-08  238.92
## 16      CAM 2010-01-04   43.43
## 17      CAM 2010-01-05   43.96
## 18      CAM 2010-01-06   44.26
## 19      CAM 2010-01-07   44.50
## 20      CAM 2010-01-08   44.86
```

We used function `rep` to replicate and facilitate the creation of the data for the `dataframe` object. Notice how all our data is now stored in a single object, facilitating access and organization of the resulting code. The content of `my.df` can be viewed in RStudio. To do so, click on the object name in the *environment* tab, top right of the screen. After that, a viewer will appear on the main screen of the program, as in 4.1.

The advantages of using the viewer is that you can explore the data and sort the columns easily, by just clicking in their names. For those who like to use the prompt, you can open the viewer with function `View`, as in `View(my.df)`.

4.3.2   Accessing Information from a `dataframe`

A `dataframe` object makes use of same commands and symbols used for object of type `matrix` and `list`. These functions are generic and can be customized for different objects, including user-created classes.

To find out the names of the columns of a `dataframe`, we have two functions, `names` and `colnames`, with the exact same behaviour:

```
# get names of columns with names
names(my.df)
```

```
## [1] "ticker" "date"    "prices"
```

Figure 4.1: Example of viewing a dataframe in RStudio

```
# get names of columns with colnames
colnames(my.df)
```

```
## [1] "ticker" "date"    "prices"
```

To access a particular column of a **dataframe**, we can use operator **$** or the name/position of the column with brackets. See next:

```
# get column ticker from my.df
my.ticker <- my.df$ticker
```

```
# get column price from my.df
my.prices <- my.df['prices']
```

```
# get second column from my.df
my.date <- my.df[ ,2]
```

```
# print the results
print(my.ticker)
```

```
##  [1] AAP AAP AAP AAP AAP COG COG COG COG COG BLK BLK BLK BLK
## [15] BLK CAM CAM CAM CAM CAM
## Levels: AAP BLK CAM COG
```

```
print(my.prices)
```

```
##     prices
## 1    40.38
## 2    40.14
## 3    40.49
## 4    40.48
## 5    40.64
## 6    46.23
## 7    46.17
## 8    45.97
## 9    45.56
## 10   45.46
## 11  238.58
## 12  239.61
## 13  234.67
## 14  237.25
## 15  238.92
## 16   43.43
## 17   43.96
## 18   44.26
## 19   44.50
## 20   44.86
```

```
print(my.date)
```

```
##  [1] "2010-01-04" "2010-01-05" "2010-01-06" "2010-01-07"
##  [5] "2010-01-08" "2010-01-04" "2010-01-05" "2010-01-06"
##  [9] "2010-01-07" "2010-01-08" "2010-01-04" "2010-01-05"
## [13] "2010-01-06" "2010-01-07" "2010-01-08" "2010-01-04"
## [17] "2010-01-05" "2010-01-06" "2010-01-07" "2010-01-08"
```

Another important piece of information about `dataframe` objects is, internally, they are stored as `lists`, where each element is a column. This is important because some properties of `lists` also work for `dataframes`. One example is using double bracket (`[[ ]]`) for selecting columns:

```
# select column in dataframe with list notation
print(my.df[[2]])
```

```
##  [1] "2010-01-04" "2010-01-05" "2010-01-06" "2010-01-07"
##  [5] "2010-01-08" "2010-01-04" "2010-01-05" "2010-01-06"
##  [9] "2010-01-07" "2010-01-08" "2010-01-04" "2010-01-05"
## [13] "2010-01-06" "2010-01-07" "2010-01-08" "2010-01-04"
```

```
## [17] "2010-01-05" "2010-01-06" "2010-01-07" "2010-01-08"
```

To access specific rows and columns of a **dataframe**, use single brackets together with atomic vectors that indicate positions:

```
# accessing rows 1:5, column 2
print(my.df[1:5, 2])
```

```
## [1] "2010-01-04" "2010-01-05" "2010-01-06" "2010-01-07"
## [5] "2010-01-08"
```

```
# accessing rows 1:5, columns 1 and 2
print(my.df[1:5, c(1,2)])
```

```
##   ticker       date
## 1    AAP 2010-01-04
## 2    AAP 2010-01-05
## 3    AAP 2010-01-06
## 4    AAP 2010-01-07
## 5    AAP 2010-01-08
```

```
# accessing rows 1:5, all columns
print(my.df[1:5, ])
```

```
##   ticker       date prices
## 1    AAP 2010-01-04  40.38
## 2    AAP 2010-01-05  40.14
## 3    AAP 2010-01-06  40.49
## 4    AAP 2010-01-07  40.48
## 5    AAP 2010-01-08  40.64
```

Column selection can also be performed using names. Look at the following example:

```
# selecting rows 1 to 3, columns 'ticker' and 'prices'
print(my.df[1:3, c('ticker','prices')])
```

```
##   ticker prices
## 1    AAP  40.38
## 2    AAP  40.14
## 3    AAP  40.49
```

4.3.3 Modifying a `dataframe`

To create a new column in a **dataframe**, simply allocate an atomic vector of any class with the same length as the number of rows in the existing **dataframe**. If we want to insert a sequence of values as a new column in `my.df`, we could do it as follows:

```
# add a sequence to my.df
my.df$my.seq <- 1:nrow(my.df)

# print result
print(my.df)
```

```
##    ticker       date prices my.seq
## 1     AAP 2010-01-04  40.38      1
## 2     AAP 2010-01-05  40.14      2
## 3     AAP 2010-01-06  40.49      3
## 4     AAP 2010-01-07  40.48      4
## 5     AAP 2010-01-08  40.64      5
## 6     COG 2010-01-04  46.23      6
## 7     COG 2010-01-05  46.17      7
## 8     COG 2010-01-06  45.97      8
## 9     COG 2010-01-07  45.56      9
## 10    COG 2010-01-08  45.46     10
## 11    BLK 2010-01-04 238.58     11
## 12    BLK 2010-01-05 239.61     12
## 13    BLK 2010-01-06 234.67     13
## 14    BLK 2010-01-07 237.25     14
## 15    BLK 2010-01-08 238.92     15
## 16    CAM 2010-01-04  43.43     16
## 17    CAM 2010-01-05  43.96     17
## 18    CAM 2010-01-06  44.26     18
## 19    CAM 2010-01-07  44.50     19
## 20    CAM 2010-01-08  44.86     20
```

You can also perform this modification of a `dataframe` with single brackets or the position of the new column:

```
# set new col by name
my.df['my.seq.2'] <- seq(1,100, length.out = nrow(my.df))

# set new col by position
my.df[[6]] <- seq(1,10, length.out = nrow(my.df))
print(my.df)
```

```
##    ticker       date prices my.seq   my.seq.2       V6
## 1     AAP 2010-01-04  40.38      1   1.000000 1.000000
## 2     AAP 2010-01-05  40.14      2   6.210526 1.473684
```

```
## 3     AAP 2010-01-06  40.49       3  11.421053  1.947368
## 4     AAP 2010-01-07  40.48       4  16.631579  2.421053
## 5     AAP 2010-01-08  40.64       5  21.842105  2.894737
## 6     COG 2010-01-04  46.23       6  27.052632  3.368421
## 7     COG 2010-01-05  46.17       7  32.263158  3.842105
## 8     COG 2010-01-06  45.97       8  37.473684  4.315789
## 9     COG 2010-01-07  45.56       9  42.684211  4.789474
## 10    COG 2010-01-08  45.46      10  47.894737  5.263158
## 11    BLK 2010-01-04 238.58      11  53.105263  5.736842
## 12    BLK 2010-01-05 239.61      12  58.315789  6.210526
## 13    BLK 2010-01-06 234.67      13  63.526316  6.684211
## 14    BLK 2010-01-07 237.25      14  68.736842  7.157895
## 15    BLK 2010-01-08 238.92      15  73.947368  7.631579
## 16    CAM 2010-01-04  43.43      16  79.157895  8.105263
## 17    CAM 2010-01-05  43.96      17  84.368421  8.578947
## 18    CAM 2010-01-06  44.26      18  89.578947  9.052632
## 19    CAM 2010-01-07  44.50      19  94.789474  9.526316
## 20    CAM 2010-01-08  44.86      20 100.000000 10.000000
```

When using column position for setting a new column into a `dataframe`, its name becomes V6, i.e. *variable 6*. In R, when no name is entered by the user, this is the default allocation. However, it is always good policy to name all columns of the `dataframe` with some hint to its content. As for columns that will not be used, simply remove them prior to processing. In our example, we can rename the columns using function `colnames`:

```
# rename colnames
colnames(my.df) <- c('ticker', 'date', 'prices',
                     'my.seq', 'my.seq.2', 'my.seq.3')

# print result
print(my.df)
```

```
##    ticker       date prices my.seq   my.seq.2  my.seq.3
## 1     AAP 2010-01-04  40.38      1   1.000000  1.000000
## 2     AAP 2010-01-05  40.14      2   6.210526  1.473684
## 3     AAP 2010-01-06  40.49      3  11.421053  1.947368
## 4     AAP 2010-01-07  40.48      4  16.631579  2.421053
## 5     AAP 2010-01-08  40.64      5  21.842105  2.894737
## 6     COG 2010-01-04  46.23      6  27.052632  3.368421
## 7     COG 2010-01-05  46.17      7  32.263158  3.842105
## 8     COG 2010-01-06  45.97      8  37.473684  4.315789
## 9     COG 2010-01-07  45.56      9  42.684211  4.789474
## 10    COG 2010-01-08  45.46     10  47.894737  5.263158
```

```
## 11     BLK 2010-01-04 238.58       11  53.105263  5.736842
## 12     BLK 2010-01-05 239.61       12  58.315789  6.210526
## 13     BLK 2010-01-06 234.67       13  63.526316  6.684211
## 14     BLK 2010-01-07 237.25       14  68.736842  7.157895
## 15     BLK 2010-01-08 238.92       15  73.947368  7.631579
## 16     CAM 2010-01-04  43.43       16  79.157895  8.105263
## 17     CAM 2010-01-05  43.96       17  84.368421  8.578947
## 18     CAM 2010-01-06  44.26       18  89.578947  9.052632
## 19     CAM 2010-01-07  44.50       19  94.789474  9.526316
## 20     CAM 2010-01-08  44.86       20 100.000000 10.000000
```

R allows using spaces in the names of columns. If we wanted a column to be named My Column 1, you could set it as:

```
# set df
temp.df <- data.frame('My Column 1' = runif(5), check.names=FALSE)


# set columns name "My Column 2" with grave accent
temp.df$`My column 2` <- runif(5)


# set columns name "My Column 3" with apostrophe
temp.df$'My column 3' <- runif(5)


#print result
print(temp.df)


##    My Column 1 My column 2 My column 3
## 1    0.3151841  0.55032776   0.1472167
## 2    0.2826696  0.64836951   0.8223904
## 3    0.7131957  0.23478670   0.4135184
## 4    0.8621379  0.07629721   0.6125206
## 5    0.1063235  0.92309504   0.0681205
```

Within function data.frame, we need to use check.names=FALSE for custom column names, otherwise the spaces in the are converted to dots. When using $ or brackets, we use the grave accent and apostrophe to encapsulate the column name. You can access the custom column using the same notation or with brackets (temp.df['My column 1']). This is a great feature because it allows us to create the final version of tables directly in R. We set the names of the columns as they should appear in the final version of the report and export the dataframe to a spreadsheet-like tool. Within this software, you can format your table to your needs and later export it to the final report. In later section, we will discuss a more elegant way of exporting tables from R using specialized packages.

To remove the columns of a dataframe, just set the column to a NULL value:

```
# removing columns
my.df$my.seq <- NULL
my.df$my.seq.2 <- NULL
my.df$my.seq.3 <- NULL
my.df$V6 <- NULL

# print final result
print(my.df[1:5, ])
```

```
##   ticker       date prices
## 1    AAP 2010-01-04  40.38
## 2    AAP 2010-01-05  40.14
## 3    AAP 2010-01-06  40.49
## 4    AAP 2010-01-07  40.48
## 5    AAP 2010-01-08  40.64
```

You can also remove columns using negative indices. For example, in the following code, we create a new **dataframe** without the first and third columns of `my.df`:

```
# create new dataframe without cols 1 and 3 of my.df
new.df <- my.df[ ,c(-1,-3)]

# print result
print(new.df)
```

```
##  [1] "2010-01-04" "2010-01-05" "2010-01-06" "2010-01-07"
##  [5] "2010-01-08" "2010-01-04" "2010-01-05" "2010-01-06"
##  [9] "2010-01-07" "2010-01-08" "2010-01-04" "2010-01-05"
## [13] "2010-01-06" "2010-01-07" "2010-01-08" "2010-01-04"
## [17] "2010-01-05" "2010-01-06" "2010-01-07" "2010-01-08"
```

Just as we have done for matrices, indexing **dataframes** with a logical condition is also possible. If we are only interested in stock AAP, we can create a new **dataframe** by selecting the rows where information for this stock is found:

```
# set logical index for selecting data about stock
my.idx <- my.df$ticker == 'AAP'

# create new df with index
my.df.stock <- my.df[my.idx, ]

# print result
print(my.df.stock)
```

```
##   ticker       date prices
```

```
## 1      AAP 2010-01-04   40.38
## 2      AAP 2010-01-05   40.14
## 3      AAP 2010-01-06   40.49
## 4      AAP 2010-01-07   40.48
## 5      AAP 2010-01-08   40.64
```

We can also interact different columns using logical objects. If we wanted to find out the date where the stock had its highest historical value, we can use the following code:

```
# find index with which.max
my.idx <- which.max(my.df.stock$price)

# get date
my.date <- my.df.stock$date[my.idx]

# print result
print(my.date)
```

```
## [1] "2010-01-08"
```

Therefore, in our dataset, the highest price of stock AAP was 40.64, and it happened in date 2010-01-08.

4.3.4   Sorting a dataframe

After creating or importing a dataframe, you can sort its rows according to the values of any column. A common case where a sort operation is needed is when financial data is imported, but the dates are not ascending. Depending on the situation, it may be easier (or expected) to deal with data where the dates are always increasing along the rows. The sorting operation in dataframes is performed using function order.

Consider creating a data.frame with the following values:

```
# set new df
my.df <- data.frame(col1 = c(4,1,2),
                    col2 = c(1,1,3),
                    col3 = c('a','b','c'))

# print it
print(my.df)
```

```
##   col1 col2 col3
## 1    4    1    a
```

```
## 2    1    1    b
## 3    2    3    c
```

Function `order` returns the position of the elements for the sorted vector. With the first column of `my.df`, the positions of the elements in an ascending order are:

```
# set index with positions of ascending order in col1
idx <- order(my.df$col1)

# print it
print(idx)
```

```
## [1] 2 3 1
```

Therefore, when using the output of function `order` as an index of an existing `dataframe`, you get a new version of the `dataframe`, where all rows are set according to the ascending values of a particular column. See next:

```
# order my.df by col1
my.df.2 <- my.df[order(my.df$col1), ]

# print result
print(my.df.2)
```

```
##   col1 col2 col3
## 2    1    1    b
## 3    2    3    c
## 1    4    1    a
```

This operation may also be performed considering more than one column. See the following example, where we sort the rows of `my.df` using columns `col2` and `col1`.

```
# sort df with col2 and col1
my.df.3 <- my.df[order(my.df$col2, my.df$col1), ]

# print result
print(my.df.3)
```

```
##   col1 col2 col3
## 2    1    1    b
## 1    4    1    a
## 3    2    3    c
```

4.3.5   Combining and Aggregating `dataframes`

Sometimes, it is necessary to join different **dataframes**. This usually happens when the data is imported from different sources, and we need to combine them into a single object in R. In the simplest case of combining data frames, we join them according to the rows (vertically) or columns (horizontally). For that, we have functions `rbind` (row bind) and `cbind` (column bind). Examples of usage are given next.

```
# set two dfs with same colnames
my.df.1 <- data.frame(col1 = 1:5, col2 = rep('a', 5))
my.df.2 <- data.frame(col1 = 6:10, col2 = rep('b', 5))

# bind them by rows
my.df <- rbind(my.df.1, my.df.2)

# print result
print(my.df)
```

```
##      col1 col2
## 1      1    a
## 2      2    a
## 3      3    a
## 4      4    a
## 5      5    a
## 6      6    b
## 7      7    b
## 8      8    b
## 9      9    b
## 10    10    b
```

Notice, in the previous example, the names of the columns are the same. Function `rbind` searches for equal names in both **dataframes**. This means, if we swapped the positions of the columns, there would be no change in the result of the bind operation. If the names of the columns don't match, an error is returned. See next:

```
# set two df with different colnames
my.df.1 <- data.frame(col1 = 1:5,
                       col2 = rep('a', 5))
my.df.2 <- data.frame(col1 = 6:10,
                       col3 = rep('b', 5))

# bind them by rows (ERROR)
my.df <- rbind(my.df.1, my.df.2)
```

```
## ##Error in match.names(clabs, names(xi)) :
##   names do not match previous names
```

In the case where you have various `dataframes` with different column names and a row bind operation is necessary, one solution is to use function `bind_rows` of package `dplyr`, which places `NA` values whenever a missing column is found. Have a look:

```r
# load package
library(dplyr)

# bind them by rows
my.df <- bind_rows(my.df.1,
                   my.df.2)

# print result (NAs where there should be a column)
print(my.df)
```

```
##      col1 col2
## 1      1    a
## 2      2    a
## 3      3    a
## 4      4    a
## 5      5    a
## 6      6    b
## 7      7    b
## 8      8    b
## 9      9    b
## 10    10    b
```

For the case of column bind with function `cbind`, the names of the columns must be different, but the number of rows must be the same. See an example next.

```r
# set two dfs
my.df.1 <- data.frame(col1 = 1:5, col2 = rep('a', 5))
my.df.2 <- data.frame(col3 = 6:10, col4 = rep('b', 5))

# column bind dfs
my.df <- cbind(my.df.1, my.df.2)

# print result
print(my.df)
```

```
##   col1 col2 col3 col4
## 1    1    a    6    b
## 2    2    a    7    b
```

```
## 3     3     a     8     b
## 4     4     a     9     b
## 5     5     a    10     b
```

If the number of rows don't match, an error is returned by cbind. But, if the names of columns are the same, the function still accepts the inputs. Have a look:

```
# set two dfs with same name in one
my.df.1 <- data.frame(col1 = 1:5, col2 = rep('a', 5))
my.df.2 <- data.frame(col1 = 6:10)

# column bind dfs
my.df <- cbind(my.df.1, my.df.2)

# print result (!)
print(my.df)
```

```
##    col1 col2 col1
## 1     1     a     6
## 2     2     a     7
## 3     3     a     8
## 4     4     a     9
## 5     5     a    10
```

Yes, we have two columns named col1, but in different positions. If we accessed my.df$col1, it returns the first column. This is a strange behaviour of R. You should pay attention to these cases to avoid bugs in the code.

For more complex cases, where the binding process must happen according to some index, such as dates, it is possible to combine two dataframes using function merge:

```
# set dfs
my.df.1 <- data.frame(date = as.Date('2016-01-01')+0:10,
                      x = 1:11)

my.df.2 <- data.frame(date = as.Date('2016-01-05')+0:10,
                      y = seq(20,30, length.out = 11))

# merge dfs by date
my.df <- merge(my.df.1, my.df.2, by = 'date')

# print result
print(my.df)
```

```
##          date  x  y
## 1 2016-01-05  5 20
## 2 2016-01-06  6 21
## 3 2016-01-07  7 22
## 4 2016-01-08  8 23
## 5 2016-01-09  9 24
## 6 2016-01-10 10 25
## 7 2016-01-11 11 26
```

From the result, we can see the resulting `dataframe` retained only the information shared between the two objects, the rows where columns `date` are equal in both `dataframes`.

Another usefull function is `match`, which does a look up operation in vectors. For example, if we wanted to find the indices in `my.df.2` that match the dates in `my.df.1`, we can write:

```
# set lookup index
idx <- match(my.df.1$date, my.df.2$date)

# print result
print(idx)
```

```
##  [1] NA NA NA NA  1  2  3  4  5  6  7
```

Now we can use the index to set a new column in `my.df.1` with data from `my.df.2`:

```
# use idx to set col in my.df.1
my.df.1$y.2 <- my.df.2$y[idx]

# print result
print(my.df.1)
```

```
##           date  x y.2
## 1  2016-01-01  1  NA
## 2  2016-01-02  2  NA
## 3  2016-01-03  3  NA
## 4  2016-01-04  4  NA
## 5  2016-01-05  5  20
## 6  2016-01-06  6  21
## 7  2016-01-07  7  22
## 8  2016-01-08  8  23
## 9  2016-01-09  9  24
## 10 2016-01-10 10  25
## 11 2016-01-11 11  26
```

A different from the use of `merge` is that `NA` values are set where there is not matching date.

4.3.6   Reporting a Dataframe Table

`Dataframes` can be used to represent and export tables to text editing softwares, such as Word and LaTeX. The simplest way of exporting a table from a `dataframe` object is to write it in a spreadsheet-like tool, format it, and export the final version to the report. Specific packages can write a `dataframe` table in an Excel file. We will study these packages in chapter 6.

A more elaborate way is to remove the middle man and export the table directly from R to a LaTeX or Word file. Let's start with an example for LaTeX. In the next chunk of code, we will create a print-ready table as a `dataframe` and export it to a LaTeX file using package `xtable`.

```
# set number of rows in table
N = 10

# create artifitial data
set.seed(20)
my.returns <- matrix(rnorm(50*N), ncol = N)

# set columns of df
my.names <- paste('Stock',1:N)
my.mean.return <- colMeans(my.returns)
my.sd.return <- apply(my.returns, sd, MARGIN = 2)
my.max.return <- apply(my.returns, max, MARGIN = 2)
my.min.return <- apply(my.returns, min, MARGIN = 2)

# set table
my.table <- data.frame('Stocks' = my.names,
                       'Mean Ret.' = my.mean.return,
                       'StDev. of Ret.' = my.sd.return,
                       'Max. Ret.' = my.max.return,
                       'Min. Ret.' = my.min.return,
                       check.names = F)
```

The artificial data was set as a `matrix` object containing random values from the Normal distribution. Each stock has its returns as a column in `my.returns`. Several statistics for each column are calculated using function `apply`. This function allows the user to apply a procedure to several columns of a `matrix`. We will study it further in chapter 9.

In the creation of the `dataframe`, notice how we used column names with space by encapsulating the text with apostrophes. It was also necessary to use input `check.names = FALSE`, so R does not change the original name of the columns. Now that we have our data, let's export it to LaTeX.

```
library(xtable)

# set xtable object
my.xtable <- xtable(x = my.table,
                    label = 'tab:DescRetStats',
                    caption = 'Descriptive Statistics for Returns')

# check if folder exists
if (!dir.exists('tabs')) {
    dir.create('tabs')
}

# print output to latex file
my.f.tex <- 'tabs/MyTable.tex'

# save it
print(my.xtable,
      include.rownames = FALSE,
      file = my.f.tex,
      type='latex')
```

In function `xtable`, we kept it simple by only using arguments `caption` and `label`. The resulting LaTeX file is saved in folder `tabs` of the current directory. If it doesn't exist, you can create it with `dir.create('tabs')`. There are many more options for customization. The result in a compiled latex file will be identical to 4.2, a print-ready material for an scientific article or report.

Another interesting package worth mentioning at this stage is **stargazer**. Like **texreg**, it provides many options for customizing a table and exporting it. One innovation over **texreg** is it offers templates for journals, such as a table template for *American Economic Review, Quarterly Journal of Economics*, and others. Let's give it a try by replicating the previous table. In the next code, we again use object `my.table` to export a LaTeX table. The result is reported in 4.3.

```
library(stargazer)

my.stargazer <- stargazer(my.table,
                          summary = FALSE,
                          title = 'Descriptive Statistics for Returns',
```

Stocks	Mean Ret.	StDev. of Ret.	Max. Ret.	Min. Ret.
Stock 1	-0.16	1.04	1.79	-2.89
Stock 2	0.17	0.92	2.21	-1.97
Stock 3	0.04	1.01	1.92	-1.79
Stock 4	0.14	1.01	1.76	-1.79
Stock 5	-0.04	1.18	2.93	-2.31
Stock 6	0.11	0.94	2.25	-2.52
Stock 7	0.00	0.86	2.02	-2.63
Stock 8	-0.27	1.04	1.76	-2.65
Stock 9	-0.04	0.89	2.16	-1.45
Stock 10	0.03	1.06	2.74	-2.17

Figure 4.2: Example of table with xtable

```
type = 'latex',
style = 'qje',
font.size = 'footnotesize',
rownames = FALSE,
out.header = FALSE,
header = FALSE,
label = 'tab:DescRetStats_stargazer' )
```

Stocks	Mean Ret.	StDev. of Ret.	Max. Ret.	Min. Ret.
Stock 1	-0.160	1.042	1.785	-2.890
Stock 2	0.170	0.915	2.208	-1.968
Stock 3	0.043	1.006	1.916	-1.789
Stock 4	0.137	1.007	1.759	-1.793
Stock 5	-0.043	1.178	2.932	-2.310
Stock 6	0.108	0.937	2.246	-2.520
Stock 7	0.002	0.862	2.022	-2.633
Stock 8	-0.270	1.045	1.756	-2.646
Stock 9	-0.040	0.890	2.160	-1.447
Stock 10	0.034	1.057	2.738	-2.175

Figure 4.3: Example of table with stargazer

As for exporting tables to Word (Microsoft) or Writer (Libreoffice) files, there is no direct way of doing so using xtable or stargazer. But, a simple workaround is to use either package to output a table to a temporary *.html* or *.doc* file and then copy and paste the result in the final report. This operation works because *.html* and *.doc* files share a similar format for tables. Let's try it. First, we will save the table in a new file with the *.html* extension:

```
# set html file for output
my.f.html <- 'tabs/MyTable.html'

# write it!
print(x = my.xtable,
      file = my.f.html,
      type = 'html',
      include.rownames = FALSE )
```

Once the file is available, we can open tabs/MyTable.html with any web browser, select and copy the table and, finally, paste it in our *.docx* document. The result should look like Figure 4.4.

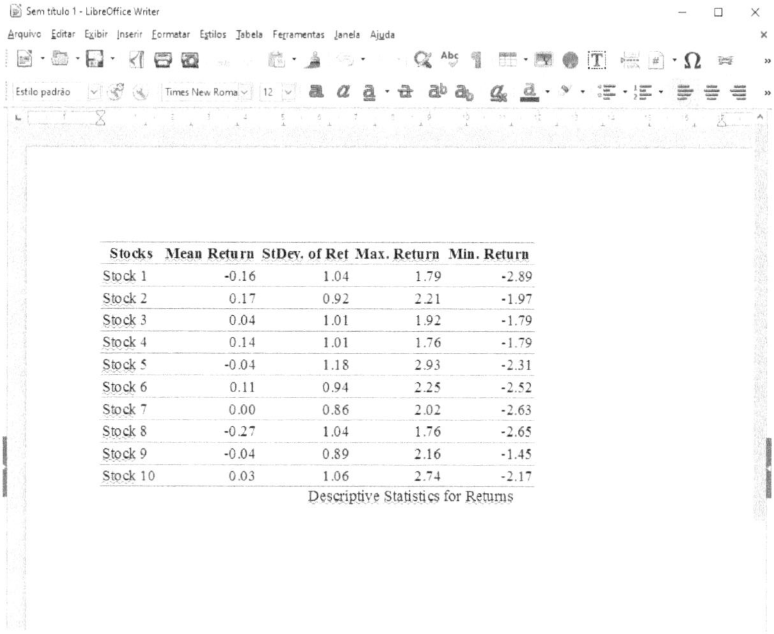

Figure 4.4: Example of table in Writer (LibreOffice)

If you deal with lots of figures and tables in *.docx* (Word/Writer) or *.ppt* (Power-point/Impress) files, packages `knitr` (Xie, 2015) and `ReporteRs` (Gohel, 2017) can save you a lot of time and effort. Both have extensive capabilities of automating the process of creating reports.

4.3.7 The Format of the `dataframe` (*long* and *wide*)

After understanding the basics of `dataframe` manipulation, it is important to discuss the format of the object and how it facilitates future work. This is a relatively new topic that came up with the introduction of specific packages for data manipulation and graphics. At the heart of the debate, we discuss whether the data should be guided by columns (*wide* format) or lines (*long* format).

In the wide format, the rows are usually indexed by a single factor, such as a date, and the columns indicate the different variables. As new information is added to the database, it usually grows in the number of columns. An example:

refdate	STOCK1	STOCK2	STOCK3
2017-05-06	10.02	3.15	5.19
2017-05-07	9.79	3.34	5.06
2017-05-08	8.08	2.74	5.61
2017-05-09	7.33	2.56	5.99

Note, the above table has three distinct pieces of information for each data point: ticker, price, and date. If we added one more stock, the table would be incremented by one column. If we wanted to include a new variable such as traded volume, we would need to create a new table or a structured naming system for the columns.

In the long format, each row of the `dataframe` is new information and each column is a variable. Table rows may or may not be unique (does not repeat). As new data is added, the table usually grows in the number of rows. Example:

refdate	ticker	price
2017-05-06	STOCK1	10.02
2017-05-07	STOCK1	9.79
2017-05-08	STOCK1	8.08
2017-05-09	STOCK1	7.33
2017-05-06	STOCK2	3.15
2017-05-07	STOCK2	3.34
2017-05-08	STOCK2	2.74
2017-05-09	STOCK2	2.56
2017-05-06	STOCK3	5.19
2017-05-07	STOCK3	5.06
2017-05-08	STOCK3	5.61
2017-05-09	STOCK3	5.99

This argument may seem trivial since the information is the same in both formats. But, make no mistake: the format of the data is very important and may facilitate the analysis of the data. Specialized packages, such as `dplyr` (Wickham and Francois, 2016) and `ggplot2` (Wickham, 2009), expect a `dataframe` in the *long* format; therefore, this structure must be prioritized if one is using these packages.

In finance, the wide format is used in the creation and manipulation of investment portfolios with the creation of a matrix of returns. This matrix separates the different assets by columns and rows representing different time periods. Each value in the matrix is the return (percent change) of a particular asset from one period to the other. The wide format is justified as the matrix notation facilitates matrix calculations. I emphasize, however, these same calculations could also be performed with the *long* format. Conversion between formats is also possible, as we will see next.

4.3.7.1 Converting a `dataframe` Structure (long and wide)

The conversion from one format to the other is possible with the `tidyr` package (Wickham, 2016c). See the following example, where we change the *wide* format of the previous table for the *long* format using function `gather`. Here, it is necessary to know the variable `id` that will index the lines (in this case, the dates) and the names of the new columns.

```
library(tidyr)

# set dates and stock vectors
refdate <- as.Date('2015-01-01') + 0:3
STOCK1 <- c(10, 11, 10.5, 12)
STOCK2 <- c(3, 3.1, 3.2, 3.5)
STOCK3 <- c(6, 7, 7.5, 6)

# create wide dataframe
my.df.wide <- data.frame(refdate, STOCK1, STOCK2, STOCK3)

# convert wide to long
my.df.long <- gather(data = my.df.wide,
                     key = 'ticker',
                     value = 'price',
                     - refdate)

# print result
print(my.df.long)

##          refdate ticker price
## 1     2015-01-01 STOCK1  10.0
## 2     2015-01-02 STOCK1  11.0
## 3     2015-01-03 STOCK1  10.5
## 4     2015-01-04 STOCK1  12.0
## 5     2015-01-01 STOCK2   3.0
## 6     2015-01-02 STOCK2   3.1
```

```
## 7   2015-01-03 STOCK2    3.2
## 8   2015-01-04 STOCK2    3.5
## 9   2015-01-01 STOCK3    6.0
## 10 2015-01-02 STOCK3    7.0
## 11 2015-01-03 STOCK3    7.5
## 12 2015-01-04 STOCK3    6.0
```

To perform the reverse conversion, *long* to *wide*, we can use the **spread** function from the same package, **tidyr**:

```
# convert from long to wide
my.df.wide.converted <- spread(data = my.df.long,
                               key = 'ticker',
                               value = 'price')


# print result
print(my.df.wide.converted)
```

```
##       refdate STOCK1 STOCK2 STOCK3
## 1 2015-01-01   10.0    3.0    6.0
## 2 2015-01-02   11.0    3.1    7.0
## 3 2015-01-03   10.5    3.2    7.5
## 4 2015-01-04   12.0    3.5    6.0
```

With more complex conversions, where it is necessary to aggregate some variables, I recommend package **reshape2** (Wickham, 2007), which offers more features than **tidyr**. The syntax, however, is different. See the following code, where we use the functions of the package **reshape2** for the same procedure performed previously.

```
library(reshape2)


# use melt to change from wide to long
my.df.long <- melt(data = my.df.wide,
                   id.vars = 'refdate',
                   variable.name = 'ticker',
                   value.name = 'price')


# print result
print(my.df.long)
```

```
##       refdate ticker price
## 1   2015-01-01 STOCK1  10.0
## 2   2015-01-02 STOCK1  11.0
## 3   2015-01-03 STOCK1  10.5
## 4   2015-01-04 STOCK1  12.0
```

```
## 5  2015-01-01 STOCK2    3.0
## 6  2015-01-02 STOCK2    3.1
## 7  2015-01-03 STOCK2    3.2
## 8  2015-01-04 STOCK2    3.5
## 9  2015-01-01 STOCK3    6.0
## 10 2015-01-02 STOCK3    7.0
## 11 2015-01-03 STOCK3    7.5
## 12 2015-01-04 STOCK3    6.0
```

```
# use melt to change from long to wide
my.df.wide.converted <- dcast(data = my.df.long,
                              formula = refdate ~ ticker,
                              value.var = 'price')
print(my.df.wide.converted)
```

```
##      refdate STOCK1 STOCK2 STOCK3
## 1 2015-01-01   10.0    3.0    6.0
## 2 2015-01-02   11.0    3.1    7.0
## 3 2015-01-03   10.5    3.2    7.5
## 4 2015-01-04   12.0    3.5    6.0
```

It is important to know these functions when working with R, because often, the researcher has no control over the format of the imported data. When necessary, convert the data to the *long* format after importing it. This will facilitate the further processing of the data with specialized packages.

4.3.8   Extensions of the `dataframe` Class

As mentioned in the previous chapter, one of the benefits of using R is the existence of packages designed to deal with specific problems. This is also true for extensions of the basic data structure. While the `dataframe` class is a good solution for most cases, sometimes, it can make more sense to store the data in a specific type of custom object. Over time, several solutions that improve the base `dataframe` have been developed.

For example, it is common in research to work with numeric data indexed by time. We can store this dataset in a matrix format, so each line represents dates and each column represents a variable. With this format, time operations, such as period aggregations, are easier to perform. This is the main idea of package `xts` (Ryan and Ulrich, 2014). The great benefit of this alternative `dataframe` is that several functions for time aggregation and manipulation are available. We can turn a whole set of daily data for several variables to the weekly frequency in one line of code. In addition, various other functions automatically recognize the time index and adapt accordingly. One example is the creation of a figure with the values of a variable over time. The horizontal axes of the figure are automatically arranged as dates, without the need of an explicit definition.

See the following example, where we represent the same stock data as a **xts** object:

```
# load pkg
library(xts)

# set ticker symbols as a vector
ticker <- c('AAP', 'COG', 'BLK', 'CAM')

# set a date vector
date <- as.Date(c("2010-01-04", "2010-01-05", "2010-01-06",
                   "2010-01-07", "2010-01-08"))

# set prices as  matrix
price.mat <- matrix(c(40.38,   40.13,   40.49,   40.48,   40.63,
                      46.23,   46.16,   45.97,   45.56,   45.45,
                      238.58, 239.61, 234.66, 237.25, 238.91,
                      43.43,   43.95,   44.25,   44.5,    44.86),
                    nrow = length(date))

# set xts object
my.xts <- xts(price.mat, order.by = date)

# set colnames
colnames(my.xts) <- ticker

# print it
print(my.xts)
```

```
##               AAP    COG    BLK    CAM
## 2010-01-04 40.38 46.23 238.58 43.43
## 2010-01-05 40.13 46.16 239.61 43.95
## 2010-01-06 40.49 45.97 234.66 44.25
## 2010-01-07 40.48 45.56 237.25 44.50
## 2010-01-08 40.63 45.45 238.91 44.86
```

```
# show its class
class(my.xts)
```

```
## [1] "xts" "zoo"
```

In creating the `xts` object, notice how the time index is explicitly defined using argument `order.by`. This is a necessary step in creating every `xts` object.

The previous code can give the impression that object `my.xts` is similar to a native `dataframe`. However, make no mistake. By having an explicit time index, object `my.xts` can be used for several temporal procedures. See the following example, where we create a new `xts` object with two columns and calculate their average for each week.

```
# set number of time periods
N <- 500

# create matrix with data
my.mat <- matrix(c(seq(1, N), seq(N, 1)), nrow=N)

# set xts object
my.xts <- xts(my.mat, order.by = as.Date('2016-01-01')+1:N)

# apply mean function for each weel
my.xts.weekly.mean <- apply.weekly(my.xts, mean)

# print result
print(head(my.xts.weekly.mean))

##                [,1]  [,2]
## 2016-01-03   1.5  499.5
## 2016-01-10   6.0  495.0
## 2016-01-17  13.0  488.0
## 2016-01-24  20.0  481.0
## 2016-01-31  27.0  474.0
## 2016-02-07  34.0  467.0
```

In finance, these time aggregations with `xts` objects are useful when working with data in different time frequencies. It is common to aggregate transaction data in the financial market for high frequency intervals of 5 by 5 minutes. Such procedure is easily accomplished in R through the correct representation of the data as `xts` objects. There are several other features in this package. Users that work frequently with time indexed data are encouraged to read the manual and learn more about it.

Package `xts` is not alone as an alternative to `dataframes`. For example, the data structure proposed by package `data.table` (Dowle et al., 2015) prioritizes processing time and using a compact notation. Package `dplyr` (Wickham and Francois, 2016) and `tibble` (Wickham et al., 2017) also provide alternatives to the native `dataframe` with similar goals. If the user is working with large-scale datasets, using these packages is strongly recommended. Throughout the book, whenever needed, we will work with these packages for fast data processing and easier notation. The use of package `dplyr` will be discussed in chapter 9.

Most basic functions of accessing and handling `dataframes` work equivalently for these alternative objects. So, everything you learned before can be used in the same way for other types of tabular data structures.

4.3.9   Other Useful Functions for Handling `dataframes`

- **head** Returns the first n rows of a `dataframe`. This function is mostly used for showing only a small part of a `dataframe` in the prompt.

```
# set df
my.df <- data.frame(col1 = 1:5000, col2 = rep('a', 5000))

# print its first 5 rows
print(head(my.df, 5))
```

```
##   col1 col2
## 1    1    a
## 2    2    a
## 3    3    a
## 4    4    a
## 5    5    a
```

- **tail** - Returns the last n rows of a `dataframe`. Also used to glimpse a `dataframe`.

```
# print its last 5 rows
print(tail(my.df, 5))
```

```
##        col1 col2
## 4996 4996    a
## 4997 4997    a
## 4998 4998    a
## 4999 4999    a
## 5000 5000    a
```

- **complete.cases** - Returns a logical vector with the same length as the number of rows of the `dataframe`, containing `TRUE` when all columns have non `NA` values and `FALSE` otherwise.

```
# create df
my.df <- data.frame(x = c(1:5, NA, 10),
                    y = c(5:10, NA))
```

```
# show df
print(my.df)
```

```
##     x  y
## 1   1  5
## 2   2  6
## 3   3  7
## 4   4  8
## 5   5  9
## 6 NA 10
## 7 10 NA
```

```
# print logical test of complete.cases
print(complete.cases(my.df))
```

```
## [1]  TRUE  TRUE  TRUE  TRUE  TRUE FALSE FALSE
```

```
# print all rows where there is at least one NA
print(which(!complete.cases(my.df)))
```

```
## [1] 6 7
```

- **na.omit** - Returns a `dataframe` without the rows where a `NA` is found.

```
print(na.omit(my.df))
```

```
##   x y
## 1 1 5
## 2 2 6
## 3 3 7
## 4 4 8
## 5 5 9
```

- **unique** - Returns a `dataframe` where all duplicated rows are removed and only the unique cases, row wise, are left.

```
# set df with repeating rows
my.df <- data.frame(col1 = c(1,1,2,3,3,4,5),
                    col2 = c('A','A','A','C','C','B','D'))
```

```
# print it
print(my.df)
```

```
##   col1 col2
## 1    1    A
## 2    1    A
```

```
## 3     2     A
## 4     3     C
## 5     3     C
## 6     4     B
## 7     5     D
```

```
# print unique df
print(unique(my.df))
```

```
##    col1 col2
## 1    1     A
## 3    2     A
## 4    3     C
## 6    4     B
## 7    5     D
```

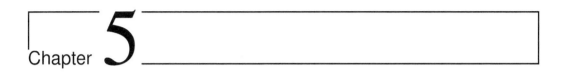

Chapter **5**

Financial Data and Common Operations

Before learning how to import data into R, it is wise to discuss the types and properties of the typical cases of financial data. These are datasets you are likely to encounter in your work. This chapter will provide you context and help you understand where the data is coming from and what it represents. Let's start by looking into datasets from financial markets.

5.1 Data from Financial Markets

Without a doubt, the most popular dataset in finance is related to the prices of financial contracts. In financial markets, investors can buy contracts that entitle a claim to a cash flow. An example, governments fund their operations by issuing bonds (debt contracts). When you buy a government bond, what you acquire is a contract where the government promises to pay you a value, in specified dates and within a period of time. From the viewpoint of the investor, money is spent today to acquire a cash flow in the future.

What differs one financial contract to the other is the underlying uncertainty, the structure of how payments are set and the rights acquired by the buyer. With stock markets, when a company needs money, it can raise capital by selling ownership. Several rights, including a share of future profits, are granted to whoever buy its new stocks. Since it is difficult to forecast future profits, the usual equity contract is far riskier than the usual debt contract.

Issuing stocks is an elaborate process. For most financial exchanges, when a company opens its capital, it first sells it through the primary market, composed of selected investors. This is where the *initial public offering* (IPO) takes place. At this stage, the company usually retains part of the shares in its treasury, so it can sell later for another raise of capital. In the second stage of the IPO, the secondary market, shares are traded in the *common* market, such as NYSE, where everyone has access. This is where most of the financial data for capital markets comes from.

Prices in financial markets move according to supply and demand. For example, if many investors buy a stock, its price is likely to rise. Every time that a seller meets a buyer, a trade is recorded, and a cash transaction occurs. New information and market expectations about future performance play a prominent role in the dynamics of demand. If the market understands that a company will do well in the future, investors will likely buy the stock, and its price will rise. The prices of the financial contracts are, therefore, an indication of how the market perceives the future.

Certain events can also alter the price of a stock, even though no new information or shift in the demand is seen. This is the typical case of a *split* operation, where a single stock is fractioned into several. For a one to two split, an investor with 100 stocks at 10$ will now have 200 shares at 5$ each. The value of the portfolio stays the same. When looking at the price series, a split operation results in a big drop of price.

Another event that impacts price is the payment of dividends. In the date previous to the payment, a stock will drop its price regarding the value of the dividend per share. This happens because a new buyer loses its right to the upcoming dividend payment and, therefore, a discount is expected. It is important to understand and recognize these events as you may have to deal with raw price data. In general, data providers give the option for *adjusted prices*, that is, the price is already adjusted to these events.

In its raw form, price data is sampled whenever there is a trade. Sites like Yahoo Finance and Google finance offers daily statistics about share prices such as highest/lowest price, traded volume and closing prices for the day. The variety of datasets is wide, covering almost every financial exchange in the world. Anyone can download this data using the website or a custom access point. Many of the CRAN packages that imports financial data from the web offer functions that make it easy to download datasets from these websites.

The data from Yahoo Finance or others is in the daily frequency. Obtaining information about trades within the day is far more difficult.[1] This is usually called tick-by-tick, or high-frequency data (HFD). For liquid markets, the size of this database can be restrictive. One exchange that offers free access to tick-by-tick

---

[1]Some companies, such as kibot, pitrading and backtestmarket, sell this data to the public.

data is Bovespa, the Brazilian exchange. We will discuss this dataset in chapters 6 and 11.

From the viewpoint of data analysis, price datasets usually have three dimensions, an identifier (ticker), a date/time reference and a price. This means that, in the long format, you can represent this data in R with a three column `dataframe`. When new stocks are added to the dataset, this `dataframe` will increase in rows. When new variables, such as traded volume, are inserted, a new column can be added. As we saw in chapter 4, the long format facilitates data processing tasks and is recommended. While we only discussed data for equity markets, other types of markets have similar datasets, but with extra information. For example, financial contracts from the debt and derivative markets usually have an expiration (maturity) date. Option contracts have a strike price. Additional information regarding debt and derivative contracts can be easily added to a long `dataframe` with extra columns.

5.1.1 Calculating Returns for a Single Asset

After importing price data, one of the most common operation is to calculate returns based on prices. Nominal prices are not usually used for research as they are difficult to compare for different assets. A price change of 1$ is almost insignificant to an 800$ stock, but not to 10 dollar stock. Very few methods in finance use prices as input. Almost all research in capital markets uses the return vector as the primary information in the analysis.

Returns are simply the percentage difference of prices from one day to the next. By calculating it to several stocks, it normalizes the price differences, allowing a cross section analysis. From the financial side, the intuition behind calculating returns is that they provide the percentage return of an investor that bought the stock in day t and sold it in next day, $t+1$. We can use these percentages to calculate the nominal profit or loss for an investment of any size.

There are two types of returns, arithmetic and logarithmic. The simplest one is the arithmetic return, or percentage. Its formula is given by:

$$AritRet_t = \frac{P_t - P_{t-1}}{P_{t-1}} = \frac{P_t}{P_{t-1}} - 1$$

So, based on a series of prices, we can create a return vector by calculating the percentage increase or decrease of prices from one period to the next. An important information here is that we always lose the first observation when calculating returns. So, if you have a price series with 10 elements, the resulting return vector will have 9 elements. My recommendation is to always match the size of the original vector by adding one extra element. An `NA` value for the first observation of a return series seems appropriate. By using vectors with the same size, the organization of the objects and code is simpler, and that can avoid errors in the code.

In R, let's first simulate a price series with the following code:

```
set.seed(10)
# simulate artificial prices
nT <- 5
P <- 10*(cumprod(1+rnorm(nT,
                         mean = 0,
                         sd = 0.1)))

# print prices
print(P)
```

```
## [1] 10.018746  9.834148  8.485561  7.977134  8.212097
```

Now, we can calculate a return vector based on the artificial price series with:

```
# calculate arit. return
arit.ret <- c(NA, P[2:length(P)]/
                  P[1:(length(P)-1)] -1)

# print result
print(arit.ret)
```

```
## [1]          NA -0.01842525 -0.13713305 -0.05991677
## [5]  0.02945451
```

Arithmetic returns can also be compounded, which tell how much return over time one would get by keeping the investment. Compounding arithmetic returns are given by this formula:

$$AcumAritRet_t = \prod (1 + AritRet_t)$$

In R, we can calculate it using function `cumprod`:

```
# calculate accumulated arit. return
acum.arit.ret <- c(1, cumprod(1+na.omit(arit.ret)))

# print result
print(acum.arit.ret)
```

```
## [1] 1.0000000 0.9815747 0.8469684 0.7962208 0.8196731
```

Notice how it was necessary to omit all `NA` values from object `arit.ret` using function `na.omit`. We also set value 1 for the first element of `acum.arit.ret`.

The second return is the logarithmic (or log-return). This is commonly used in academic research as some properties facilitate modelling. For example, if prices follow a log-Normal distribution, the log-returns will follow a Normal distribution. This property is convenient as some statistical procedures assume a Normal distribution. Another property of log-returns is they can be accumulated in a much simpler way than arithmetic returns. First, let's have a look in its formula. A log return is given by:

$$LogRet_t = \log\left(\frac{P_t}{P_{t-1}}\right)$$

The biggest difference between arithmetic and log returns is the use of the log function. In R, we can calculate log returns using the following code, in two versions:

```
# using indexing
log.ret <- c(NA, log(P[2:length(P)]/
                      P[1:(length(P)-1)]))


# using diff
log.ret <- c(NA, diff(log(P)))
```

As for compounding log returns, the additive property makes it much simpler. You can compound a log return vector by simply summing its elements. Have a look.

$$AcumLogRet_t = 1 + \sum(LogRet_t)$$

We can use function `cumsum` to calculate the compound log return:

```
# calculate accumulated log. return
acum.log.ret <- c(1, 1+cumsum(na.omit(arit.ret)))


# print result
print(acum.log.ret)


## [1] 1.0000000 0.9815747 0.8444417 0.7845249 0.8139794
```

The conversion from log to arithmetic return is simple. Consider the following conversion formulas:

$$AritRet_t = \exp(LogRet_t) - 1$$

$$LogRet_t = \log(1 + AritRet_t)$$

Let's try it out:

```
# converting arit ret to log ret and vice-versa
arit.ret.from.log <- exp(log.ret)-1
log.ret.from.arit <- log(arit.ret+1)

# print result as df
print(data.frame(arit.ret, arit.ret.from.log,
                 log.ret, log.ret.from.arit))
```

```
##         arit.ret arit.ret.from.log      log.ret
## 1             NA                NA           NA
## 2  -0.01842525       -0.01842525  -0.01859711
## 3  -0.13713305       -0.13713305  -0.14749478
## 4  -0.05991677       -0.05991677  -0.06178687
## 5   0.02945451        0.02945451   0.02902906
##     log.ret.from.arit
## 1                  NA
## 2         -0.01859711
## 3         -0.14749478
## 4         -0.06178687
## 5          0.02902906
```

As you can see from the printed **dataframe**, the returns from the conversion match the ones from the log or arithmetic return formula.

5.1.2   Calculating Returns for a Portfolio

Another common operation in using data from financial markets is to calculate returns for a portfolio, where an investor divides its capital in different assets. For a portfolio with total value V, each investment i will have m_i invested. I.e, The percentage position of each investment is $w_i = m_i/V$. Based on these percentages, we can calculate the return of the portfolio as a weighted average of the returns of the assets individually. Formally:

$$R_{P,t} = \sum_{i=1}^{N} w_i R_{i,t}$$

Now, let's try an example where the investor has its capital evenly divided within three assets. First, we will create a `dataframe` in the long format with the price information.

```
# set seed for reproducibility
set.seed(10)

# set number of time periods
nT <- 5

# simulate prices
P.1 <- 10*(cumprod(1+rnorm(nT,mean = 0, sd = 0.1)))
P.2 <- 20*(cumprod(1+rnorm(nT,mean = 0, sd = 0.1)))
P.3 <- 30*(cumprod(1+rnorm(nT,mean = 0, sd = 0.1)))

# gather info in df
my.df <- data.frame(ref.date = Sys.Date()+1:nT,
                    prices = c(P.1,P.2,P.3),
                    ticker = paste('Stock ',c(rep('A',nT),
                                              rep('B',nT),
                                              rep('C',nT))))

# print result
print(my.df)
```

```
##       ref.date    prices   ticker
## 1  2017-05-06 10.018746 Stock  A
## 2  2017-05-07  9.834148 Stock  A
## 3  2017-05-08  8.485561 Stock  A
## 4  2017-05-09  7.977134 Stock  A
## 5  2017-05-10  8.212097 Stock  A
## 6  2017-05-06 20.779589 Stock  B
## 7  2017-05-07 18.269256 Stock  B
## 8  2017-05-08 17.604847 Stock  B
## 9  2017-05-09 14.741115 Stock  B
## 10 2017-05-10 14.363037 Stock  B
## 11 2017-05-06 33.305339 Stock  C
## 12 2017-05-07 35.822494 Stock  C
## 13 2017-05-08 34.969082 Stock  C
## 14 2017-05-09 38.422086 Stock  C
## 15 2017-05-10 41.270661 Stock  C
```

As mentioned before, using a matrix notation facilitates calculations for the portfolio. With that in mind, we will first transform the long `dataframe` in a `matrix` of prices:

```
# set price matrix
my.price.mat <- matrix(my.df$prices, nrow = nT)

# set row and col names
colnames(my.price.mat) <- unique(my.df$ticker)
rownames(my.price.mat) <- as.character(unique(my.df$ref.date))

# print result
print(my.price.mat)
```

```
##              Stock  A Stock  B Stock  C
## 2017-05-06 10.018746 20.77959 33.30534
## 2017-05-07  9.834148 18.26926 35.82249
## 2017-05-08  8.485561 17.60485 34.96908
## 2017-05-09  7.977134 14.74111 38.42209
## 2017-05-10  8.212097 14.36304 41.27066
```

Now, from the price matrix, we can calculate a return matrix using simple element by element operation with the whole matrix:

```
# apply return formula for each column
my.ret.mat <- my.price.mat[2: nrow(my.price.mat)    , ]/
              my.price.mat[1:(nrow(my.price.mat)-1), ] -1

# print it!
print(my.ret.mat)
```

```
##               Stock  A     Stock  B     Stock  C
## 2017-05-07 -0.01842525 -0.12080762  0.07557815
## 2017-05-08 -0.13713305 -0.03636760 -0.02382336
## 2017-05-09 -0.05991677 -0.16266727  0.09874447
## 2017-05-10  0.02945451 -0.02564784  0.07413901
```

Finally, we use the weight vector in a `matrix` object to calculate the return of the portfolio over time:

```
# set weight of portfolio (evenly weighted)
w <- matrix(rep(1/3,3), nrow = 3)

# calculate return of portfolio over time
ret.port <- my.ret.mat %*% w

# print result
print(ret.port)
```

```
##                       [,1]
## 2017-05-07 -0.02121824
## 2017-05-08 -0.06577467
## 2017-05-09 -0.04127986
## 2017-05-10  0.02598190
```

Vector `ret.port` show the return an investor would receive if the total value of the portfolio is evenly divided between the stocks.

5.2 Data from the Financial Evaluation of Projects

In corporate finance, we can evaluate a project by looking at its future cash-flow, that is, the predicted amount of cash to be spent and gained from the project. Based on these cash flows, we calculate measures such as NPV (net present value), IRR (internal rate of return) and payback time, that help indicate whether a project has financial merit and should be executed. We will not go into the theoretical details that pertain each measure. If this is the first time hearing about these measures, I suggest looking into Ross et al. (2008), which provides excellent material about project evaluation.

As for the data side, the cash-flow of projects is a one dimensional information and can be represented as atomic vectors of the `numeric` type, where the first element is the initial investment at time 0. An example:

```
# set project cashflow
CF <- c(-8000, 2500, 3000, 3000, 5000)
names(CF) <- paste('Year', 0:(length(CF)-1))

# print result
print(CF)
```

```
## Year 0 Year 1 Year 2 Year 3 Year 4
##  -8000   2500   3000   3000   5000
```

Notice how the first element is negative. This means that, at time zero, cash will be spent. Now, we can use package `FinCalc` (Fan, 2016) to evaluate the project using NPV and IRR.

```
library(FinCal)

# set discount rate
r <- 0.1

# calculate npv
```

```r
my.NPV <- npv(r = r, cf = CF)

# calculate irr
my.IRR <- irr(cf = CF)

# calculate payback
my.payback <- min(which(cumsum(CF) > 0)) - 1

# print results
cat('NPV = ', my.NPV )
```

```
## NPV =   2421.078
```

```r
cat('IRR = ', my.IRR)
```

```
## IRR =   0.2183874
```

```r
cat('Payback = ', my.payback, 'years')
```

```
## Payback =   3 years
```

In this simple example, the net present value of the project is positive and equal to 2421, the internal rate of return is 21.84%. The initial investment is paid back in 3 years. From the financial side, this fictional project creates value and should be accepted.

Package `FinCal` offers many more functions for standard operations in cash flow analysis, such as the calculation of present and future values. It also includes functions for manipulating fixed income datasets. If analyzing financial cash flows or fixed income markets is part of your job, I strongly suggest studying the functions from this package.

5.3   Data from Financial Statements

Another popular dataset in finance relates to financial statements from companies. In most financial exchanges, companies must report their financial result on a quarterly basis. This is related to balance sheets, the assets and liabilities of the company and cash flow statements, its financial performance in the last period. These documents are important to keep markets aware of the current financial health of each traded company and any other event that might be of interest of current and potential investors. You can find more details about financial statements in Penman and Penman (2007) and Ittelson (1998). Most of the data for financial statements is available on the financial exchange site or research and government agencies. As we will see in a later chapter, several packages are available for downloading this type of financial data.

When looking at data for just one company in one period of time, financial statements are one dimensional and using simple vectors suffice. Then we have a single company and many periods of time, this data has two dimensions, and it should be represented as a `dataframe` in R. As for the case of financial statements from several companies and many time periods, we can use a `dataframe` in the long format with five columns:

- RefTime - reference date or time period
- CompanyID - unique identifier for companies
- TypeOfFinStatement - the type of financial statement (balance sheets, cash-flows, ..)
- TypeAccount - type/name of account (total assets, net profit, ...)
- Value - the value of the account

The previous format is flexible and can hold a large number of different financial statements from different companies and different time periods.

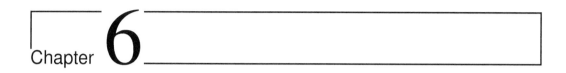

## Chapter 6

Importing and Exporting Data from Local Files

In chapter 4, we studied the main types of R objects and the many ways to manipulate them. In particular, we looked at **dataframes**, an efficient storage type to represent our data in a tabular format. We learned more about the types of financial data in chapter 5. In this chapter, we will study the process of importing and exporting datasets with R. In most cases of data analysis, the database will be contained in an external source, such as a local file.

6.1 Importing Data from Local Files

The easiest way to import data into R is using a local file. Here, we will discuss four main formats and their file extensions: the *comma separated values* format (*.csv*), Microsoft Excel files (*.xls*, *.xlsx*), R native data (*.RData*), SQLITE (*.SQLITE*) and unstructured text files (*.txt*). These are the most common cases one will find in a data analysis situation. As with the previous chapters, all data used in the examples is publicly available in the book website.

Throughout this chapter, we will assume the imported files are located within a subdirectory called **data**, available in the current working directory. If you are not sure about the current working folder, just call command `print(getwd())` so it shows it in the prompt. This step is important, as you must provide the exact address of the imported file to R. If no address is informed, R assumes the file is available in the working directory. If you are not working in the same directory as your data file, you'll need to inform its full address, as in `my.f <- 'C:/My Data/MyData.csv'`.

However, keeping the R script in a different root folder than the data file is not recommended.

Since R allows the use of relative paths, using a folder for the script and a sub-folder for the data files is good policy. For example, if you are working in a script located at directory `C:/My Research` and you placed all data files inside `C:/My Research/data/`, you could first use function `setwd` at the beginning of *script* to change the directory and then use the relative path of the file, as in `my.f <- 'data/my_data.csv'`, to load the information. The resulting script would look like the next code:

```
# set working directory
my.d <- 'C:/My Research/'
setwd(my.d)


# set file to be imported
my.f <- 'data/my_data.csv'
```

Notice how the code is self-contained and portable. If you sent the code to someone else as a compressed *.zip* file, the receiver only has to unzip the file, open the main script, change the directory in `my.d` and *source* (execute) the script. Given the relative paths were used in the rest of the code, R will be able to find all data files, and the code will run without problems.

6.1.1   Importing Data from a *.csv* File (*comma separated values*)

Consider the data file called SP500.csv, located in folder `data` from the current working directory. This file contains daily closing prices of the SP500 index from 2010-01-04 until 2017-02-28. Since SP500.csv is a simple text file, you can open it in any text editor.

The first lines of SP500.csv, also called header lines, shows the column names. Rows are set using line breaks, and all columns are separated by commas (`,`). This is an international standard. For some countries, the international standard is confusing, because the comma symbol can also indicate decimal values. If this is your case, my suggestion is to give preference to the international notation. Since a *.csv* file is editable, you can manually replace all commas with a point. Programs, such as Notepad and Notepad++, perform this task easily with *search and replace* functions. Another solution is to use the capabilities of the import function in R and set the decimal and column separator in the R code.

To load the contents of file SP500.csv in R, use the `read.csv` function.

```
# set file to read
my.f <- 'data/SP500.csv'

# read file
my.df.sp500 <- read.csv(my.f)

# print it
print(head(my.df.sp500))
```

```
##           date   price
## 1 2010-01-04 1132.99
## 2 2010-01-05 1136.52
## 3 2010-01-06 1137.14
## 4 2010-01-07 1141.69
## 5 2010-01-08 1144.98
## 6 2010-01-11 1146.98
```

The contents of the imported file are set as a `dataframe` object in R. As mentioned in the previous chapter, each column of a `dataframe` has a class. We can check the class of `my.df.sp500` using functions `class` and `sapply`. The latter is a special type of function that applies a procedure to several elements of a `list` or `dataframe`. In this case, we apply function `class` to each column of `my.df.sp500`. The use of `sapply` will be detailed in the chapter 9. The classes of the columns are presented next.

```
# print classes of all columns of my.df.sp500
print(sapply(my.df.sp500, class))
```

```
##      date      price
##  "factor"  "numeric"
```

Note that the column of dates (`date`) was imported as a `factor` vector, not as a `Date` object. This is a common mistake because, by default, function `read.csv` imports text data as factors. The problem is `factors` do not have the same properties as a `Date` object, and a bug is likely to occur once the user tries to manipulate the column.

The solution for the problem is simple: indicate the class of columns with the `colClasses` input, as in the following code:

```
# read csv file with correct col classes
my.df.sp500 <- read.csv(my.f,  colClasses = c('Date', 'numeric'))

# print column classes
print(sapply(my.df.sp500, class))
```

```
##      date     price
##     "Date" "numeric"
```

As we can see, the result is now correct. Another way to do it is to change the class of columns with the conversion functions `as.Date` and `as.numeric`:

```
# load raw data
my.df.sp500 <- read.csv(my.f)

# convert columns to correct classes
my.df.sp500$date <- as.Date(my.df.sp500$date)
my.df.sp500$price <- as.numeric(my.df.sp500$price)

# print column classes
print(sapply(my.df.sp500, class))
```

```
##      date     price
##     "Date" "numeric"
```

Again, we got the desired result. As a rule of thumb, **whenever data is imported into R, it is essential to verify the classes of the columns**. You'll be able to avoid many problems by simply checking the imported data.

Going further, function `read.csv` has several other features in addition to those presented here. Using its inputs, you can set the column names, ignore the first **n** lines of the file, among many other possibilities. In most cases, however, the direct use of the function suffices.

Another possibility for importing *.csv* files as **dataframes** in R is using function `read_csv` from package **readr** (Wickham et al., 2016). The biggest benefit of this function is it reads the data very quickly, and it uses a clever format for defining the classes of the columns. If you are dealing with many large files with several columns, using `readr::read_csv` is strongly advised. Consider the next example.

```
library(readr)
```

```
# read file with readr::read_csv
my.df.sp500 <- read_csv(my.f)
```

```
## Parsed with column specification:
## cols(
##    date = col_date(format = ""),
##    price = col_double()
## )
```

Notice how the previous code presented a message, entitled **Parsed with column** specification:. This message shows how the function set the attributes of the columns by reading the first 1000 lines of the file. We can use this information in our own code by copying the text and assigning it to a variable. Have a look:

```
library(readr)
```

```
# set cols from import message
my.cols <- cols(date = col_date(format = ""),
                price = col_double() )
```

```
# read file with readr::read_csv
my.df.sp500 <- read_csv(my.f, col_types = my.cols)
```

Now, let's check the classes of the column:

```
# print column classes
print(sapply(my.df.sp500, class))
```

```
##      date     price
##    "Date" "numeric"
```

As expected, it looks good. Both columns have the expected format. So, a possible set of steps using `readr::read_csv` is, first, to read the file without arguments in `read_csv`, copy the default column classes from the output message, add it as argument `col_types`, and re-execute the script. This is handy when the imported file has several columns and manually defining each column class requires lots of typing.

6.1.2 Importing Data from an *Excel* File

In many situations, the data to be analysed is contained in a Microsoft Excel file, with *.xls* or *.xlsx* extension. Although it is not an efficient or portable data storage format, Excel is a very popular software in finance because of it spreadsheet-like capacities. It is not uncommon for data to be stored and distributed in this format.

R does not have a native function for importing Excel files; therefore, we must install and use packages to perform this operation. There are several options, but the main packages are `XLConnect` (Mirai Solutions GmbH, 2016), `xlsx` (Dragulescu, 2014), `readxl` (Wickham, 2016a) and `tidyxl` (Garmonsway, 2017).

Although the previous cited packages have similar goals, each has its peculiarities. If reading Excel files is important to your work, I strongly advise you study the differences between these packages. For example, package `tidyxl` was specially designed to read unstructured Excel files, where the desired information is not contained in the tabular format. Package `XLConnect` allows the user to open a live connection and control an Excel file from R, making it possible to export and send data, format cells, create graphics in Excel, and more.

In this section, we will give priority to package `readxl`, one of the easiest and most straightforward packages to use. It also does not require the installation of external software such as *Java*. Let's start with an example. Consider a file, called `SP500-Excel.xlsx`, that contains the same SP500 data as the previous example. We can import the information from the file using function `read_excel` from `readxl`:

```
library(readxl)

# set excel file
my.f <- 'data/SP500-Excel.xlsx'

# read excel file
my.df <- read_excel(my.f, sheet = 'sp500-prices')

# print classes
print(sapply(my.df, class))
```

```
## $date
## [1] "POSIXct" "POSIXt"
##
## $price
## [1] "numeric"
```

```
# print with head (first five rows)
print(head(my.df))
```

```
## # A tibble: 6 × 2
##          date   price
##         <dttm>   <dbl>
## 1 2010-01-04 1132.99
## 2 2010-01-05 1136.52
## 3 2010-01-06 1137.14
## 4 2010-01-07 1141.69
## 5 2010-01-08 1144.98
## 6 2010-01-11 1146.98
```

As we can see, one of the benefits of using Excel files is the classes of the columns are taken from the classes in the Excel file. That is, if the classes are correct in Excel, then they will automatically be correct in R. In our case, the date column of file data/SP500-Excel.xlsx was correctly set as a `POSIXct` object. Likewise, even if the Excel file used commas for decimals, the import process would still be successful as the conversion is handled internally.

The downside of using Excel files for storing data is its low portability and the longer time required to read it. This may not be a problem for small datasets, but when handling a large volume of data, using Excel files can be very frustrating, and it is not advised.

6.1.3 Importing Data from a *.RData* File

R has a native format to save objects from the environment to a local file with extension *.RData*. The great benefit in using this format is the saved file is compact, and its access is fast. The downside is it has low portability, i.e., it can be difficult to use the files in other software.

To create a new *.RData* file, use the **save** function, and to load the data file, use the **load** function. See the following example, where we create a *.RData* file with some content, clear R's memory, and then load the previously created file:

```r
# set a object
my.x <- 1:100

# set name of RData file
my.file <- 'data/temp.RData'

# save it
save(list = c('my.x'), file = my.file)
```

We can verify the existence of the file with the **list.files** function:

```r
# print contents of data folder
print(list.files('data'))
```

```
##  [1] "AdjustedPrices-InternacionalIndices.RDATA"
##  [2] "BovStocks_2011-12-01_2016-11-29.csv"
##  [3] "BovStocks_2011-12-01_2016-11-29.RData"
##  [4] "example_getfhdata.RDATA"
##  [5] "FileWithLatinChar.txt"
##  [6] "grunfeld.csv"
##  [7] "HFData.csv"
##  [8] "HFData_6_Assets_15 min.RData"
##  [9] "MktIndices_and_Symbols.csv"
## [10] "MySQLiteDatabase.SQLITE"
## [11] "SP500-Excel.xlsx"
## [12] "SP500-Stocks-WithRet.RData"
## [13] "SP500-Stocks_long.csv"
## [14] "SP500-Stocks_wide.csv"
```

```
## [15] "SP500.csv"
## [16] "SP500_2011-11-13_2016-11-11.csv"
## [17] "TDData.csv"
## [18] "temp.csv"
## [19] "temp.RData"
## [20] "temp.txt"
## [21] "temp.xlsx"
## [22] "temp_xts.RData"
```

As expected, the data/temp.RData file is available, along with several others. Now, let's clear the memory and load the *.RData* file created in the previous step.

```
# clear environment
rm(list=ls())

# load file
load(file = 'data/temp.RData')

# print all objects in environment
print(ls())
```

```
## [1] "my.x"
```

We can see object `my.x` was recovered, and it is available in the environment.

6.1.4 Importing Data from SQLITE

The use of *.csv* or *.RData* files for storing datasets has its limits as the size of the files increases. If you are waiting a long time to read a `dataframe` from a file, you should look for alternatives. Likewise, if you are working in a network of computers and many people are using the same data, it makes sense to keep and distribute the information from a central server. This way, every user can have access to the same information concurrently.

This brings us to the topic of *database software*. These specific programs usually work with a query language, called *SQL (Structured Query Language)*. It allows the user to read portions of the data and even manipulate it efficiently. There are many options of database software that integrates nicely with R. The list includes **mySQL**, **SQLite** and **MariaDB**. Here, we will provide a quick tutorial on this topic, using SQLITE, which is the easiest one to work with, as it doesn't need any server configuration.

Before moving to the examples, we need to understand how to use database software. First, R will connect to the database and return a connection object. Based on this connection, we will send queries for importing data from this database using a *SQL* language. The main advantage is we can have a large database of, let's say, 10 GB and only load a small portion of it in R. This operation is also very quick, allowing efficient access to the available tables.

As an example, let's first create a SQLITE database. For that, we will set two large `dataframes` with random data and save both in a SQLITE file using package `RSQLite`.

```
library(RSQLite)

# set number of rows in df
N = 10^6

# create simulated dataframe
my.large.df.1 <- data.frame(x=runif(N),
                            G= sample(c('A','B'),
                                      size = N,
                                      replace = TRUE))

my.large.df.2 <- data.frame(x=runif(N),
                            G = sample(c('A','B'),
                                       size = N,
                                       replace = TRUE))

# set name of SQLITE file
f.sqlite <- 'data/MySQLiteDatabase.SQLITE'

# open connection
my.con <- dbConnect(drv = SQLite(), f.sqlite)

# write df to sqlite
dbWriteTable(conn = my.con, name = 'MyTable1', value = my.large.df.1)
```

```
## [1] TRUE
```

```
dbWriteTable(conn = my.con, name = 'MyTable2', value = my.large.df.2)
```

```
## [1] TRUE
```

```
# disconnect
dbDisconnect(my.con)
```

The `TRUE` output of `dbWriteTable` indicates everything went well. A connection was opened using function `dbConnect`, and the `dataframes` were written to a

SQLITE file, called data/MySQLiteDatabase.SQLITE. Unlike other database software, SQLITE stores data and configurations from a single file, without the need of
a formal server. Also, notice how we disconnected from the database with function
dbDisconnect.

Now, let's use the previously created file to read the tables back into R.

```
# set name of SQLITE file
f.sqlite <- 'data/MySQLiteDatabase.SQLITE'

# open connection
my.con <- dbConnect(drv = SQLite(), f.sqlite)

# read table
my.df <- dbReadTable(conn = my.con, name = 'MyTable1')

# print with str
print(str(my.df))
```

```
## 'data.frame':     1000000 obs. of  2 variables:
##  $ x: num   0.5356 0.0931 0.1698 0.8998 0.4226 ...
##  $ G: chr   "B" "B" "A" "A" ...
## NULL
```

It worked. The dataframe is exactly as expected.

Another example of using SQLITE is with the actual SQL statements. Notice, in
the previous code, we used function dbReadTable to get the contents of all rows in
table MyTable1. Now, lets use an SQL command to get only the rows where the G
column is equal to A.

```
# set sql statement
my.SQL <- "select * from myTable2 where G='A'"

# get query
my.df.A <- dbGetQuery(conn = my.con, statement = my.SQL)

# disconnect from db
dbDisconnect(my.con)

# print with str
print(str(my.df.A))
```

```
## 'data.frame':     500154 obs. of  2 variables:
##  $ x: num   0.0064 0.4769 0.4825 0.1253 0.7501 ...
```

```
## $ G: chr  "A" "A" "A" "A" ...
## NULL
```

It also worked as expected.

In this simple example, we can see how easy it is to create a connection to a database, retrieve tables, and disconnect. If you have to work with large datasets, which, in my opinion is any database that occupies more than 4 GB of your computer memory, it is worth moving it to proper database software. You'll be able to retrieve data fast, without the need of loading the whole database in the computer's memory. If you have a server available in your workplace, I strongly advise learning how to connect to it and use the SQL language to your advantage. There are many other ways you can query and manipulate data using SQL. Several tutorials are available in the internet.

6.1.5 Importing Data from a Text File

In some cases, we are faced with data stored in a non-structured format, usually as raw text files. You can read the contents of a text file with function `readLines`. See next:

```
# set file to read
my.f <- 'data/SP500.csv'

# read file line by line
my.txt <- readLines(my.f)

# print first five lines
print(my.txt[1:5])
```

```
## [1] "\"date\",\"price\""      "2010-01-04,1132.98999"
## [3] "2010-01-05,1136.52002"   "2010-01-06,1137.140015"
## [5] "2010-01-07,1141.689941"
```

In this example, we imported the entire content of file `SP500.csv` as a `character` vector named `my.txt`. Each element of `my.txt` is a line of `SP500.csv`. If needed, we could write a routine to process each line, separating the columns with the `strsplit` function and saving the information of interest to another object.

6.1.6 Other File Formats

Using the import functions for files with extensions *.csv*, *.xlsx* and *.RData* is sufficient in most situations. Nonetheless, it is worth noting R has specific functions for other, less popular, formats. This includes files exported from other statistical software, such as SPSS, SAS, Matlab, Eviews, among many others. If you are required to read files from different software, I suggest a thorough study of package `foreign` (R Core Team, 2015).

6.2 Exporting to Local File

A very common operation in the use of R is to write data to files. Exporting data from R involves a decision regarding the format. The user must take into account three points in this decision: the resulting file size, the speed of the export process, and the compatibility with other softwares.

In most situations, the use of *.csv* files satisfies all points. Since it is simply a text file that can be opened and imported into any system, sharing it with others is straightforward. Moreover, the resulting *.csv* file size is not excessive. And, if the size of the generated file is large, you can compress it using the *zip* function. For these reasons, in most situations, the use of *.csv* files in importing and exporting information is preferable. However, if the user will only use R and he is not interested in portability, the next best solution is exporting the information in the *RData* format. Both options are described next.

6.2.1 Exporting Data to a *.csv* File

To write a *.csv* file, use the `write.csv` function.

```
# set the number of rows
N <- 100

# set dataframe
my.df <- data.frame(y = runif(N), z = rep('a',N))

# set file out
f.out <- 'data/temp.csv'

# write to files
write.csv(x = my.df, file = f.out)
```

In the previous example, we save the object `my.df` into a file, called `temp.csv`, located in the `data` working directory. We can check its contents using `read.csv`:

```
# read it
my.df.import <- read.csv(f.out)
```

```
# print first five rows
print(head(my.df.import))
```

```
##   X          y z
## 1 1 0.51089782 a
## 2 2 0.38012799 a
## 3 3 0.04965114 a
## 4 4 0.19958776 a
## 5 5 0.36816402 a
## 6 6 0.94310436 a
```

Note that a column called x, containing the name/number of lines, has been added. If you do not want this new column, just set option row.names = FALSE as in write.csv(x = my.df, file = f.out, row.names = FALSE). See the difference in the following example.

```
# set the number of rows
N <- 100
```

```
# set dataframe
my.df <- data.frame(y = runif(N), z = rep('a',N))
```

```
# set file out
f.out <- 'data/temp.csv'
```

```
# write to files (without rownames)
write.csv(x = my.df, file = f.out, row.names=FALSE)
```

```
# check result
my.df.import <- read.csv(f.out)
print(head(my.df.import))
```

```
##           y z
## 1 0.9141985 a
## 2 0.9240226 a
## 3 0.8307530 a
## 4 0.2948835 a
## 5 0.5214990 a
## 6 0.4476653 a
```

As we can see, the row numbers are no longer saved as a column in the *.csv* file.

6.2.2   Exporting Data to a *RData* File

The native solution for exporting R objects is function **save**. It usage is simple; just name the objects to save and the name of the local file. Have a look:

```
# set random data
my.x <- runif(100)
my.df <- data.frame(y = runif(100),
                    z = runif(100))

my.f <- 'data/temp.RData'
save(list = c('my.x', 'my.df'),
     file = my.f)
```

After saving it, the contents of file data/temp.RData includes objects **my.df** and **my.x**. A note here is important. If you are saving custom classes of objects into a *.RData* file, you must first load the package before reading the file. Otherwise, R will not understand the custom format.

6.2.3   Exporting Data to an Excel File

Exporting a **dataframe** to an Excel file is also easy. Again, there is no native function in R that performs this procedure. We can, however, use package **xlsx**. A requisite for using this package is the installation of Java in the operating system. For Windows users, visit the Java site and install the software. After that, install **xlsx** with command **install.packages('xlsx')** and try loading it with **library(xlsx)**. If you got an error message about *Java* , try rebooting your system.

An example of usage is given next.

```
library(xlsx)

# create dataframe
N <- 50
my.df <- data.frame(y = seq(1,N), z = rep('a',N))

# set excel file
f.out <- 'data/temp.xlsx'

# write to excel
write.xlsx(x = my.df, file = f.out, sheetName = "my df")
```

If you want to save several **dataframes** into several worksheets of the same Excel file, you must use input option `append=TRUE` in the call to `write.xlsx`. Otherwise, the function will create a new file on each call and erase all previous content. See the following example, where we export two *dataframes* for two different sheets in the same Excel file:

```
# create two dataframes
N <- 25
my.df.A <- data.frame(y = seq(1,N),
                      z = rep('a',N))

my.df.B <- data.frame(z = rep('b',N))

# set file out
f.out <- 'data/temp.xlsx'

# write in different sheets
write.xlsx(x = my.df.A,
           file = f.out,
           sheetName = "my df A")

write.xlsx(x = my.df.B,
           file = f.out,
           sheetName = "my df B",
           append = TRUE )
```

6.2.4 Exporting Data to a Text File

In some situations, you may need to export an output to a file, for example, when you need to save the log record of a procedure, or when you need to record information in a specific format not supported by R. This procedure is quite simple. Using function `cat`, use input `file` to set the name of the local file. All the text supplied in function `cat` will be written in the corresponding text file. See next:

```
# set file
my.f <- 'data/temp.txt'

# set some string
my.str <- paste(letters[1:5], '\n', collapse = '')

# save string to file
cat(my.str, file = my.f, append = FALSE)
```

In the previous example, we created a text object with the first five letters of the alphabet, separated by the symbol \n, which indicates a line break. We then execute a call to `cat` with arguments `file` and `append`. The latter sets the option to add new text to the end of the file or not. We can check the result with the `readLines` function:

```
print(readLines(my.f))
```

```
## [1] "a " "b " "c " "d " "e "
```

As we can see, it worked as expected.

## Chapter 7

Importing Financial Data from the Internet

One of the great advantages of using R for data analysis is the amount of data that can be imported over the web. This is practical because a database can be downloaded or updated with a simple command, avoiding all the manual and tedious work of collecting data manually. It is also easy to share code, as anyone can download the exact same dataset with a single line of code.

7.1 CRAN Packages

In most cases, the importation of financial data from the web is performed using specific packages. For Finance, there are several packages with this purpose. Here, we will describe the main packages available in CRAN: `quantmod`, `BatchGetSymbols`, `finreportr`, `tidyquant`, `GetHFData`, `ustyc`, `Quandl` and `Rbitcoin`.

7.1.1 Package `quantmod`

To import daily trade data of stocks, one of the most popular packages is `quantmod` (Ryan, 2015). You can download information for a huge number of stocks from different sources, such as *Yahoo Finance* and *Google Finance*.

In the following example, we will get data for the FTSE equity index using function `getSymbols`. In this case, a simple search on the Yahoo Finance site shows its code is `^FTSE`. See the next example.

```
library(quantmod)

# get data for FTSE
my.df <- getSymbols(Symbols = '^FTSE', auto.assign = FALSE)

# print last rows
print(tail(my.df))
```

```
##              FTSE.Open FTSE.High FTSE.Low FTSE.Close
## 2017-04-26    7275.6    7302.6    7262.3    7288.7
## 2017-04-27    7288.7    7289.4    7224.4    7237.2
## 2017-04-28    7237.2    7243.3    7197.3    7203.9
## 2017-05-02    7203.9    7254.3    7203.9    7250.1
## 2017-05-03    7250.1    7250.1    7218.6    7234.5
## 2017-05-04    7234.5    7280.7    7226.1    7248.1
##              FTSE.Volume FTSE.Adjusted
## 2017-04-26    860455200       7288.7
## 2017-04-27   1094741200       7237.2
## 2017-04-28   1148718800       7203.9
## 2017-05-02    910924000       7250.1
## 2017-05-03    766336200       7234.5
## 2017-05-04    918713600       7248.1
```

In the call to getSymbols, we used argument auto.assign = F. This forces the function to save the data to object my.df and not auto-assign the data to a new object with the name of the asset. Notice the last date of the imported data is 2017-05-04, which is the last date when markets were opened in the UK at the time of the compilation of the book. The imported data includes the opening price (Open), maximum price (High), minimum price (Low), closing price (Close), trading volume (Volume), and the adjusted price (Adjusted). All data is in the daily frequency, and each column shows different information about the trade prices of a stock. In my.df, the only column with not so obvious content is Adjusted. It contains closing prices adjusted to dividends, split, and inplits. These are events that can artificially change a stock price. We discussed these issues in chapter 5.

Some attention is required when downloading trade data for some exchanges. Yahoo Finance has specific codes for specific markets. As an example, all tickers from the Brazilian equity market have the .SA text attached to their original ticker. So, stock PETR4 becomes PETR4.SA. You should investigate if Yahoo Finance has a particular format for the market you are interested. You can do that by looking for the tickers in the website.

While downloading data for one asset can be useful, in most data analysis cases, we will be interested in downloading and analyzing information for several stocks. To perform a batch download of stock data with `quantmod`, it is necessary to create a new *enviroment*. This process, however, is quite simple. See the next example, where we download data for Microsoft (MSFT), Google (GOOGL), JP-Morgan (JPM), and General Electric (GE):

```
# set tickers
my.tickers <- c('MSFT','GOOGL','JPM','GE')

# create new environment
my.env <- new.env()

# download fin data and save to my.env
getSymbols(Symbols = my.tickers, env = my.env)
```

```
## [1] "MSFT"  "GOOGL" "JPM"    "GE"
```

```
# print objects in my.env
print(names(my.env))
```

```
## [1] "JPM"         "GOOGL"        "GE"           ".getSymbols"
## [5] "MSFT"
```

```
# print contents of MSFT
print(tail(my.env$MSFT))
```

```
##             MSFT.Open MSFT.High MSFT.Low MSFT.Close
## 2017-04-27     68.15     68.38    67.58      68.27
## 2017-04-28     68.91     69.14    67.69      68.46
## 2017-05-01     68.68     69.55    68.50      69.41
## 2017-05-02     69.71     69.71    69.13      69.30
## 2017-05-03     69.38     69.38    68.71      69.08
## 2017-05-04     69.03     69.08    68.64      68.81
##             MSFT.Volume MSFT.Adjusted
## 2017-04-27    33464900         68.27
## 2017-04-28    39423500         68.46
## 2017-05-01    31789300         69.41
## 2017-05-02    23519500         69.30
## 2017-05-03    28751500         69.08
## 2017-05-04    21502600         68.81
```

The previous code downloads data for all tickers in `my.tickers`. The resulting `dataframe` objects are available in environment `my.env`, and we can access them using operator `$`. There are easier ways of organizing financial data for several tickers, as we will soon learn. Ideally, we should have all stocks in a long `dataframe`.

7.1.2   Package BatchGetSymbols

Another possibility for downloading financial data from Yahoo Finance and Google Finance is package BatchGetSymbols (Perlin, 2016). The main difference between BatchGetSymbols and quantmod is it organizes the dataset in a structured way. All the financial data from different tickers is kept in the same dataframe, facilitating further analysis.

Look at the following example, where we download financial data regarding four stocks for the previous 30 days using function BatchGetSymbols.

```
library(BatchGetSymbols)

# set tickers
my.tickers <- c('MSFT','GOOGL','JPM','GE')

# set dates
first.date <- Sys.Date()-30
last.date <- Sys.Date()

l.out <- BatchGetSymbols(tickers = my.tickers,
                         first.date = first.date,
                         last.date = last.date)


##
## Running BatchGetSymbols for:
##    tickers = MSFT, GOOGL, JPM, GE
##    Downloading data for benchmark ticker
## Downloading Data for MSFT from yahoo (1|4) - Got it!
## Downloading Data for GOOGL from yahoo (2|4) - Good job!
## Downloading Data for JPM from yahoo (3|4) - Good stuff!
## Downloading Data for GE from yahoo (4|4) - Good job!
```

The output of BatchGetSymbols is a list, where element df.control contains a dataframe with the result of the download process. The package not only downloads the data, but also keeps track of possible errors and missing values. Let's see the content of this dataframe.

```
# print result of download process
print(l.out$df.control)

##    ticker   src download.status total.obs
## 1    MSFT yahoo              OK        21
## 2   GOOGL yahoo              OK        21
## 3     JPM yahoo              OK        21
```

```
## 4        GE yahoo              OK        21
##    perc.benchmark.dates threshold.decision
## 1                    1                KEEP
## 2                    1                KEEP
## 3                    1                KEEP
## 4                    1                KEEP
```

Object `df.control` shows all tickers were valid, and we got 21 observations (rows) for each.

As for the actual financial data, it is contained in element `df.tickers` of `l.out`. Let's look:

```
# print df.tickers
print(tail(l.out$df.tickers))
```

```
##    price.open price.high price.low price.close    volume
## 79      29.29      29.31     29.02       29.08 32777900
## 80      29.10      29.16     28.93       28.99 23929100
## 81      29.01      29.17     28.93       28.94 23695700
## 82      29.01      29.05     28.91       28.99 31475900
## 83      28.92      29.29     28.85       29.23 26774100
## 84      29.27      29.31     29.05       29.20 19544100
##    price.adjusted   ref.date ticker
## 79          29.08 2017-04-27     GE
## 80          28.99 2017-04-28     GE
## 81          28.94 2017-05-01     GE
## 82          28.99 2017-05-02     GE
## 83          29.23 2017-05-03     GE
## 84          29.20 2017-05-04     GE
```

As expected, the information about prices and volume is there. Notice it also includes a column, called `ticker`, containing the symbols of the stocks. Later, in chapter 9, we will use this column to make calculations for each stock in our dataset.

Another useful function of `BatchGetSymbols` is `GetSP500Stocks`, which imports the current composition of the SP500 index, including the tickers of the stocks. So, by using `GetSP500Stocks` and `BatchGetSymbols` together, you can easily download a large amount of stock data for the US market. Consider the following chunk of code, where we performed such operation:

```
library(BatchGetSymbols)
```

```
# set tickers
my.tickers <- GetSP500Stocks()$ticker
```

```
# set dates
first.date <- Sys.Date()-30
last.date <- Sys.Date()

l.out <- BatchGetSymbols(tickers = my.tickers,
                         first.date = first.date,
                         last.date = last.date)
```

Be aware running the previous code takes time, but once you have the data, you can save it locally and use it in a future study.

7.1.3   Package `finreportr`

Package `finreportr` (Lee, 2016) is designed to download financial data from the U.S. Securities and Exchange Commission. Every company with traded assets in the American market is required to file information with government agencies, including financial statements (see chapter 5). What `finreportr` does is use webscraping tools to access and acquire this information from the SEC website. First, let's look at the available functions.

```
library(finreportr)

# print available functions in finreportr
ls('package:finreportr')
```

```
## [1] "AnnualReports"   "CompanyInfo"       "GetBalanceSheet"
## [4] "GetCashFlow"     "GetIncome"
```

We have 5 functions at our disposal. Let's try function `CompanyInfo` for Facebook (FB):

```
my.ticker <- 'FB'
info <- CompanyInfo(my.ticker)
print(info)
```

```
##          company        CIK  SIC state state.inc FY.end
## 1 Facebook Inc 0001326801 7370    CA        DE   1231
##      street.address           city.state
## 1 1601 WILLOW ROAD MENLO PARK CA 94025
```

As we can see, the formal name of Facebook is Facebook Inc, and its registered address is 1601 WILLOW ROAD, MENLO PARK CA 94025. We can access the income statement of a traded company using function `GetIncome`. Let's give it a try:

```
# set final year
my.year <- 2016

# get income for FB
my.income <- GetIncome(my.ticker, my.year)

# print result
print(head(my.income))
```

```
##             Metric Units     Amount  startDate     endDate
## 1          Revenues   usd  7872000000 2013-01-01 2013-12-31
## 2          Revenues   usd 12466000000 2014-01-01 2014-12-31
## 3          Revenues   usd 17928000000 2015-01-01 2015-12-31
## 4  Cost of Revenue   usd  1875000000 2013-01-01 2013-12-31
## 5  Cost of Revenue   usd  2153000000 2014-01-01 2014-12-31
## 6  Cost of Revenue   usd  2867000000 2015-01-01 2015-12-31
```

Let's see what types of financial information we find in the Metric column. We will cut off the size of the text so it fits the book page nicelly.

```
# get unique fields
unique.fields <- unique(my.income$Metric)

# cut size of string
unique.fields <- substr(unique.fields,1, 60)

# print result
print(unique.fields)
```

```
##  [1] "Revenues"
##  [2] "Cost of Revenue"
##  [3] "Research and Development Expense"
##  [4] "Selling and Marketing Expense"
##  [5] "General and Administrative Expense"
##  [6] "Costs and Expenses"
##  [7] "Operating Income (Loss)"
##  [8] "Nonoperating Income (Expense)"
##  [9] "Income (Loss) from Continuing Operations before Income Taxes"
## [10] "Income Tax Expense (Benefit)"
## [11] "Net Income (Loss) Attributable to Parent"
## [12] "Undistributed Earnings (Loss) Allocated to Participating Sec"
## [13] "Net Income (Loss) Available to Common Stockholders, Basic"
## [14] "Earnings Per Share, Basic"
```

```
## [15] "Earnings Per Share, Diluted"
## [16] "Weighted Average Number of Shares Outstanding, Basic"
## [17] "Weighted Average Number of Shares Outstanding, Diluted"
## [18] "Allocated Share-based Compensation Expense"
```

We have not only revenues and earnings per share but plenty more. We could use function `GetIncome` to download and store income information about US companies in a large scale.

Let's see how each Facebook investor was financially compensated in the previous years:

```
# set col and date
my.col <- 'Earnings Per Share, Basic'

# print earnings per share
print(my.income[my.income$Metric == my.col, ])
```

```
##                        Metric       Units  Amount   startDate
## 40 Earnings Per Share, Basic usdPerShare    0.62  2013-01-01
## 41 Earnings Per Share, Basic usdPerShare    1.12  2014-01-01
## 42 Earnings Per Share, Basic usdPerShare    1.31  2015-01-01
##        endDate
## 40 2013-12-31
## 41 2014-12-31
## 42 2015-12-31
```

From the data, we can see Facebook investors received an increasing earning per share throughout the years. This is interesting as, in the past, there was some disbelief in the capacity of the company in generating cash flow. The financial data indicates that this was not the case.

An interesting aspect of `finreportr` is it works using tickers as input. You can easily merge information from this package with information in other datasets, such as equity prices from Yahoo Finance.

7.1.4   Package `tidyquant`

Package `tidyquant` provides functions related to financial data acquisition and processing. It is an ambitious project that offers many solutions in the field of finance. The package is designed to interact well with the *tidyverse* format, also know as the *long* format, discussed in chapter 4.

The package includes functions for obtaining financial data from the web, manipulation of financial data, and the calculation of performance measures of portfolios. It also integrates nicely with the pipeline operator, which will be discussed in chapter 9.

In its current version, `tidyquant` has 47 functions. Let's look at its main function-alities. First, we will obtain price data for Apple stocks (AAPL) using function `tq_get`.

```
library(tidyquant)

# set stock and dates
my.ticker <- 'AAPL'
first.date <- '2017-01-01'
last.date <-  Sys.Date()

# get data with tq_get
my.df <- tq_get(my.ticker,
                get = "stock.prices",
                from = first.date,
                to = last.date)

print(tail(my.df))
```

```
## # A tibble: 6 × 7
##          date  open  high   low close   volume adjusted
##        <date> <dbl> <dbl> <dbl> <dbl>    <dbl>    <dbl>
## 1 2017-04-27 143.92 144.16 143.31 143.79 14106100   143.79
## 2 2017-04-28 144.09 144.30 143.27 143.65 20763500   143.65
## 3 2017-05-01 145.10 147.20 144.96 146.58 33424500   146.58
## 4 2017-05-02 147.54 148.09 146.84 147.51 40290100   147.51
## 5 2017-05-03 145.59 147.49 144.27 147.06 45404200   147.06
## 6 2017-05-04 146.52 147.14 145.81 146.53 23309300   146.53
```

As we can see, the price data is the same as using `quantmod` and `BatchGetSymbols`. In fact, the origin of it is the same, Yahoo Finance. One interesting aspect of `tidyquant` is the same function, `tq_get`, can be used to download other financial information from different sources, such as Google Finance, Morning Star, FRED, and Oanda. For example, we can download key financial ratios from Morning Star by setting get='key.ratios' in `tq_get`.

```
# get key financial rations of AAPL
df.key.ratios <- tq_get("AAPL",get = "key.ratios")

# print it
print(df.key.ratios)
```

```
## # A tibble: 7 × 2
##               section              data
##                 <chr>            <list>
## 1          Financials <tibble [150 × 5]>
## 2       Profitability <tibble [170 × 5]>
## 3              Growth <tibble [160 × 5]>
## 4           Cash Flow <tibble [50 × 5]>
## 5    Financial Health <tibble [240 × 5]>
## 6 Efficiency Ratios   <tibble [80 × 5]>
## 7  Valuation Ratios   <tibble [40 × 5]>
```

Object `df.key.ratios` offers fundamental information about Apple. In this case, the output is an object of class `tibble`, a special type of `dataframe`. Column `data` in `df.key.ratios` is a `list-column`, allowing objects other than single values to take an element in the table. Its behaviour is the same as for other `list` objects. For example, we can look into the profitability section with the following notation:

```
# get profitability table
df.profitability <- df.key.ratios$data[[2]]

# print it
print(tail(df.profitability))
```

```
## # A tibble: 6 × 5
##     sub.section group          category       date    value
##           <chr> <dbl>             <chr>     <date>    <dbl>
## 1 Profitability    32 Interest Coverage 2011-09-01       NA
## 2 Profitability    32 Interest Coverage 2012-09-01       NA
## 3 Profitability    32 Interest Coverage 2013-09-01   369.79
## 4 Profitability    32 Interest Coverage 2014-09-01   140.28
## 5 Profitability    32 Interest Coverage 2015-09-01    99.93
## 6 Profitability    32 Interest Coverage 2016-09-01    43.15
```

A novel and noteworthy aspect of `tidyquant` is the access to information about US stock exchanges using function `tq_exchange`. Look at the next example, where we access information about all stocks traded in AMEX.

```
# get stocks in AMEX
print(head(tq_exchange('AMEX')))
```

```
## # A tibble: 6 × 7
##    symbol
##     <chr>
## 1    XXII
## 2     FAX
```

```
## 3      IAF
## 4       CH
## 5      ABE
## 6      FCO
## # ... with 6 more variables: company <chr>,
## #   last.sale.price <dbl>, market.cap <chr>,
## #   ipo.year <dbl>, sector <chr>, industry <chr>
```

We can also get information about components of an index using function `tq_index`. The available market indices are:

```
# print available indices
print(tq_index_options())
```

```
##  [1] "DOWJONES"    "DJI"         "DJT"         "DJU"
##  [5] "SP100"       "SP400"       "SP500"       "SP600"
##  [9] "RUSSELL1000" "RUSSELL2000" "RUSSELL3000" "AMEX"
## [13] "AMEXGOLD"    "AMEXOIL"     "NASDAQ"      "NASDAQ100"
## [17] "NYSE"        "SOX"
```

Let's get information for `"DOWJONES"`.

```
# get components of "DOWJONES"
print(tq_index("DOWJONES"))
```

```
## # A tibble: 65 × 2
##    symbol                     company
##    <chr>                        <chr>
## 1     MMM                         3M
## 2     ALK            ALASKA AIR GROUP
## 3     AAL AMERICAN AIRLINES GROUP INC.
## 4     AEP       AMERICAN ELECTRIC POWER
## 5     AXP             AMERICAN EXPRESS
## 6     AWK          AMERICAN WATER WORKS
## 7    AAPL                       APPLE
## 8     CAR            AVIS BUDGET GROUP
## 9     CAT                  CATERPILLAR
## 10    CNP            CENTERPOINT ENERGY
## # ... with 55 more rows
```

These functions are useful because they give the user access to the current tickers for each market. By using functions `tq_exchange` or `tq_index` with `tq_get`, downloading comprehensive information for American stock exchanges becomes very easy.

We only looked into a few functions from package **tidyquant** related to importing datasets. It also offers solutions for the usual manipulations, such as calculating returns and functions for portfolio analytics, among others. You can find more details about this package in its website.

7.1.5   Package `GetHFData`

Package `GetHFData` (Perlin and Ramos, 2016) is designed to facilitate the importation and analysis of high frequency trading data from Bovespa, the Brazilian Financial exchange. It allows access to trade data in the equity and derivative market. At the time of this book, `GetHFData` is the only available package in CRAN that allows direct and free access to high frequency data. The functions from the package allow the user to get information from the ftp site and download raw or aggregate datasets. In section 11.3.3 we provide a full example of processing and manipulating high frequency data using `GetHFData`.

Let's try a simple example by downloading trade data for the last available date for the two most traded stocks in the Brazilian financial market, Petrobras (PETR4) and Vale do Rio Doce (VALE5).

```
library(GetHFData)

# set tickers and type of market
my.ticker <- c('PETR4','VALE5')
my.type.market <- 'equity'

# get available dates from ftp
df.available.dates <- ghfd_get_ftp_contents(my.type.market)

##
## Reading ftp contents for equity (attempt = 1|10)
# set last date
last.date <- max(df.available.dates$dates)

# get data!
my.df <- ghfd_get_HF_data(my.assets = my.ticker,
                          type.market = 'equity',
                          first.date = last.date,
                          last.date = last.date,
                          type.output = 'agg',
                          agg.diff = '5 min')

##
## Running ghfd_get_HF_Data for:
```

```
##      type.market = equity
##      my.assets = PETR4, VALE5
##      type.output = agg
##        agg.diff = 5 min
## Reading ftp contents for equity (attempt = 1|10)
##    Found  555  files in ftp
##    First available date in ftp:  2015-03-02
##    Last available date in ftp:   2017-05-04
##    First date to download:  2017-05-04
##    Last date to download:   2017-05-04
## Downloading ftp files/NEG_20170504.zip (1|1) Attempt 1
##    -> Reading files - Imported  1093119 lines, 432 unique tickers
##    -> Processing file - Found 93681 lines for 2 selected tickers
##    -> Aggregation resulted in dataframe with 166 rows
```

```
# print results
print(head(my.df))
```

```
##   InstrumentSymbol SessionDate        TradeDateTime n.trades
## 1           PETR4  2017-05-04 2017-05-04 10:00:00      248
## 2           PETR4  2017-05-04 2017-05-04 10:05:00      377
## 3           PETR4  2017-05-04 2017-05-04 10:10:00      576
## 4           PETR4  2017-05-04 2017-05-04 10:15:00      691
## 5           PETR4  2017-05-04 2017-05-04 10:20:00      622
## 6           PETR4  2017-05-04 2017-05-04 10:25:00      577
##   last.price weighted.price   period.ret period.ret.volat
## 1      13.97        13.98443 -0.002142857     0.0005178093
## 2      13.97        13.97799  0.000000000     0.0003911436
## 3      13.90        13.95730 -0.005010737     0.0003922858
## 4      13.87        13.86272 -0.001439885     0.0004579248
## 5      13.82        13.83004 -0.003604903     0.0003567767
## 6      13.81        13.81749 -0.001446132     0.0003467844
##    sum.qtd  sum.vol n.buys n.sells Tradetime
## 1   375700  5253941     65     183  10:00:00
## 2   398000  5563238    136     241  10:05:00
## 3  1582200 22083094    181     395  10:10:00
## 4   718200  9956191    179     512  10:15:00
## 5   669100  9253666    221     401  10:20:00
## 6   855200 11816689    181     396  10:25:00
```

The output of `ghfd_get_HF_data` is a `dataframe` with several columns, such as time frame, last price, volatility, number of buyer/seller initiated trades, among other information. The user can also download raw data, without aggregation, by setting option `type.output='raw'`. Let's give it a try:

```
library(GetHFData)

# set tickers and type of market
my.ticker <- c('PETR4','VALE5')
my.type.market <- 'equity'

# get available dates from ftp
df.available.dates <- ghfd_get_ftp_contents(my.type.market)

##
## Reading ftp contents for equity (attempt = 1|10)
# set last date
last.date <- max(df.available.dates$dates)

# get data!
my.df <- ghfd_get_HF_data(my.assets = my.ticker,
                          type.market = 'equity',
                          first.date = last.date,
                          last.date = last.date,
                          type.output = 'raw')

##
## Running ghfd_get_HF_Data for:
##     type.market = equity
##     my.assets = PETR4, VALE5
##     type.output = raw
## Reading ftp contents for equity (attempt = 1|10)
##     Found  555  files in ftp
##     First available date in ftp:  2015-03-02
##     Last available date in ftp:   2017-05-04
##     First date to download:  2017-05-04
##     Last date to download:   2017-05-04
## Downloading ftp files/NEG_20170504.zip (1|1) Attempt 1
##     -> Reading files - Imported  1093119 lines, 432 unique tickers
##     -> Processing file - Found 93681 lines for 2 selected tickers
# print results
print(head(my.df))

##    SessionDate InstrumentSymbol TradePrice TradedQuantity
## 1   2017-05-04            PETR4         14            700
## 2   2017-05-04            PETR4         14            100
## 3   2017-05-04            PETR4         14           1000
```

```
## 4   2017-05-04               PETR4          14                900
## 5   2017-05-04               PETR4          14                300
## 6   2017-05-04               PETR4          14                100
##        Tradetime CrossTradeIndicator BuyMember SellMember
## 1 10:04:13.925                    0       386         72
## 2 10:04:13.925                    0        86         39
## 3 10:04:13.925                    0        86         39
## 4 10:04:13.925                    0       386         85
## 5 10:04:13.925                    0       262         39
## 6 10:04:13.925                    0       262         39
##          TradeDateTime TradeSign
## 1 2017-05-04 10:04:13        -1
## 2 2017-05-04 10:04:13        -1
## 3 2017-05-04 10:04:13        -1
## 4 2017-05-04 10:04:13        -1
## 5 2017-05-04 10:04:13        -1
## 6 2017-05-04 10:04:13        -1
```

In the chapter about research scripts, we will use this package for studying the intraday pattern of liquidity in the stock market. More details about the package can be found in Perlin and Ramos (2016).

7.1.6 Package ustyc

Package ustyc allows the download of yield curve data from the US Treasury data feed system. The yield curve is the nominal return an investor would receive for different maturities. The values of yields are based on prices of US government debt instruments traded on the secondary market. Since US bonds have minimal default risk, these values are commonly used as benchmarks for risk free returns in financial markets.

Using package ustyc is very simple. All you need to do is call function getYieldCurve. In the following example, we will download the yield curve for year 2016.

```
library(ustyc)
```

```
# get yield curve
my.yield.curve <- getYieldCurve(year = 2016)
```

The return object is a list, where the yield curve data is contained in slot df. Each row represents a date, and each column represents a different maturity:

```
# print result
print(head(my.yield.curve$df))
```

```
##             BC_1MONTH BC_3MONTH BC_6MONTH BC_1YEAR BC_2YEAR
## 2016-01-04     0.17      0.22      0.49     0.61     1.02
## 2016-01-05     0.20      0.20      0.49     0.68     1.04
## 2016-01-06     0.21      0.21      0.47     0.67     0.99
## 2016-01-07     0.20      0.20      0.46     0.66     0.96
## 2016-01-08     0.20      0.20      0.45     0.64     0.94
## 2016-01-11     0.19      0.21      0.48     0.63     0.94
##             BC_3YEAR BC_5YEAR BC_7YEAR BC_10YEAR BC_20YEAR
## 2016-01-04    1.31     1.73     2.06     2.24      2.64
## 2016-01-05    1.32     1.73     2.06     2.25      2.67
## 2016-01-06    1.26     1.65     1.98     2.18      2.59
## 2016-01-07    1.22     1.61     1.94     2.16      2.56
## 2016-01-08    1.20     1.57     1.91     2.13      2.55
## 2016-01-11    1.20     1.58     1.94     2.17      2.59
##             BC_30YEAR BC_30YEARDISPLAY
## 2016-01-04    2.98          2.98
## 2016-01-05    3.01          3.01
## 2016-01-06    2.94          2.94
## 2016-01-07    2.92          2.92
## 2016-01-08    2.91          2.91
## 2016-01-11    2.96          2.96
```

In section 8.3, we will learn how to use this data to plot the US yield curve.

7.1.7 Package `Quandl`

Another major source of financial data is the *Quandl* platform. It is an established and comprehensive system that provides access to a series of free and paid data. It provides information for several types of financial markets, such as equity, options, futures, currencies, commodities, and more. Several central banks and research institutions also provide economic and financial information in this platform. I strongly recommend browsing the available datasets from the Quandl website.

The first step in using `Quandl` is to register a new user at the website. Soon after, go to *account settings* and click *API KEY*. This page should show a code, such as `Asv8Ac7zuZzJSCGxynfG`. Copy this text to the clipboard (*Control + c*) and, in R, define a character object containing the copied content as follows:

```
# set api key to quandl
my.api.key <- 'Asv8Ac7zuZzJSCGxynfG'
```

This API key is unique to each user, and the one presented here will not work in your computer. You need to get your own to run the examples. After finding and setting your own API key, go to Quandl's website and look for the symbol of the time series of interest. As an example, we will use the symbol WGC/GOLD_DAILY_EUR, which represents the time series of gold prices in euro. Another, more practical way of finding the Quandl symbol is to use funtion Quandl.search to lookup a search string directly from R.

```
library(Quandl)
```

```
# search string in quandl
df.search <- Quandl.search('Gold in Euro', silent = TRUE)
```

In our case, the function returned a dataframe with 10 rows and 13 columns. Let's have a look in the names of the columns:

```
# print columns from
print(colnames(df.search))
```

```
##  [1] "id"                    "dataset_code"
##  [3] "database_code"         "name"
##  [5] "description"           "refreshed_at"
##  [7] "newest_available_date" "oldest_available_date"
##  [9] "column_names"          "frequency"
## [11] "type"                  "premium"
## [13] "database_id"
```

The description column gives information about the available datasets matching the search string. The actual Quandl code is given by combining database_id with dataset_code.

With the API key and the Quandl symbol, we use function Quandl.api_key from package Quandl to register our key and function Quandl to download the data. See the full example next:

```
library(Quandl)
```

```
# register api key
Quandl.api_key(my.api.key)
```

```
# set symbol and dates
my.symbol <- 'WGC/GOLD_DAILY_EUR'
first.date <- as.Date('2000-01-01')
last.date <- Sys.Date()
```

```
# get data!
my.df <- Quandl(code = my.symbol,
                type='raw',
                start_date = first.date,
                end_date = last.date)

print(tail(my.df))

##            Date     Value
## 4519 2000-01-10  274.3301
## 4520 2000-01-07  274.1764
## 4521 2000-01-06  269.9777
## 4522 2000-01-05  271.3069
## 4523 2000-01-04  273.2482
## 4524 2000-01-03  280.2000
```

Notice how we used `type = 'raw'` in the inputs of `Quandl`. This option forces the function to output a `dataframe`. Other options include the output of objects of type `ts`, `zoo`, `xts` and `timeSeries`. If using `Quandl` will become part of your data analysis routine, I strongly recommend reading the help manual of the package. Several parameters can be passed to function `Quandl`, including the choice for applying transformations in the resulting dataset. You can find more details about using `Quandl` in R from its website.

7.1.8   Package `Rbitcoin`

Given the popularity of cripto-currencies, another package worth mentioning is `RBitcoin`. It allows access to trade data from several Bitcoin exchanges. Here, let's show a simple example of importing trade data from the `'kraken'` exchange, using Euro as the currency.

```
library(Rbitcoin)

# set mkt, currency pair and type of action
my.mkt <- "kraken"
my.currency <- c("BTC","EUR")
my.action <- 'trades'

# import data
my.l <- market.api.process(market = my.mkt,
                           currency_pair = my.currency,
                           action = my.action)
```

```
# print it
print(my.l)

## $market
## [1] "kraken"
##
## $base
## [1] "BTC"
##
## $quote
## [1] "EUR"
##
## $timestamp
## [1] "2017-05-05 14:17:20 BRT"
##
## $market_timestamp
## [1] NA
##
## $trades
##                        date     price      amount
##    1: 2017-05-05 17:01:07 1366.032 0.07871112
##    2: 2017-05-05 17:01:07 1367.914 0.00830200
##    3: 2017-05-05 17:01:07 1367.951 0.00154166
##    4: 2017-05-05 17:01:11 1370.000 0.01730000
##    5: 2017-05-05 17:01:11 1374.000 0.00458442
##   ---
##  996: 2017-05-05 17:17:07 1385.567 0.03620793
##  997: 2017-05-05 17:17:18 1384.501 0.45299199
##  998: 2017-05-05 17:17:19 1385.567 0.01339636
##  999: 2017-05-05 17:17:22 1385.567 0.10539408
## 1000: 2017-05-05 17:17:22 1385.567 0.04400000
##                        tid type
##    1:                  NA  bid
##    2:                  NA  bid
##    3:                  NA  bid
##    4:                  NA  bid
##    5:                  NA  bid
##   ---
##  996:                  NA  ask
##  997:                  NA  ask
##  998:                  NA  bid
##  999:                  NA  bid
```

```
## 1000: 1494004642362940051  bid
```

The output of `market.api.process` is a `list` object with information about Bitcoin in the `'kraken'` market. The actual trades are available in the `trade` slot of `my.l`. Let's have a look at its content:

```
print(tail(my.l$trades))
```

```
##                      date    price      amount
## 1: 2017-05-05 17:17:07 1385.567 0.12100000
## 2: 2017-05-05 17:17:07 1385.567 0.03620793
## 3: 2017-05-05 17:17:18 1384.501 0.45299199
## 4: 2017-05-05 17:17:19 1385.567 0.01339636
## 5: 2017-05-05 17:17:22 1385.567 0.10539408
## 6: 2017-05-05 17:17:22 1385.567 0.04400000
##                      tid type
## 1:                   NA  ask
## 2:                   NA  ask
## 3:                   NA  ask
## 4:                   NA  bid
## 5:                   NA  bid
## 6: 1494004642362940051  bid
```

It includes price and time information for the past 1000 trades. The package also includes functions for looking into the order book of each market and managing Bitcoin wallets. More details about the functionalities of the package are found in its website.

7.1.9   Other Packages

In CRAN, you'll find many more packages for importing financial datasets in R. In this section, we focused on packages that are free and easy to use. Interface to commercial data sources is also possible. Several companies provide APIs for serving data to their clients. Packages such as `Rblpapi` (Bloomberg), `IBrokers` (Interactive Brokers), `TFX` (TrueFX), `rdatastream` (Thomson Dataworks) can make R communicate with these APIs and allow importation of datasets. If the company you use is not presented here, the list of CRAN packages can help you find a package for other data vendors.

7.2 Accessing Data from Web Pages (*webscraping*)

The previous packages are useful, as they make it easy to import data directly from the web. In many cases, however, the information of interest is not available in packages, but in a web page - usually in a tabular format. The main advantage of using information from a webpage is that, every time we run the code, we can get current information as the site is updated. By doing this on a large scale, we can build complex systems to help make decisions.

The process of extracting information from web pages is called *webscraping*. Depending on the structure and technology used in the internet page, importing its content can be as trivial as a single line in R or a complex process as a full script. Let's look at two examples; first, we will retrieve tabular information about SP500 index from Wikipedia and, second, we will extract current inflation and interest rate from the Reserve Bank of Australia (RBA) website.

7.2.1 Scraping the Components of the SP500 Index from Wikipedia

In its website, Wikipedia offers a section about the components of the SP500 index. This information is presented in a tabular format, Figure 7.1.

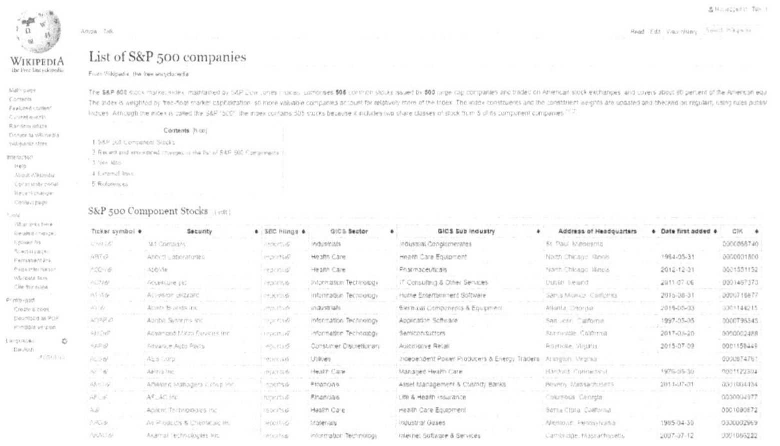

Figure 7.1: Mirror of Wikipedia page on SP500 components

The information in this web page is constantly updated, and we can use it to import information about the stocks belonging to the SP500 index. Before delving into the R code, we need to understand how a webpage works. In a nutshell, a webpage is nothing more than a lengthy *html* code interpreted by your browser. A numerical value or text presented in the website can usually be found within the code. This code has a particular structure with classes and formats. Every element of a webpage has an address, called *xpath* . In chrome and firefox browsers, you can see the actual code of a webpage by using the mouse to right-click any part of the webpage and selecting *show source code.*

The first step in webscraping is finding out where the information you want is located. You can do that by right clicking in the specific location of the number/text in the website and selecting *inspect*. This will open an extra window in the browser. Once you do that, right click in the selection and chose *copy* and *copy xpath*. In Figure 7.2, we see a mirror of what you should be seeing in your browser.

Figure 7.2: Finding xpath from website

In this case, the copied *xpath* is:

```
'//*[@id="mw-content-text"]/table[1]/thead/tr/th[2]'
```

This is the address of the header of the table. We can go to an upper level and get all the content of the table, including header, rows, and columns. This is equivalent to address `//*[@id="mw-content-text"]/table[1]`.

Now that we have the location of what we want, let's load package `rvest` (Wickham, 2016b) and use functions `read_html`, `html_nodes` and `html_table` to import the desired table into R:

```
library(rvest)
```

```
# set url and xpath
my.url <- 'https://en.wikipedia.org/wiki/List_of_S%26P_500_companies'
my.xpath <- '//*[@id="mw-content-text"]/table[1]'
```

```
# get nodes from html
out.nodes <- html_nodes(read_html(my.url),
                        xpath = my.xpath)
```

```
# get table from nodes (each element in
# list is a table)
df.SP500Stocks <- html_table(out.nodes)

# isolate it and print it
df.SP500Stocks <- df.SP500Stocks[[1]]
print(head(df.SP500Stocks))
```

```
##   Ticker symbol                Security SEC filings
## 1          MMM              3M Company      reports
## 2          ABT   Abbott Laboratories       reports
## 3         ABBV             AbbVie Inc.      reports
## 4          ACN           Accenture plc      reports
## 5         ATVI     Activision Blizzard      reports
## 6          AYI      Acuity Brands Inc      reports
##              GICS Sector                GICS Sub Industry
## 1            Industrials       Industrial Conglomerates
## 2            Health Care          Health Care Equipment
## 3            Health Care                Pharmaceuticals
## 4 Information Technology    IT Consulting & Other Services
## 5 Information Technology      Home Entertainment Software
## 6            Industrials Electrical Components & Equipment
##     Address of Headquarters Date first added      CIK
## 1       St. Paul, Minnesota                       66740
## 2   North Chicago, Illinois       1964-03-31      1800
## 3   North Chicago, Illinois       2012-12-31   1551152
## 4           Dublin, Ireland       2011-07-06   1467373
## 5 Santa Monica, California       2015-08-31    718877
## 6           Atlanta, Georgia       2016-05-03   1144215
```

Object `df.SP500Stocks` contains a mirror of the data from the Wikipedia website. The names of the columns require a bit of work, but the data is intact and could be further used in a script.

7.2.2 Scraping the Website of the Reserve Bank of Australia

As another example of webscraping with R, let's import information from the Reserve Bank of Australia. When accessed in 2017-03-24, its home page mirrors Figure 7.3.

As you can see, the website offers financial information, such as news and market rates. Let's assume we are interested in the information about current cash/bank

Figure 7.3: Website for the Reserve Bank of Australia

rate and inflation, right upper corner of the webpage. The first step is finding out the *xpath* of the information we want. Using the procedure described in previous example, we find out the address of both values, market rate and current inflation:

```
my.xpath.inflation <- '//*[@id="content"]/section[1]/div/div[2]/p'
my.xpath.int.rate <- '//*[@id="content"]/section[1]/div/div[1]/p'
```

A difference from the previous example is we are not importing a table, but a simple text from the website. For that, we use function `html_text` and not `html_table`. The full code and its output is presented next.

```
library(rvest)

# set address of RBA
my.url <- 'http://www.rba.gov.au/'

# read html
html.code <- read_html(my.url)

# set xpaths
my.xpath.inflation <- '//*[@id="content"]/section[1]/div/div[2]/p'
my.xpath.int.rate <- '//*[@id="content"]/section[1]/div/div[1]/p'

# get inflation from html
my.inflation <- html_text(html_nodes(html.code,
```

```
                                    xpath = my.xpath.inflation ))

# get interest rate from html
my.int.rate <- html_text(html_nodes(x = html.code,
                                     xpath = my.xpath.int.rate ))

# print result
cat("\nCurrent inflation in AUS:", my.inflation)
cat("\nCurrent interest rate AUS:", my.int.rate)

##
## Current inflation in AUS:   1.5%

##
## Current interest rate in AUS:   1.50%
```

The use of *Webscraping* techniques becomes a strong ally of the researcher. They give you access to an immense amount of information available on the web. However, each scenario of *webscraping* is particular. It is not always the case that you can import data directly and easily as in the previous examples. Readers interested in this topic should study the functionalities of packages **rvest** (Wickham, 2016b), **XML** (Lang and the CRAN Team, 2016), **RSelenium** (Harrison, 2016) and **splashr** (available in Github). Each one of these is best suited to particular webscraping problems.

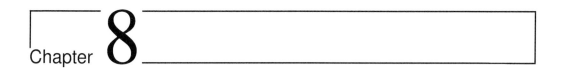

Chapter 8

Creating and Saving Figures with ggplot2

Using graphical resources in technical reports and academic documents is widespread. Sometimes, this is simply what your audience expects. R has built-in functions for creating figures, such as `plot` and `hist`. Using the native plotting functions, however, is not recommended. The customization of the graphic is not straightforward and the options are limited. This deficiency was remedied by users. In 2005, Hadley Wickham, author of many other packages featured in this book, proposed a new way of structuring and creating figures in R, with a package called `ggplot2` (Wickham, 2009). It provides functions to generate graphics, structuring the process with an accessible and intuitive *layer* notation. This means graphics can be customized quickly and easily.

In this book, we will not go deep into `ggplot2` and all the details of its capacity. We will show the main features of the package for most situations of data analysis in finance. For advanced users who want to know more about `ggplot2`, my advice is to consult the author's own book (Wickham, 2009).

For most examples given here, we will work with the data available in file `SP500-Stocks-WithRet.RData`. It contains daily closing prices and returns data for all components of the SP500 index. This file was created in chapter 9.

First, let's load the data.

```r
# set file and load data
my.f <- 'data/SP500-Stocks-WithRet.RData'
load(my.f)
```

```
# print first 5 rows
print(head(my.df))
```

```
## # A tibble: 6 × 4
##    price.adjusted   ref.date ticker          ret
##             <dbl>     <date> <chr>         <dbl>
## 1        68.72509 2010-01-05    MMM -0.006263503
## 2        69.69973 2010-01-06    MMM  0.014181794
## 3        69.74972 2010-01-07    MMM  0.000717162
## 4        70.24120 2010-01-08    MMM  0.007046423
## 5        69.95798 2010-01-11    MMM -0.004032220
## 6        70.01629 2010-01-12    MMM  0.000833529
```

8.1   Using Graphic Windows

Before studying the use of `ggplot2`, we need to understand how these images are handled within the RStudio platform. When a new figure is created, as in `plot(1:20)`, it appears in the *Plots* panel (bottom right corner of RStudio). This panel, however, is small, making it difficult to visualize the figure in standard monitors. You can increase the panel's size manually, but this creates unnecessary work, as you might need to resize it later to give space for other panels.

A more intelligent approach to managing figures is to create an external window in RStudio, so the graphic can be displayed and resized independently of the main interface. To create a window, just use command `x11()` before the line of code that creates the figure, as in:

```
x11()
plot(1:10)
```

The visual result in RStudio should be similar to Figure 8.1.

Each call to `x11()` will create a new window. Therefore, we can create various figures and allocate them in different windows, making it easy to analyze each individually or together, side by side.

After creating so many windows, it is best to close them. You can use `graphics.off` for that. This function, called with no argument, as in `graphics.off()`, will close all opened windows. It is common practice to use it in the beginning of a research script, so all graphic windows are closed.

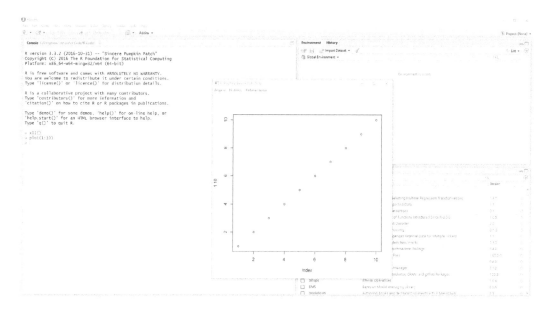

Figure 8.1: Screen of RStudio with the use of command x11()

8.2   Creating Figures with Function `qplot`

Package `ggplot2` has an introductory function, called `qplot` (*quick plot*), that mimics the behaviour of the native R function `plot`. To use it, all you need to know are the points that define the horizontal axis (x), the points of the vertical axis (y), and the geometric shape used in the plot.

To build a time series plot with the prices of stock MMM, we use the following code:

```
library(ggplot2)

# filter stock data
temp.df <- my.df[my.df$ticker == 'MMM', ]

# plot its prices
qplot(data = temp.df,
      x = ref.date,
      y = price.adjusted,
      geom = 'line')
```

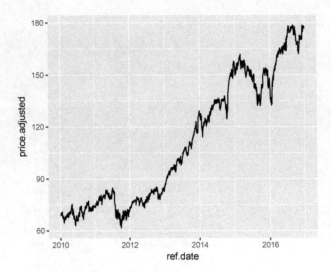

In the previous example, the name of the axis corresponds to the names of the columns in `temp.df`. If we want to customize it for a given text, we use arguments `xlab` and `ylab`:

```
qplot(data = temp.df,
      x = ref.date,
      y = price.adjusted,
      geom = 'line',
      xlab = 'Dates',
      ylab = 'Adjusted closing prices')
```

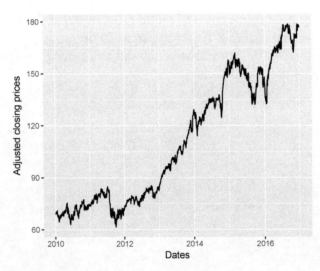

Notice how the horizontal axis of dates in the previous figures is formatted to show only the years. It adapts automatically according to the length of time in the plot. This only happened because the `ref.date` column is correctly defined as a `Date`

object.

8.3 Creating Figures with Function ggplot

Using function qplot is recommended when you want to create a plot quickly for immediate viewing. This function has restrictions in the way it works, making it more difficult to customize the output.The recommended function to use in ggplot2 is ggplot. It uses a specific framework that allows a series of complex graphical constructions.

Before presenting examples using ggplot, let's discuss the philosophy behind how ggplot works. First, every figure has horizontal and vertical coordinates. These points define where the symbols or lines should be drawn. Second, we have a geometric shape placed in the coordinates. It can be a circle, a point or a line, as in the previous figures. We set the size and colour of these objects and, finally, by combining all these elements, we create the full figure.

The distinction between the steps of creating a figure is important, because it is precisely this way that ggplot2 works. We make choices for x, y, colour, and size based on data, and then chose the desired format of the graphic. Everything works within each step, as if we are drawing layers in the figure.

Look at the syntax of the following example that recreates the figure previously created with qplot.

```
p <- ggplot(data = temp.df, aes(x = ref.date, y = price.adjusted))
p <- p + geom_line()
p <- p + labs(x = 'Dates', y = 'Adjusted closing prices')
print(p)
```

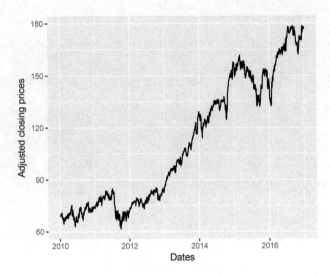

In using ggplot, it is always necessary to provide a dataframe. If you want to create figures from atomic vectors, you must allocate them to a dataframe first. After defining the data, we use function aes to set the aesthetics of the graph with the x and y coordinates. Here, we set the horizontal axis using column date and the vertical axis as prices (column price.adjusted). As we will soon see, it is possible to use other information in aes, such as colour and shapes.

Once the data and axis are defined, we save it in object p. This object registers the current information as new layers are added with the + sign. The second line of the code, p <- p + geom_line(), defines the type of figure. Here, we used function geom_lines, which is a simple line graph that connects the points. In ggplot2, the functions that define the geometric type begins with geom_ character. So, using the *autocomplete* function of RStudio, you can see there a lot of options. We can use stringr to find the list of functions in ggplot2, version 2.2.1 (2017-05-05), that starts with geom_:

```
library(ggplot2)
library(stringr)

# get names of functions in ggplot2
fcts <- ls('package:ggplot2')

# select those that starts with geom_
idx <- str_sub(fcts, 1, 5) == 'geom_'
fcts <- fcts[idx]

# print result
print(fcts)
```

```
##  [1] "geom_abline"     "geom_area"        "geom_bar"
##  [4] "geom_bin2d"      "geom_blank"       "geom_boxplot"
##  [7] "geom_col"        "geom_contour"     "geom_count"
## [10] "geom_crossbar"   "geom_curve"       "geom_density"
## [13] "geom_density_2d" "geom_density2d"   "geom_dotplot"
## [16] "geom_errorbar"   "geom_errorbarh"   "geom_freqpoly"
## [19] "geom_hex"        "geom_histogram"   "geom_hline"
## [22] "geom_jitter"     "geom_label"       "geom_line"
## [25] "geom_linerange"  "geom_map"         "geom_path"
## [28] "geom_point"      "geom_pointrange"  "geom_polygon"
## [31] "geom_qq"         "geom_quantile"    "geom_raster"
## [34] "geom_rect"       "geom_ribbon"      "geom_rug"
## [37] "geom_segment"    "geom_smooth"      "geom_spoke"
## [40] "geom_step"       "geom_text"        "geom_tile"
## [43] "geom_violin"     "geom_vline"
```

As you can see, there are plenty of options. Package `ggplot2` offers a significant quantity of geometrics shapes in creating figures. Going back to our example, the third line of the code defines the name of axis x and y with function `labs`. Finally, we print the figure stored in `p` with function `print`. It is important to highlight this modular approach in using `ggplot`: each layer of the figure was created in a line of code. For example, if we did not want to set the axes as *Dates* and *Adjusted closing prices*, we can simply comment the line in the script, as in:

```
p <- ggplot(data = temp.df, aes(x = ref.date, y = price.adjusted))
p <- p + geom_line()
#p <- p + labs(x = 'Dates', y = 'Adjusted closing prices')
print(p)
```

One of the great advantages of using `ggplot` is when creating figures for different groups. Let's create a figure that shows, on the same axis, prices of four stocks selected randomly. The first step is to create a temporary `dataframe` that contains these stocks only.

```
# fix seed
set.seed(10)

# select 4 stocks randomly
my.tickers <- sample(unique(my.df$ticker), 4)

# find all rows that contain the stocks
idx <- my.df$ticker %in% my.tickers

# create temporary df
```

```
temp.df <- my.df[idx, ]
```

In this code, first, we set a random seed, so anyone can reproduce the result. We use operator `%in%` to find out the rows of `my.df` that contain data for the tickers in `my.tickers`. It returns `TRUE` when any *ticker* in `my.tickers` is found and `FALSE` otherwise. After finding the rows, we create a temporary `dataframe` that contains the data of the selected stocks. Now, we create the figure with the following code:

```
p <- ggplot(data = temp.df, aes(x = ref.date,
                                y = price.adjusted,
                                colour=ticker))
p <- p + geom_line()
p <- p + labs(x = 'Dates', y = 'Adjusted closing prices')
print(p)
```

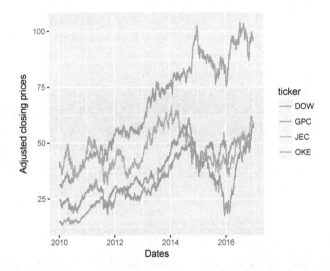

A difference from the previous examples is that we defined the colour of the lines using argument `colour` in `aes`. Each line colour is defined by the elements in column `ticker` of `temp.df`. The actual choices of colour, e.g., red, blue, and so on, is automatically defined by `ggplot`.

Now, let's use what we learned so far to create the current yield curve of the US market. The yield curve is one of the standard plots in finance, showing the market assessment of interest rates according to different time horizons. In the following code, we will first download the related data using package `ustyc`, structure and clean the raw data, and plot the yields for the last available date in 2016 using ggplot2.

```
library(ustyc)
library(tidyr)
```

```r
library(ggplot2)
library(stringr)

# get yield curve
my.df.yc <- getYieldCurve(year = 2016)$df

# set date.col
my.df.yc$ref.date <- as.Date(rownames(my.df.yc))

# change to long format and convert to factor
my.df.yc <- gather(data=my.df.yc, key =ref.date)
names(my.df.yc) <- c('ref.date', 'maturity', 'rate')
my.df.yc$maturity <- as.factor(my.df.yc$maturity)

# keep only longer term yields (names with YEAR)
idx <- str_detect(my.df.yc$maturity, 'YEAR')
my.df.yc <- my.df.yc[idx, ]

# change name to year number with
# obs: regex ([0-9]+) extracts all numbers within a string
out <- str_extract_all(string = my.df.yc$maturity,
                       pattern = '([0-9]+)')
my.df.yc$maturity <- as.numeric(out)

# keep only last date of each
last.date <- max(my.df.yc$ref.date)
my.df.yc.last.date <- my.df.yc[my.df.yc$ref.date == last.date, ]

# plot it!
p <- ggplot(my.df.yc.last.date, aes(x=maturity, y=rate))
p <- p + geom_point(size=2)
p <- p + geom_line(size=1)
p <- p + labs(x = 'Maturity (years)',
              y='Yield Rate',
              title = paste0('US Yield Curve (',last.date,')' ))

print(p)
```

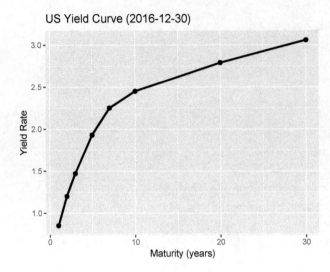

As expected, the current yield curve is upward rising, meaning the yield rate increases with the maturity of the debt. As an extension of the example, we can add some dynamic to the figure by using several dates. Have a look in the following code, where we use five yield curves covering the whole year of 2016.

```r
# set number of periods
n.periods <- 5

# set sequence of observations
my.seq <- floor(seq(1,nrow(my.df.yc), length.out = n.periods))

# get actual dates from sequence
my.dates <- my.df.yc$ref.date[my.seq]

# find rows for dates in df
idx <- my.df.yc$ref.date %in% my.dates
my.df.yc.periods <- my.df.yc[idx, ]

# plot it!
p <- ggplot(my.df.yc.periods, aes(x=maturity,
                                  y=rate,
                                  color= factor(ref.date)))
p <- p + geom_point(size=2)
p <- p + geom_line(size=1)
p <- p + labs(x = 'Maturity (years)',
              y='Yield Rate',
              title = 'US Yield Curve')
```

```
print(p)
```

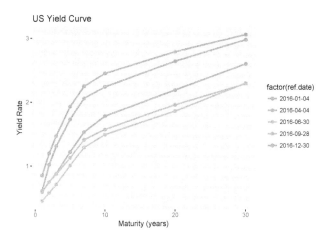

The US yield curve changed significantly in 2016. In empirical applications, the information in the US yield curve can be used as a benchmark for the calculation of cost of capital.

As another example of geometric shape in `ggplot`, let's create a bar plot with the daily sharpe ratio, mean divided by standard deviation of returns, for 10 assets from the database, ordered from high to low. First, we need to calculate the sharpe ratio for each stock. This is easily done with `dplyr`. Once the data is available, we use `geom_bar` to create the bar figure. Notice input `x` in `aes` is set using `reorder(ticker, -sharpe.ratio)`. It forces the horizontal axis to display descending values of sharpe ratio.

```
library(dplyr)
# fix seed
set.seed(10)

# select 10 stocks randomly
my.tickers <- sample(unique(my.df$ticker), 10)

# find all rows that contain the stocks
idx <- my.df$ticker %in% my.tickers

# create temporary df
temp.df <- my.df[idx, ]

plot.df <- temp.df %>%
  group_by(ticker) %>%
  summarise(sharpe.ratio = mean(ret)/sd(ret))
```

```
p <- ggplot(data = plot.df,
            aes(x = reorder(ticker, -sharpe.ratio),
            y = sharpe.ratio))
p <- p + geom_bar(stat = 'identity')
p <- p + labs(x = 'Tickers', y = 'Daily Sharpe Ratio')
print(p)
```

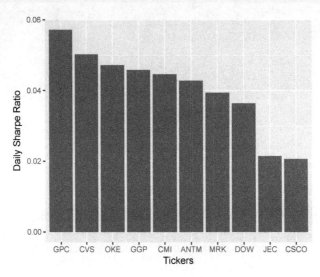

8.3.1   Using Themes

One way of customizing graphics in `ggplot2` is using themes. A theme is a collection of options that defines the organization of the figure, its points and line colours, notation of axis, background colour, and several other features. Package `ggplot` has a collection of functions for setting themes, and their name start with text *theme*. Next, we show the list of theme related functions in `ggplot`, version 2.2.1 (2017-05-05).

```
library(ggplot2)
library(stringr)

# get all functions
fcts <- ls('package:ggplot2')

# find out those that start with theme_
idx <- str_sub(fcts, 1, 6) == 'theme_'
fcts <- fcts[idx]
```

```
# print result
print(fcts)
```

```
## [1] "theme_bw"      "theme_classic"  "theme_dark"
## [4] "theme_get"     "theme_gray"     "theme_grey"
## [7] "theme_light"   "theme_linedraw" "theme_minimal"
## [10] "theme_replace" "theme_set"     "theme_update"
## [13] "theme_void"
```

Let's try it with the theme of function `theme_bw`. From the manual: "theme_bw sets the classic dark-on-light ggplot2 theme. May work better for presentations displayed with a projector." Let's look at it visually. We need only to add a new line `p <- p + theme_bw()` in the previous code.

```
p <- ggplot(data = temp.df, aes(x = ref.date,
                                y = price.adjusted,
                                colour=ticker))
p <- p + geom_line()
p <- p + labs(x = 'Dates', y = 'Adjusted closing prices')
p <- p + theme_bw()
```

```
print(p)
```

As you can see, the new theme was a white background and a frame box. You can try other themes on your computer and see which one you like the most. You can also create your own theme. Have a look at Wickham (2009) for instructions on this specific task.

In the previous example, notice how the structure of the figure has changed, but not the colours of the lines. These selection of the colours follows a cycle. When the whole sequence of colours ends, it restarts. Sometimes, especially in the submission to scientific journals, it is expected that all figures have a grey theme; they must be in black and white. We can use function `scale_colour_grey` to set a colour cycle between white and black in our previous figure:

```
p <- p + scale_colour_grey(start = 0.0, end = 0.6)
print(p)
```

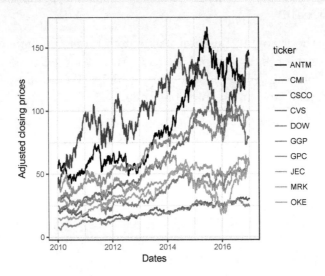

The lines of the plot are now in grey. The inputs `start` and `end` at `scale_color_grey` set the minimum and maximum of "whiteness". So, never use `end=1` with a white background. Otherwise, some lines will will not be visible.

8.3.2 Creating Panels with `facet_wrap`

Another possibility in creating graphics for different groups is to use panels. It allocates each group in a different part of the figure. When placed side by side and with the same axis, the visual comparison is straightforward.

Facets are possible with function `facet_wrap`, which takes as input a formula containing the name of a column with groups that will define each panel. In the following example, we use `facet_wrap` with option `facets = ~ ticker` to create a panel of prices for four selected assets.

```
library(dplyr)
# fix seed
set.seed(20)

# select 4 stocks randomly
```

```
my.tickers <- sample(unique(my.df$ticker), 4)

p <- my.df %>%
  filter(ticker %in% my.tickers) %>%
  ggplot(aes(x = ref.date, y = price.adjusted)) +
  geom_line() +
  labs(x = 'Date',
       y = 'Adjusted closing prices') +
  facet_wrap(facets = ~ticker)

print(p)
```

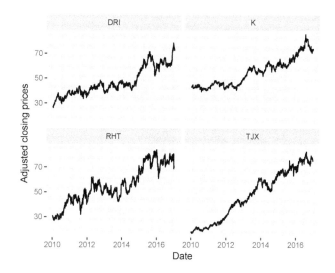

Using panels is recommended when the data of the groups are similar and tend to agglomerate. This makes it difficult to analyze the differences between the groups in a single graphic. This is the case of stock returns of different assets. Consider the following example, where we create a panel for the returns of four randomly selected shares.

```
# fix seed
set.seed(25)

# select 4 stocks randomly
my.tickers <- sample(unique(my.df$ticker), 4)

p <- my.df %>%
  filter(ticker %in% my.tickers) %>%
  ggplot(aes(x = ref.date, y = ret)) +
  geom_line(size=1) +
```

```
labs(x = 'Date',
    y = 'Returns') +
facet_wrap(facets = ~ticker)

print(p)
```

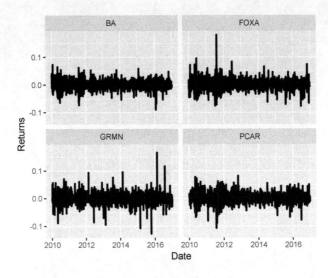

Notice how the vertical axis of the panels is fixed for all stocks, facilitating the visual analysis. We can also set the scales free by using option scales='free' in facet_wrap:

```
p <- p + facet_wrap(facets = ~ticker, scales = 'free')

print(p)
```

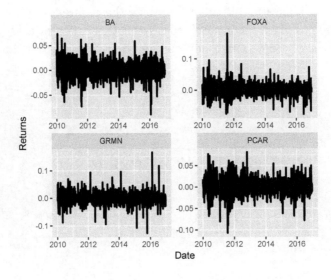

8.4 Using Pipelines for Data Analysis and Figures

Another great thing about `ggplot2` is you can use the pipeline operator and write a code where data processing and plotting are integrated. Look at the next example, where we plot the average return and standard deviation of all stocks from the dataset available in `my.df`.

```
library(dplyr)
library(ggplot2)

# calculated mean and sd of returns, plot result
p <- my.df %>%
  group_by(ticker) %>%
  summarise(mean.ret = mean(ret),
            std.ret = sd(ret)) %>%
  ggplot(aes(x = std.ret, y = mean.ret)) +
  geom_point() +
  labs(x = 'Standard deviation of returns',
       y = 'Average Returns')
```

```
print(p)
```

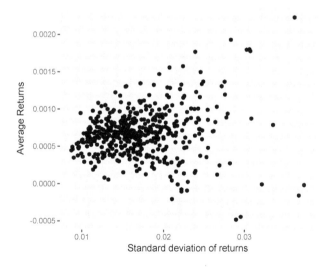

Notice how the previous code is self-contained, easy to read, and elegant. It goes from raw data to the plot, with no object created in the intermediate steps. Anyone can clearly see the steps taken to build the plot. Modifications in the data processing stage are also straightforward. One detail about using pipelines with `ggplot` is the steps in the plot creation are incremented with the + sign, not %>%. From this section on, we will use the pipeline notation to simplify the code, whenever possible.

We only scratched the surface of ggplot2. Many other aspects of the resulting figure can be controlled. Users with a specific need may consult the manual or the main reference of the package, Wickham (2009). Forums and *mailing lists* are also a great source of information.

8.5   Creating Statistical Graphics

Package ggplot has several options for creating graphs with statistical content. This includes histograms, *boxplot* graphics, QQ plots, and more.

8.5.1   Creating Histograms

A histogram shows the empirical distribution of the data. We can easily create them with ggplot and function geom_histogram. An example is given in the following code, where we generate a histogram for all returns found in my.df.

```
p <- ggplot(data = my.df, aes(x = ret))
p <- p + geom_histogram(bins = 25)

print(p)
```

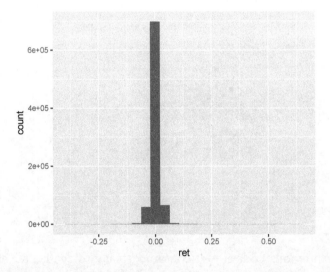

Here, we only need to define the x value, without the y. The size of the intervals in the histogram is defined by input bins.

We can also use groups and facets as we did for point and line plots. Have a look.

```
# fix seed
set.seed(30)

# select 4 stocks randomly
my.tickers <- sample(unique(my.df$ticker), 4)

p <- my.df %>%
  filter(ticker %in% my.tickers) %>%
  ggplot(aes(x = ret)) +
  geom_histogram(bins = 50) +
  facet_wrap(facets = ~ticker)

print(p)
```

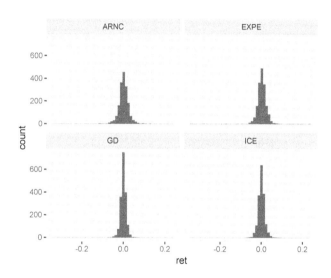

A histogram with the empirical densities of the data can be created using function `geom_density`. While histograms built with `geom_histogram` count the number of times the data is located within an interval, a density histogram uses the relative frequency and interpolates the values, resulting in a more visually appealing representation of a distribution. See an example next.

```
p <- my.df %>%
  filter(ticker %in% my.tickers) %>%
  ggplot(aes(x = ret)) +
  geom_density() +
  facet_wrap(facets = ~ticker)

print(p)
```

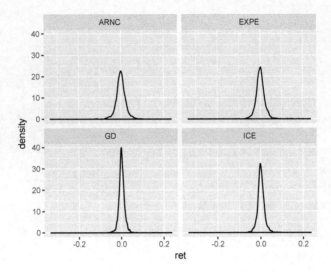

The previous figure allows a clear visual comparison of the differences between the distributions of returns of the different stocks.

8.5.2   Creating *boxplot* Figures

Figures of type *boxplot* (or box and whisker diagram) show the distribution of a variable conditional on some category or group. Using the median, maximum, minimum, and quartiles of the data, this statistical display highlights the distribution of a variable in a specific visual pattern. We can easily create them with `ggplot`. See an example next, where we show the price distribution of four randomly selected stocks.

```
# fix seed
set.seed(35)

# select 4 stocks randomly
my.tickers <- sample(unique(my.df$ticker), 4)

p <- my.df %>%
  filter(ticker %in% my.tickers) %>%
  ggplot(aes(x = ticker, y = price.adjusted)) +
  geom_boxplot()

print(p)
```

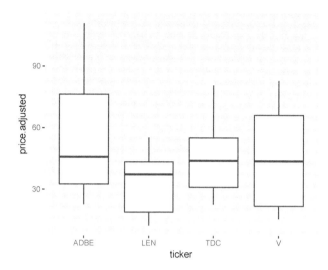

As we can see from the previous figure, the stocks have different distributions for their prices. The middle line defines the median value, while the upper and lower lines of the box define the first and third quartile.

8.5.3   Creating *QQ* Plots

QQ plots show a comparison between the distribution of a variable and a theoretical distribution, such as the Normal. It is a scatter plot between cumulative distributions. The closest to a straight line, the more similar is the empirical distribution to the theoretical.

Let's try an example with some simulated data.

```
# fix seed
set.seed(40)

N=1000
my.mean <- 10
my.sd <- 2

temp.df <- data.frame(y=rnorm(n = N, mean = my.mean, sd = my.sd))

p <- ggplot(data = temp.df, aes(sample = y))
#p <- p + labs(title = 'QQ plot for simulated data')
p <- p + geom_qq(distribution = qnorm,
                 dparams = c(mean=my.mean, sd=my.sd))

print(p)
```

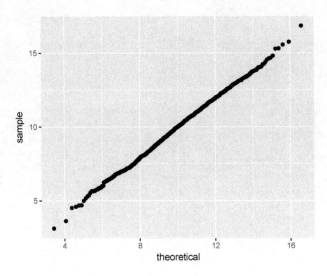

In the previous code, we simulate random normal variables with mean 10 and standard deviation equal to 2. As you can see, the QQ plot is close to a straight line, meaning the empirical distribution of the simulated data is close to a Normal distribution. Since we used artificial data from the aforementioned distribution, this result is not surprising!

Now, let's try it for our dataset of stock's returns. We will randomly select 4 stocks, create a new column, called `norm.ret`, with the normalized values of the returns. The normalization procedure works as follows; we subtract the mean for each return and divide the result by the standard deviations. This procedure must be executed on an individual basis for each stock. After that, we compare the resulting distribution against a standard Normal with mean zero and deviation equal to 1. The following code does this operation.

```r
# fix seed
set.seed(45)

# select 4 stock randomly and filter from my.df
my.tickers <- sample(unique(my.df$ticker), 4)
temp.df <- filter(my.df, ticker %in% my.tickers)

# set function for normalization
norm.vec <- function(y){
  # Normalizes a vector by subtracting mean and dividing
  # by the standard deviation
  #
  # Args:
  #   y - numerical vector
```

```
#
# Returns:
#   A normalized vector

  y.norm <- (y-mean(y, na.rm = TRUE))/sd(y, na.rm = TRUE)
  return(y.norm)
}

# apply function
my.l <- tapply(X = temp.df$ret,
               INDEX = factor(temp.df$ticker),
               FUN = norm.vec)

# reorder list (tapply sorts alphabetically)
my.l <- my.l[as.character(unique(temp.df$ticker))]

# save new column norm.ret
temp.df$norm.ret <- unlist(my.l)

# plot it!
p <- ggplot(data = temp.df, aes(sample = norm.ret))
p <- p + geom_qq()
p <- p + facet_wrap(~ticker)

print(p)
```

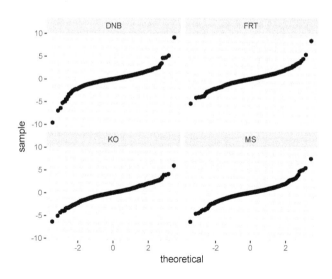

As you can see, the result is not visually similar to the result found for the simulated distribution. In the extreme values of the normalized returns distributions, we see a higher proportion of cases, when comparing to the theoretical distribution. Such a result is well-known and called *fat tails*. This means the Normal distribution does a bad job describing empirical returns from the stock market. This issue is particularly important in the calculation of risk estimates, where a *fat tail* will underestimate the likelihood of an extreme loss.

8.6   Saving Graphics to a File

To save pictures created with `ggplot`, use function `ggsave`. It takes as input the name of the file, including path and extension (*.jpg*, *.png*, etc). If the figure object `p` is not explicitly set, the last generated graph will be saved. One suggestion is to give preference to the *png* format, which is more commonly accepted for publication due to its higher printing quality. If necessary, you can set the resolution using argument `dpi`.

Consider the following example, where we create a graph and save it to a file, called `MyPrices.png`, available at folder `fig_ggplot`:

```
library(dplyr)
# fix seed
set.seed(40)

# select 4 stocks randomly
my.tickers <- sample(unique(my.df$ticker), 4)

p <- my.df %>%
  filter(ticker %in% my.tickers) %>%
  ggplot(aes(x = ref.date, y = price.adjusted, color = ticker)) +
  geom_line() +
  labs(x = 'Date',
       y = 'Adjusted closing prices')

my.fig.file <- 'fig_ggplot/MyPrices.png'
ggsave(filename = my.fig.file,
       plot=p,
       dpi = 600)
```

You can verify the creation of the file with function `list.files`:

```
print(list.files('fig_ggplot'))
```

```
## [1] "MyPrices.png"
```

As expected, the file is available in folder `fig_ggplot`, and it is ready to be inserted into a technical report or scientific article.

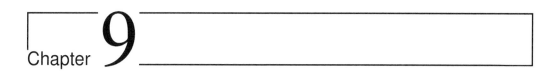

Programming and Data Analysis with R

In chapters 3, 4, and 6, we learned the ecosystem of objects in R and studied the procedures for importing datasets from local files and the web. Here, we will address programming with R and processing data. This includes the creation of custom functions, structured repetition of code (*loops*), and conditional execution. A section about one of the most popular packages in CRAN, `dplyr`, is also included. The concepts presented here are valuable. Based on it, you'll be able to solve several computational problems in your data analysis.

9.1 Creating Functions

As emphasized in an earlier chapter, **the use of functions is in the heart of R**. Any procedure can be written to a function. Using functions organizes code and increases the applicability of generic procedures. It makes it easy to fix bugs in the code. If you are using a function in many places of a script, you only need to change it in one place. For example, consider creating a procedure that cleans a database by removing outliers and `NA` cases. This procedure can be written as a function and be used in different **dataframes**. If the author of the function must apply the same procedure in the future, simply load the previously written function and use it again.

A function can be further developed, so its applicability increases. If we need to use it in a slightly different way, we can add options using arguments. By using functions in your work, you'll invest less time in rewriting repetitive tasks and more in writing new procedures. With time and experience, a baggage of previously written custom functions will be available, allowing you to write complex data operations in minutes. In this section, we will address how to create custom functions in R.

A function always has three parts: input, processing stage, and output. The inputs are the information for the solution offered by the function. Processing is the operation that will produce a result in the function output. In R, the definition of a function is structured as follows:

```
my.fct <- function(arg1 = 1, arg2 = 'abc', ...){
  # Description goes here
  #
  # Args:
  #    arg1 - description of arg1 here
  #    arg2 - description of arg2 here
  #
  # Returns:
  #    description of returned object goes here
  ...

  return(out)

}
```

And, after registering the function in the environment, we can change its input as necessary, such as in the next example:

```
out <- my.fct(arg1 = 2, arg2 = 'bcd')
```

The definition of a function is similar to the definition of an object in R. The main difference is its content is encapsulated by curly braces ({ }). Objects *arg1* and *arg2* are the inputs of the function, the information required to perform a procedure.

Using the equality symbol in this setting, as in `arg1 = 1`, defines the *default* case, determining the default value if the user does not set any in the call to the written function. Using default values is useful to define the most likely choice of the inputs of a function. This facilitates their use by speeding up the calling process by the user, who does not need to know and enter values for all possible options.

Every function will return an object with the `return` command. This is usually at the end of the function definition. There is no restriction on the type of object returned: it can be a `list`, a `numeric` array, or an object of any other class. This flexibility allows the user to return various information. Just organize it into a `list`, `vector`, or `dataframe`. The command `return` defines the end of the function and the return of the created object.

As for using the function, you'll first need to register it in the environment by executing its definition like any other code. A simple way of doing that is to place the cursor in the second curly brace and press *control + enter*. The arguments of the function can be set by position or name. So, if you called function `my.fct` as `my.fct(1,2)`, it will recognize its input as `arg1=1` and `arg2=2`. When you use names, the position of arguments is irrelevant, i.e., the previous function call is equivalent to `my.fct(arg2=2, arg1=1)`.

Now, let's create a function that does something useful: takes as input a numeric vector and outputs its mean. From previous chapters we know that there is already a function called `mean` that does this procedure, but we will write a new one as a showcase. Here is the function definition:

```
my.fct <- function(x = c(1,1,1,1)){
  # Calculates the average of input x
  #
  # Args:
  #      x: a numerical vector
  #
  # Returns:
  #   The mean of x

  out <- sum(x)/length(x)

  return(out)

}
```

Notice how we set a comment section after the first curly brace to describe the written function, including its arguments and the returned value. By giving this quick summary, the user can quickly grasp what the function does and what to expect from it. From the Google's R style manual:

> "Functions should contain a comments section immediately below the function definition line. These comments should consist of a one-sentence description of the function; a list of the function's arguments, denoted by Args:, with a description of each (including the data type); and a description of the return value, denoted by Returns:. The comments should be descriptive enough that a caller can use the function without reading any of the function's code."

> — Google's R style manual

After writing the function down, we need to execute the code to *register* the procedure in R. Notice, after running the function's definition, the name of it appears in panel *environment* of RStudio. In R, a function is an object, just like atomic vectors, `lists`, and `dataframes`.

After executing the function definition in the script, let's test it:

```
# testing function my.fct
my.mean <- my.fct(x = 1:100)

# print result
print(my.mean)
```

```
## [1] 50.5
```

The result is 50.5, as expected.

If the function `my.fct` is called without any input, it will use the *default* value of x = c (1,1,1,1). Let's try it:

```
# calling my.fct without input
my.mean <- my.fct()

# print result
print(my.mean)
```

```
## [1] 1
```

Again, as expected, the returned value is correct.

Although simple, the previous example can be further refined by introducing tests for the inputs. Notice how `my.fct` accepts any input we give. If we defined x as a `character` object, the function would still accept it and try to execute the command in out `<- sum(x)/length(x)`. The problem is the function `sum` does not accept a `character` object and it would return an error. **By not testing the types of inputs in the function, we allow for errors that can lead to problems difficult to identify**. This is especially true for complex functions with many lines of code.

Correcting this problem is simple: just use a logical test for the class of x and throw a custom error with function `stop` if the class is not `numeric` or `integer`. See next:

```
my.fct <- function(x = c(1,1,1,1)){
  # Calculates the average of input x
  #
  # Args:
  #    x - a numerical vector
  #
```

```
  # Returns:
  #    The mean of x

  if (!(class(x) %in% c('numeric','integer'))){
    stop('ERROR: x is not numeric or integer')
  }

  out <- sum(x)/length(x)

  return(out)
}
```

In the previous code, we use the `class` function to test the input type and `stop` to issue an error. If we tried to set `x` as something different than a `numeric` or `integer` object, the execution stops and an error with the message `ERROR: x is not numeric or integer` appears on the prompt. This message helps the user to understand the reason the function was not executed and give a hint on how to fix it. See an example next:

```
# using wrong inputs (ERROR)
my.fct(x = c('a','b'))
```

```
## Error in my.fct(x = c("a", "b")): ERROR: x is not numeric or integer
```

Going further in developing our function, notice how it does not deal with `NA` values in the input. As explained in previous chapter, if a numeric vector contains `NA`, the sum of it will also be a `NA` object. Have a look:

```
# sum with NA
print(sum(c(1, 2, 3, NA, 4)))
```

```
## [1] NA
```

The problem with the `NA` is this object is contagious and will turn everything it touches into a `NA`! It is possible that, in using function `my.fct`, the user will introduce a bug in his code that is difficult to identify.

To handle `NA` values in function `my.fct`, a possible solution is to issue a warning message informing the user that input `x` contains an `NA`, remove the `NA` values from the input, and proceed with the calculation. The new definition of `my.fct` will look like:

```
my.fct <- function(x = c(1,1,1,1)){
  # Calculates the average of input x
  #
  # Args:
```

```
#     x: a numerical vector
#
# Returns:
#   The mean of x

if (!(class(x) %in% c('numeric','integer'))){
  stop('ERROR: x is not numeric or integer')
}

if (any(is.na(x))){
  warning('Warning: Found NA in x. Removing it.')
  x <- na.omit(x)
}

out <- sum(x)/length(x)

return(out)
}
```

For the previous code, we used function **warning** to issue a message in the prompt, command **any(is.na(x))** to test if any element of x has a NA value, and **na.omit** to remove it from the atomic vector. Let's test it:

```
# set vector with NA
y <- c(1,2,3, NA,1)

# test function
print(my.fct(y))
```

```
## Warning in my.fct(y): Warning: Found NA in x. Removing it.

## [1] 1.75
```

As we can see, the function acknowledged the existence of a NA value, issued a warning message, and calculated the mean of x without the NA.

Using comments and input testing is a good policy in R programming. **Writing good R functions takes a lot of work and demands a great deal of knowledge about R and the underlying operation.** The great thing about it is you only need to do it once! The function can be used over and over in different scenarios. With time, you'll build a set of functions that will help you do your work, and this collection of code will be your greatest asset. If you have written something that might interest other people, package the code and send it to CRAN. The community will appreciate it.

Now, lets move to a more complete example of using functions. As emphasized in chapter 5, a very common task in financial research is to calculate the returns of one or more stocks. Notice the calculation of returns must be done for each stock, and we always lose the first observation. We will have a `dataframe` in the long format with prices for several stocks. Based on these prices, we want to calculate a vector of returns and add it as a new column.

Let's create a function that takes as input a `dataframe` in the long format and adds a new `ret` column to it. For that, we need to know only the names of the column where prices are stored and the name of the column with the ticker symbols. Once the returns are calculated for each stock, we consolidate a full vector using functions `tapply` and `unlist`. So far, we haven't discussed the use of `tapply`. For now, it is only necessary to understand it performs a function for different groups. We'll provide more detail about `tapply` in the following section.

First, let's register a function for calculating returns from a vector of prices.

```
calc.ret <- function(P) {
  # calculates arithmetic returns from a vector of prices
  #
  # Args:
  #   P - vector of prices (numeric)
  #
  # Returns:
  #   A vector of returns

  # ret = p_{t}/p_{t-1} - 1
  my.length <- length(P)
  ret <- c(NA, P[2:my.length]/P[1:(my.length - 1)] - 1)
  return(ret)
}
```

Notice how we kept it simple. Since we will use `calc.ret` inside another function, we can leave the error checking process to the main function. This can take care of `NA` values or wrong input class. In the function definition, we set a `NA` value in the first element of the return series. We do that because it is important the return object has the same length as the input, and we always lose the first observation when calculating returns. So, we need to replace it with something. We could have simply set a 0 value or the mean of the returns, but a `NA` value seems more appropriate.

Now, let's write a function that, using a `dataframe` as input, adds a new column with the arithmetic returns based on the column of prices and tickers. The definition is given next.

```r
df.calc.ret <- function(df.in, colname.price, colname.tickers){
  # Calculates an arithmetic return series and adds it to input
  #
  # Args:
  #   df.in - a dataframe with columns for prices and tickers
  #   colname.price -  the name of the column in input df.in with prices
  #   colname.tickers - the name of the column with tickers
  #
  # Returns:
  #     A copy of the input dataframe, but with a new column ret

  # error checking (classes)
  if ( !('data.frame' %in% class(df.in)) ) {
    stop('ERROR: df.in should be a data.frame!')
  }

  if ( class(colname.price) != 'character') {
    stop('ERROR: colname.price should be a character object!')
  }

  if ( class(colname.tickers) != 'character') {
    stop('ERROR: colname.tickers should be a character object!')
  }

  # error checking (col.names)
  my.colnames <- colnames(df.in)

  if (any(!c(colname.price, colname.tickers) %in% my.colnames)) {
    stop('ERROR: column names dont match with names in df.in!')
  }

  # error checking (size of df)
  if ( nrow(df.in) < 2) {
    stop('ERROR: input df should have at least 2 rows!')
  }

  # do calc with tapply
  my.l <- tapply(X = df.in[[colname.price]],
                 INDEX = df.in[[colname.tickers]],
                 FUN = calc.ret)
```

```
# restore order of tickers in df.in
my.l <- my.l[unique(df.in[[colname.tickers]])]

# set new col in df.in
df.in$ret <- unlist(my.l)

# return df
return(df.in)
}
```

That's a lengthy code! But remember, you only need to do it one time. The function has many error checking procedures that ensure the inputs are correctly specified. Even though you spend time writing it, you can reuse it whenever you need it.

Now, let's use the function with the data available in `SP500-Stocks_long.csv`.

```
library(readr)

my.f <- 'data/SP500-Stocks_long.csv'

# set columns types
my.cols <- cols(
  price.adjusted = col_double(),
  ref.date = col_date(format = ""),
  ticker = col_character()
)

# import data
my.df <- read_csv(my.f, col_types = my.cols)

# calculate return column
my.df <- df.calc.ret(my.df,
                     colname.price = 'price.adjusted',
                     colname.tickers = 'ticker')
```

Let's look at the result:

```
print(head(my.df))
```

```
## # A tibble: 6 × 4
##   price.adjusted   ref.date ticker          ret
##            <dbl>     <date> <chr>         <dbl>
## 1       69.15826 2010-01-04    MMM           NA
## 2       68.72509 2010-01-05    MMM -0.006263503
```

```
## 3          69.69973 2010-01-06     MMM   0.014181794
## 4          69.74972 2010-01-07     MMM   0.000717162
## 5          70.24120 2010-01-08     MMM   0.007046423
## 6          69.95798 2010-01-11     MMM  -0.004032220
```

It looks great! The return vector is available in column `ret`. Going further, let's remove all `NA` rows with function `complete.cases`, so we only keep the rows with actual values in all columns.

```
idx <- complete.cases(my.df)
my.df <- my.df[idx, ]
```

For last, we save the resulting dataset as a *.RData* file. We will use the data in this `dataframe` in the following chapters.

```
save(list = 'my.df',
     file = 'data/SP500-Stocks-WithRet.RData')
```

9.2   Using Loops (`for`)

Loops are the most basic command in any programming language. Briefly, loops allow a structured repetition of code. Consider a scenario where we have a database composed of 1,000 *.csv* files in the same folder. Here, we can create a *loop* to load the data individually, process the resulting `dataframe` of each file, and finally, aggregate all imported `dataframes` into a single object of the same class.

The great thing about *loops* is the length of it is dynamically set. Using the previous example, if we had 5,000 files, the loop would process all 5,000 files. If we had just 500, the *loop* would run 500 times. That means we can encapsulate a generic procedure for processing all found files in a particular folder. With it, you have at your reach a tool for the execution of any sequential process.

The structure of a *loop* in R follows:

```
for (i in i.vec){
   ...
}
```

In the previous code, command `for` indicates the beginning of a *loop*. Object `i` in (`i in i.vec`) is the iterator of the *loop*. This iterator will change its value in each iteration, taking each individual value contained in `i.vec`. Note the *loop* is encapsulated by curly braces (`{}`). These are important, as they define where the *loop* starts and where it ends. The indentation (use of bigger margins) is also important for visual cues, but not necessary. Consider the following practical example:

```
# set seq
my.seq <- seq(-5,5)

# do loop
for (i in my.seq){
  cat(paste('\nThe value of i is',i))
}


##
## The value of i is -5
## The value of i is -4
## The value of i is -3
## The value of i is -2
## The value of i is -1
## The value of i is 0
## The value of i is 1
## The value of i is 2
## The value of i is 3
## The value of i is 4
## The value of i is 5
```

In the code, we created a sequence from -5 to 5 and presented a text for each element with the cat function. Notice how we also broke the prompt line with '\n'. The *loop* starts with i=-5, execute command cat(paste('\nThe value of i is', -5)), proceed to the next iteration by setting i=-4, rerun the cat command, and so on. At its final iteration, the value of i is 5.

The iterated sequence in the *loop* is not exclusive to numerical vectors. Any type of vector or list may be used. See next:

```
# set char vec
my.char.vec <- letters[1:5]

# loop it!
for (i.char in my.char.vec){
  cat(paste('\nThe value of i.char is', i.char))
}


##
## The value of i.char is a
## The value of i.char is b
## The value of i.char is c
## The value of i.char is d
## The value of i.char is e
```

The same goes for `lists`:

```
# set list
my.l <- list(x = 1:5,
             y = c('abc','dfg'),
             z = factor('A','B','C','D'))

# loop list
for (i.l in my.l){

  cat(paste0('\nThe class of i.l is ', class(i.l), '. '))
  cat(paste0('The number of elements is ', length(i.l), '.'))

}
```

```
##
## The class of i.l is integer. The number of elements is 5.
## The class of i.l is character. The number of elements is 2.
## The class of i.l is factor. The number of elements is 1.
```

In the definition of *loops*, the iterator does not have to be the only object incremented in each iteration. We can create other objects and increment them using a simple sum operation. See next:

```
# set vec and iterators
my.vec <- seq(1:5)
my.x <- 5
my.z <- 10

for (i in my.vec){
  # iterate "manually"
  my.x <- my.x + 1
  my.z <- my.z + 2

  cat('\nValue of i = ', i,
      ' | Value of my.x = ', my.x,
      ' | Value of my.z = ', my.z)
}
```

```
##
## Value of i =  1  | Value of my.x =   6  | Value of my.z =   12
## Value of i =  2  | Value of my.x =   7  | Value of my.z =   14
## Value of i =  3  | Value of my.x =   8  | Value of my.z =   16
## Value of i =  4  | Value of my.x =   9  | Value of my.z =   18
## Value of i =  5  | Value of my.x =   10 | Value of my.z =   20
```

Using nested *loops*, that is, a *loop* inside of another *loop* is also possible. See the following example, where we present all the elements of a matrix:

```
# set matrix
my.mat <- matrix(1:9, nrow = 3)

# loop all values of matrix
for (i in seq(1,nrow(my.mat))){
  for (j in seq(1,ncol(my.mat))){
    cat(paste0('\nElement [', i, ', ', j, '] = ', my.mat[i,j]))
  }
}
```

```
##
## Element [1, 1] = 1
## Element [1, 2] = 4
## Element [1, 3] = 7
## Element [2, 1] = 2
## Element [2, 2] = 5
## Element [2, 3] = 8
## Element [3, 1] = 3
## Element [3, 2] = 6
## Element [3, 3] = 9
```

Let's do a more complex example using data files. We will create several files with random data in our computer and save them in a folder named **many_datafiles**. This is accomplished with the following script:

```
# set number of files to create
n.files <- 10

# set first part of saved files
pattern.name <- 'myfiles_'

# set dir
out.dir <- 'many_datafiles/'

# test if out.dir exists, if not, create it
if (!dir.exists(out.dir)){
  dir.create(out.dir)
}

# clean up folder before creating new files
file.remove(list.files(out.dir, full.names = TRUE))
```

```
## logical(0)
# set vec with filenames
file.names <- paste0(out.dir, pattern.name, seq(1,n.files), '.csv')

# loop it!
for (i.file in file.names){
  # create temp df
  temp.df <- data.frame(x = runif(100))

  # write it!
  write.csv(x = temp.df, file = i.file)
}
```

In the previous example, we used function `if` in `if (!dir.exists(out.dir))` to test if folder `many_datafiles` existed. If it did not, we create it in the current working directory. Before running the loop, we remove all files in `out.dir` with command `file.remove(list.files(out.dir, full.names = TRUE))`.

In the *loop*, we used function `runif` to create 100 random numbers between *0* and *1*, so each *dataframe* created in `temp.df` differs from the other. Notice how the *loop* size is set by object `n.files`. If we wanted to create *10,000* files, all we need to do is set `n.files = 10000` and the rest of the code will adjust accordingly. It becomes clear that *loops* are a powerful and flexible procedure that can be used in many situations.

Now, let's check if the files are in the folder:

```
# check files
print(list.files(out.dir))
```

```
##  [1] "myfiles_1.csv"  "myfiles_10.csv" "myfiles_2.csv"
##  [4] "myfiles_3.csv"  "myfiles_4.csv"  "myfiles_5.csv"
##  [7] "myfiles_6.csv"  "myfiles_7.csv"  "myfiles_8.csv"
## [10] "myfiles_9.csv"
```

As expected, the files are there. To complete the example, we will import the contents of these files and aggregate all information into a single **dataframe** by using another *loop* and functions `read.csv` and `rbind`.

```
# set empty df
df.agg <- data.frame()
for (i.file in file.names){
  # read file
  temp.df <- read.csv(i.file)
```

```
  # row bind
  df.agg <- rbind(df.agg, temp.df)
}

print(head(df.agg))

##   X         x
## 1 1 0.1950091
## 2 2 0.4612009
## 3 3 0.2035352
## 4 4 0.5908492
## 5 5 0.3738881
## 6 6 0.1412981
```

In the previous code, notice how we bind all dataframes with df.agg <- rbind(df.agg, temp.df). So, the size of df.agg increases with each iteration of the *loop*. Object df.agg has 1000 rows and 2 columns. The extra column is the row names of the dataframe, which is saved by default in the *.csv* file. Looking at the contents of df.agg, we can see the code performed as expected, where column x contains numerical values between *0* and *1*, just as set in the previous chunk of code.

Another practical example of using *loops* is processing data according to groups. If we have a price dataset for several tickers and we want to calculate the average price of each stock, we can use a *loop* for that. In this example, we will again use the data from file SP500-Stocks_long.csv.

```
# read data
my.f <- 'data/SP500-Stocks_long.csv'
my.df <- read.csv(my.f, colClasses = c('numeric', 'Date','factor'))

# find unique tickers in column ticker
unique.tickers <- unique(my.df$ticker)

# create empty df
tab.out <- data.frame()

# loop tickers
for (i.ticker in unique.tickers){

  # create temp df with ticker i.ticker
  temp <- my.df[my.df$ticker==i.ticker, ]

  # row bind i.ticker and mean.price
```

```
tab.out <- rbind(tab.out,
                 data.frame(ticker = i.ticker,
                            mean.price = mean(temp$price.adjusted)))

}

# print result
print(tab.out[1:10, ])

##     ticker mean.price
## 1      MMM  110.90200
## 2      ABT   32.11558
## 3      ACN   70.60025
## 4     ATVI   19.04112
## 5      AYI  112.67233
## 6     ADBE   55.24791
## 7      AAP  103.19876
## 8      AES   11.19658
## 9      AET   65.73250
## 10     AMG  143.31837
```

In the code, we used function **unique** to find out the names of all the tickers in the
dataset. Soon after, we create an empty *dataframe* to save the results and a loop
to filter the data of each stock sequentially and average its prices. At the end of
the *loop*, we use function **rbind** to paste the results of each stock with the results of
the main table. As you can see, we can use the data to perform group calculations
with *loop*. There are, however, better ways of doing this procedure in R using native
apply functions or package **dplyr**, as we will soon learn.

9.3   Conditional Statements (`if`, `else`, `switch`)

Making binary decisions of type *yes* or *no* is common programming practice. If a
condition is found true, a specific code is executed. If it is false, other command
lines are executed. These decisions define the conditional statements. In R, we can
write them using the following structure:

```
# skeleton for if statement
if (cond){

  CodeIfTRUE...

} else {
```

```
CodeIfFALSE...

}
```

The place holder `cond` is the condition to be evaluated, taking only two values: `TRUE` or `FALSE`. The result of the condition must be a single logical element. With finding a `TRUE` value to `cond`, the code in `CodeIfTRUE` will run. Otherwise, where we find a `FALSE` value in `cond`, the code in `CodeIfFALSE` will be executed. A practical example based on a *loop* is presented next:

```
# set vec and threshold
my.x <- 1:10
my.thresh <- 5

for (i in my.x){
  if (i > my.thresh){
    cat('\nValue of ', i, ' is higher than ', my.thresh)
  } else {
    cat('\nValue of ', i, ' is lower or equal than ', my.thresh)
  }
}

##
## Value of  1  is lower or equal than  5
## Value of  2  is lower or equal than  5
## Value of  3  is lower or equal than  5
## Value of  4  is lower or equal than  5
## Value of  5  is lower or equal than  5
## Value of  6  is higher than  5
## Value of  7  is higher than  5
## Value of  8  is higher than  5
## Value of  9  is higher than  5
## Value of  10  is higher than  5
```

If we want to apply more than one logical condition, we can use command `else if` and `else`. See an example next:

```
for (i in my.x){
  if (i > my.thresh){
    cat('\nValue of ', i, ' is higher than ', my.thresh)
  } else if (i==my.thresh) {
    cat('\nValue of ', i, ' is equal to ', my.thresh)
  } else {
    cat('\nValue of ', i, ' is lower than ', my.thresh)
```

```
  }
}
```

```
##
## Value of  1   is lower than  5
## Value of  2   is lower than  5
## Value of  3   is lower than  5
## Value of  4   is lower than  5
## Value of  5   is equal to  5
## Value of  6   is higher than  5
## Value of  7   is higher than  5
## Value of  8   is higher than  5
## Value of  9   is higher than  5
## Value of  10  is higher than  5
```

Another possibility for using conditional executions is function **switch**, designed to give a better structure for a decision based on more than two choices. Let's say you want a conditional execution based on five conditions, A, B, C, and D. For each condition, you want the code to show a different message. Using **if** function, you could do that using this chunk of code:

```
# set vec
my.vec <- c('A', 'D', 'B', 'A', 'C', 'B')

for (i.vec in my.vec){
  if (i.vec == 'A'){
    cat('\nGot an A!')
  } else if (i.vec == 'B') {
    cat('\nGot a B!')
  } else if (i.vec == 'C') {
    cat('\nGot a C!')
  } else if (i.vec == 'D') {
    cat('\nGot a D!')
  }
}
```

```
##
## Got an A!
## Got a D!
## Got a B!
## Got an A!
## Got a C!
## Got a B!
```

While the previous code would do what we need, using several `else if` conditions is not visually elegant. A better way of doing it is using function `switch`. See next:

```
# set vec
my.vec <- c('A', 'D', 'B', 'A', 'C', 'B')

for (i.vec in my.vec){
  msg.out <- switch(i.vec,
                    'A' = '\nGot an A!',
                    'B' = '\nGot a B!',
                    'C' = '\nGot a C!',
                    'D' = '\nGot a D!')

  cat(msg.out)

}
```

```
##
## Got an A!
## Got a D!
## Got a B!
## Got an A!
## Got a C!
## Got a B!
```

The main benefit of using `switch` is the code becomes clear and easier to understand.

9.4 Using `apply` Functions

In R, there is an alternative to the usage of *loops*. Sometimes, you want simple procedures executed in a vector object. Writing a whole *loop* for that can be more verbose than needed. Functions from the **apply family**: `sapply`, `lapply`, `tapply`, `mapply`, `apply` and `by` can be used for that purpose.

All procedures using *loops* can be restructured using *apply* functions and vice versa. The difference of processing speed from one to the other is negligible. The choice between *loops* and *apply* functions is determined by the complexity of the operation and personal taste. Sometimes, *loops* are easier to use. The opposite can be true in other scenarios. In the author's opinion, *loops* should be used when complex procedures are performed and using the structure of an *apply* function is not straightforward. Now, let's discuss each type of *apply* function.

9.4.1   Using `lapply`

Function `lapply` takes as input a `list` and a function object. It works by passing each element of the input `list` to the object function. The output of each call is aggregated and returned as an object of class `list`. Notice how the use of `lists` in the input and output of `lapply` provides flexibility. You can use it for any object, with no restriction on its output. See the following example, where we calculate the average of a series of vectors with different sizes:

```
# set list
my.l <- list(1:10, 2:5, 10:-20)

# use lapply with mean
my.mean.vec <- lapply(X = my.l, FUN = mean)

# print result
print(my.mean.vec)
```

```
## [[1]]
## [1] 5.5
##
## [[2]]
## [1] 3.5
##
## [[3]]
## [1] -5
```

The result shows the means of each vector in `my.l`, as expected. We could also pass other options to `mean` with `lapply`. See next, where we use `na.rm=TRUE`.

```
# set list
my.l <- list(c(1,NA,2), c(2:5,NA), 10:-20)

# use lapply with mean
my.mean.vec <- lapply(X = my.l, FUN = mean, na.rm=TRUE)

# print result
print(my.mean.vec)
```

```
## [[1]]
## [1] 1.5
##
## [[2]]
## [1] 3.5
```

```
##
## [[3]]
## [1] -5
```

Using `lapply` is useful when utilizing a custom function. Let's redo the previous example of creating several *.csv* files. The first step is to create a function that generates these files as we did with the *loop*.

```
# function to generate files
create.rnd.file <- function(name.file, N=100){
  # Generates a csv file with random content
  #
  # Args:
  #     name.file - name of csv file (character)
  # N - number of rows in random dataframe (integer)
  #
  # Returns:
  #     TRUE, if successful

  if (class(name.file)!='character'){
    stop('ERROR: input name.file is not a character')
  }

  if ( !(class(N) %in% c('numeric','integer')) ){
    stop('ERROR: input N is not an integer or numeric!')
  }

  # create random df
  temp.df <- data.frame(x = runif(N))

  # write it!
  write.csv(x = temp.df, file = name.file)

  # return TRUE
  return(TRUE)
}
```

Now, we use function `create.rnd.file` with `lapply`:

```
# set options
n.files <- 5
pattern.name <- 'myfiles_with_lapply_'
out.dir <- 'many_datafiles/'
```

```
# set file names
file.names <- paste0(out.dir,pattern.name, seq(1,n.files), '.csv')

# test if out.dir exists, if not, create it
if (!dir.exists(out.dir)){
  dir.create(out.dir)
}

# clean up folder before creating new files
file.remove(list.files(out.dir, full.names = TRUE))
```

```
##   [1] TRUE TRUE TRUE TRUE TRUE TRUE TRUE TRUE TRUE TRUE
```

```
# use lapply
out.l <- lapply(X = file.names, FUN = create.rnd.file, N=100)
```

```
# print result
print(out.l)
```

```
## [[1]]
## [1] TRUE
##
## [[2]]
## [1] TRUE
##
## [[3]]
## [1] TRUE
##
## [[4]]
## [1] TRUE
##
## [[5]]
## [1] TRUE
```

Everything worked well in the previous code. The creation of the random files was a success. Notice the return of `lapply` is a `list`. Whenever you need to apply a function that returns a complex object, such as the estimation of a model, it is advised to use `lapply`.

9.4.2   Using sapply

Function `sapply` works similarly to `lapply`. The main difference is in the type of output. While `lapply` returns a list, `sapply` returns an atomic matrix or vector.

See the following example:

```
# create list
my.l <- list(1:10, 2:5, 10:-20)

# use sapply
my.mean.vec <- sapply(my.l, mean)

# print result
print(my.mean.vec)
```

```
## [1]   5.5   3.5 -5.0
```

Using `sapply` is recommended when the output of the underlying function is an atomic vector. In such cases, it is unnecessary to return a flexible object, such as a `list`.

An important aspect of using `sapply` is the underlying function can return more than one value. The result comes from the aggregation of the individual vectors into a `matrix`. See the following example, where we create a function that returns the mean and standard deviation of a numeric vector:

```
# set list
my.l <- list(runif(10), runif(15), rnorm(1000))

my.fct <- function(x){
  # Returns mean and standard deviation of a vector
  #
  # Args:
  #   x - numerical vector
  #
  # Returns:
  #   Vector as c(mean(x), sd(x))

  if (!(class(x) %in% c('numeric','integer'))){
    stop('ERROR: Class of x is not numeric or integer.')
  }

  x <- na.omit(x)

  out <- c(mean(x), sd(x))
  return(out)

}
```

```r
# use sapply
my.vec <- sapply(my.l, my.fct)

# check result
print(my.vec)

##              [,1]        [,2]         [,3]
## [1,]  0.4102478  0.4090657  0.01050914
## [2,]  0.2842762  0.3344650  0.98690967
```

When there is more than one output in the underlying function, each row in the
returned object represents a different output of the function used with **sapply**, in
this case, the mean and standard deviation of **x**. The columns indicate the different
processed items in **my.l**.

A practical use of function **sapply** in data analysis is the creation of descriptive
tables. Let's use the SP500 data and create a descriptive analysis of the prices of
the different stocks. First, let's write the function.

```r
describe.vec <- function(x){
  # Describe numerical vector with mean and other stats
  #
  # Args:
  #   x - numerical vector
  #
  # Returns:
  #   A vector with mean, maximum and minimum

  # error checking
  if (!(class(x) %in% c('numeric','integer'))){
    stop('ERROR: Class of x is not numeric or integer.')
  }

  x <- na.omit(x)

  # calc vec
  out <- c(mean.price = mean(x),
           max.price = max(x),
           min.price = min(x))

  return(out)
}
```

Now, let's load the data and apply function **describe.vec** to the different stocks.

```r
# set file and read it
my.f <- 'data/SP500-Stocks_long.csv'
my.df <- read.csv(my.f,
                  colClasses = c('numeric',
                                 'Date',
                                 'factor'))

# use split to split prices by ticker
my.l <- split(x = my.df$price, my.df$ticker)

# use sapply
my.tab <- sapply(X = my.l, FUN = describe.vec)

# check result
print(head(t(my.tab)))
```

```
##        mean.price max.price min.price
## A        33.04629  48.18046 18.329764
## AAL      23.41365  54.66265  3.893684
## AAP     103.19876 199.99451 38.418693
## AAPL     75.00174 127.96609 24.881912
## ABC      58.38558 112.10088 23.307129
## ABT      32.11558  49.33589 18.430625
```

In this example, we used function split in split(x = my.df$price, my.df$ticker)
to separate the prices of the different stocks into the different elements of a list.
We later use this object with sapply. Notice also we transposed the resulting
matrix with function t, resulting in a matrix where the rows represent the assets
and the columns indicate the different statistics.

Using a descriptive table is helpful to understand a database and identify potential
data problems, such as a large values. It is worth pointing out the user could extend
the information returned by describe.vec by adding several other statistics of
interest.

9.4.3   Using tapply

Function tapply is designed to perform group operations. See the following example,
where we create a numeric vector with a sequence of 1 to 150 and a factor with
groups A, B, and C. Using tapply, we can calculate the average of the numerical
vector for each group.

```
# set numeric vec and factor
my.x <- 1:150
my.factor <- factor(c(rep('C',50), rep('B',50), rep('A',50)))

# use tapply
my.mean.vec <- tapply(X = my.x, INDEX = my.factor, FUN = mean)

# print result
print(my.mean.vec)
```

```
##     A     B     C
## 125.5  75.5  25.5
```

A very important point about using `tapply` is the order of groups in the output is set **alphabetically**, and it does not follow the order found in `my.factor`. If keeping the same order of groups is important, you must reorder the resulting `list`.

Going back to the previous example using stock prices, we can also use `tapply` to reach the same objective of calculating several descriptive statistics for different tickers. Have a look.

```
# use tapply for descriptive stats
my.l.out <- tapply(X = my.df$price,
                   INDEX = my.df$ticker,
                   FUN = describe.vec)

# print result
print(my.l.out[1:5])
```

```
## $A
## mean.price  max.price  min.price
##    33.04629   48.18046   18.32976
##
## $AAL
## mean.price  max.price  min.price
##   23.413651  54.662650   3.893684
##
## $AAP
## mean.price  max.price  min.price
##   103.19876  199.99451   38.41869
##
## $AAPL
## mean.price  max.price  min.price
##    75.00174  127.96609   24.88191
```

```
##
## $ABC
## mean.price   max.price   min.price
##    58.38558   112.10088    23.30713
```

The output of `tapply` is a `list` of values. Each element contains a vector from `describe.vec`. Despite showing the same results we've found in the previous example, a `list` is not the recommended type of object to export data in constructing tables. Ideally, we should transform the `list` to a `dataframe`, so we can later export it. The next code will do this conversion.

```
# convert list to dataframe
my.tab <- do.call(what = rbind, args = my.l.out)

# print result
print(head(my.tab))
```

```
##        mean.price max.price min.price
## A         33.04629  48.18046 18.329764
## AAL       23.41365  54.66265  3.893684
## AAP      103.19876 199.99451 38.418693
## AAPL      75.00174 127.96609 24.881912
## ABC       58.38558 112.10088 23.307129
## ABT       32.11558  49.33589 18.430625
```

This is the first appearance of `do.call`. This is a more complex function that, recursively, will use a sequence of a pair of elements from `args` and feed it to the function defined in input `what`. In our case, `do.call` will first use elements one and two of `my.l.out` as inputs in `rbind`. This is equivalent to `rbind(my.l.out[[1]], my.l.out[[2]])`. After that, it will use the result of the previous step and feed it to `rbind` again, using the third element of `my.l.out`. Function `do.call` will continue this operation until the end of `my.l.out` is reached. As you can see, it is a recursive calculation. For our case, it is simply binding all elements of `my.l.out` into a single `dataframe`. Further details about this function can be obtained with command `help(do.call)`.

Going back to the example, we can see the result in `my.tab` is exactly as expected, with each stock showing its average, minimum, and maximum price.

9.4.4 Using `mapply`

Function `mapply` is a multivariate version of `sapply` and `lapply`. It allows the use of more than one argument to a function, so each element in the output is a combination of the inputs in `mapply`. Sounds confusing? Don't worry; an example will make this clear.

Assume we are interested in creating a `list` with the content as in `my.l <- list(1,1:2, 1:3,1:4,.., 1:10)`. One possible solution is to use a `loop`:

```
# set size
N <- 10

# prealocate list
my.l <- list()

for (i in seq(1,N)){
  my.l[[i]] <- seq(1,i)
}

# print result
print(my.l)

## [[1]]
## [1] 1
##
## [[2]]
## [1] 1 2
##
## [[3]]
## [1] 1 2 3
##
## [[4]]
## [1] 1 2 3 4
##
## [[5]]
## [1] 1 2 3 4 5
##
## [[6]]
## [1] 1 2 3 4 5 6
##
## [[7]]
## [1] 1 2 3 4 5 6 7
##
## [[8]]
## [1] 1 2 3 4 5 6 7 8
##
## [[9]]
```

```
## [1] 1 2 3 4 5 6 7 8 9
##
## [[10]]
## [1]  1  2  3  4  5  6  7  8  9 10
```

Another, less verbose and more elegant solution, is to use `mapply`:

```
# use mapply for creating list
my.l <- mapply(FUN = seq, rep(1,N), seq(1,N))

print(my.l)
```

```
## [[1]]
## [1] 1
##
## [[2]]
## [1] 1 2
##
## [[3]]
## [1] 1 2 3
##
## [[4]]
## [1] 1 2 3 4
##
## [[5]]
## [1] 1 2 3 4 5
##
## [[6]]
## [1] 1 2 3 4 5 6
##
## [[7]]
## [1] 1 2 3 4 5 6 7
##
## [[8]]
## [1] 1 2 3 4 5 6 7 8
##
## [[9]]
## [1] 1 2 3 4 5 6 7 8 9
##
## [[10]]
## [1]  1  2  3  4  5  6  7  8  9 10
```

Explaining the result, function `mapply` is calling `seq` for each pair of elements in `rep(1,N)` and `seq(1,N)`. So, the first element of `my.l` is simply `seq(1,1)`. The second element is seq(1,2), and its final element is seq(1,10). As you can see, function mapply is a more elaborate use of functions lapply and sapply, and it is useful when you have more than one argument you want to change in a call to a function.

9.4.5   Using apply

Function apply follows the same logic as the others, with the main difference it is specifically used in objects with two dimensions. Here, the user can process the object by rows or columns. Look in the following example where, based on a matrix object, we calculated the sum of the row and column values.

```
# set matrix and print it
my.mat <- matrix(1:15, nrow = 5)
print(my.mat)
```

```
##      [,1] [,2] [,3]
## [1,]    1    6   11
## [2,]    2    7   12
## [3,]    3    8   13
## [4,]    4    9   14
## [5,]    5   10   15
```

```
# sum rows with apply and print it
sum.rows <- apply(X = my.mat, MARGIN = 1, FUN = sum)
print(sum.rows)
```

```
## [1] 18 21 24 27 30
```

```
# sum columns with apply and print it
sum.cols <- apply(X = my.mat, MARGIN = 2, FUN = sum)
print(sum.cols)
```

```
## [1] 15 40 65
```

In the previous example, the MARGIN argument sets the orientation of the calculation. With MARGIN = 1, function apply separates each row as a vector and uses function sum in each. With MARGIN = 2, the calculation is column oriented.

Expanding the example, we can use apply to find the maximum values of my.mat per row and per column. Have a look at the next example:

```
# print max by row
print(apply(X = my.mat, MARGIN = 1, FUN = max))
```

```
## [1] 11 12 13 14 15
```

```
# print max by column
print(apply(X = my.mat, MARGIN = 2, FUN = max))
```

```
## [1]   5 10 15
```

9.4.6 Using by

Function by has the same objective as the other functions in the apply family. Its dataframe orientation differentiates it from the others. It splits a dataframe into smaller pieces according to a factor. Its main advantage is it allows the user to access any column available in the data, not just one. Whenever you need to process the data by groups and use information from several columns of a dataframe, the byfunction should be used.

Look at the next example, where we create a more complex descriptive table using information on prices and returns.

```
# load data
load('data/SP500-Stocks-WithRet.RData')
```

```
# set function for processing df
my.fct <- function(df.in){

  P <- df.in$price.adjusted
  ret <- df.in$ret

  out <- c(MeanPrice= mean(P),
           MaxPrice = max(P),
           MinPrice = min(P),
           MeanRet = mean(ret),
           MaxRet = max(ret),
           MinRet = min(ret))

  return(out)

}
```

```
# apply my.fct for each ticker in my.df
my.l <- by(data = my.df, INDICES = my.df$ticker, FUN = my.fct)
```

```
# convert list to dataframe
my.tab <- do.call(what = rbind, args = my.l)
```

```
# print result
print(head(my.tab))
```

```
##         MeanPrice MaxPrice  MinPrice      MeanRet     MaxRet
## A        33.05298  48.18046 18.329764 0.0006090903 0.11763059
## AAL      23.42431  54.66265  3.893684 0.0017774469 0.17316703
## AAP     103.23486 199.99451 38.418693 0.0009719157 0.16557581
## AAPL     75.02859 127.96609 24.881912 0.0009460433 0.08874137
## ABC      58.40506 112.10088 23.307129 0.0007544274 0.09532090
## ABT      32.12158  49.33589 18.430625 0.0003925589 0.06496596
##            MinRet
## A       -0.11013941
## AAL     -0.15818175
## AAP     -0.16967114
## AAPL    -0.12355795
## ABC     -0.13031447
## ABT     -0.09290837
```

Function `my.fct` needed to be created for using `by`. Notice how its input is a `dataframe` and columns `ret` and `price.adjusted` are used inside it. As explained, the `by` function is passing each smaller `dataframe` related to a particular ticker to function `my.fct` and directing the result to a `list` object.

9.5   Data Manipulation with Package `dplyr`

One of the most important assets of an experienced data analyst is the knowledge of the capabilities of different R packages. For data processing operations, one of the most useful packages is `dplyr` (Wickham and Francois, 2016). It allows complex data operations to be carried out with its own intuitive and customizable syntax. Not only that, it also decreases computational time.

Before describing functions and examples, let's load `dplyr` to show its effect in the environment.

```
library('dplyr')
```

The loading screen of `dplyr` warns the user the package replaced functions of other packages, such as `xts::first` and `stats::lag`. Therefore, the features of these functions after loading `dplyr` will change. In its current version, 0.5.0, `dplyr` has 245 functions. Describing each functionality would be too exhaustive for this book. Therefore, we will focus on the main functions of the package.

9.5.1 Manipulating a `dataframe` with `dplyr`

Package `dplyr` includes several functions for standard `dataframe` manipulations, such as adding columns, filtering rows, and ordering. The main advantage of these functions is they can be used with the pipeline operator, a way to streamline data operations. We will detail the use of the pipeline operator in the following section. For now, let's learn the `dplyr` functions for simple `dataframe` manipulations, without the use of pipelines.

To select columns, you can use function `select` with the names of the desired columns as inputs:

```
library(dplyr)
```

```
# set rnd df
set.seed(10)
N <- 5
my.df <- data.frame(COL1 = runif(N),
                     COL2 = runif(N),
                     G = runif(N),
                     B = runif(N))
```

```
# select columns with dplyr::select
my.temp.df <- select(my.df, COL1, G)
print(my.temp.df)
```

```
##          COL1         G
## 1 0.50747820 0.6516557
## 2 0.30676851 0.5677378
## 3 0.42690767 0.1135090
## 4 0.69310208 0.5959253
## 5 0.08513597 0.3580500
```

```
# unselect columns with dplyr::select
my.temp.df <- select(my.df, -COL1, -COL2)
print(my.temp.df)
```

```
##           G          B
## 1 0.6516557 0.42880942
## 2 0.5677378 0.05190332
## 3 0.1135090 0.26417767
## 4 0.5959253 0.39879073
## 5 0.3580500 0.83613414
```

One innovation from the native way of selecting columns is you can select them

based on patterns on its name. For example, you can select only those that start
with a particular text:

```
# select columnw with dplyr::select
my.temp.df <- select(my.df, starts_with('COL'))
print(my.temp.df)
```

```
##          COL1        COL2
## 1 0.50747820 0.2254366
## 2 0.30676851 0.2745305
## 3 0.42690767 0.2723051
## 4 0.69310208 0.6158293
## 5 0.08513597 0.4296715
```

This possibility is interesting when dealing with a `dataframe` with several
columns. Matching other types of column names patterns is possible with functions
`ends_with`, `contains` and `matches`.

For indexing (or filtering) rows, we use function `filter`, which allows us to select
rows based on one or more conditions. See an example:

```
# filter rows with filter() - one condition
my.temp.df. <- filter(my.df, COL1 > 0.25)
print(my.temp.df)
```

```
##          COL1        COL2
## 1 0.50747820 0.2254366
## 2 0.30676851 0.2745305
## 3 0.42690767 0.2723051
## 4 0.69310208 0.6158293
## 5 0.08513597 0.4296715
```

```
# filter rows with filter() - two conditions
my.temp.df <- filter(my.df, COL1 > 0.25,
                            COL2 < 0.75)
print(my.temp.df)
```

```
##          COL1        COL2         G          B
## 1 0.5074782 0.2254366 0.6516557 0.42880942
## 2 0.3067685 0.2745305 0.5677378 0.05190332
## 3 0.4269077 0.2723051 0.1135090 0.26417767
## 4 0.6931021 0.6158293 0.5959253 0.39879073
```

We can add columns to a `dataframe` using `mutate` and sort the rows using `arrange`:

```
# add new columns with mutate
my.temp.df <- mutate(my.df, COL3 = COL1 + COL2,
                             COL4 = COL3 + runif(N) )

my.temp.df <- arrange(my.temp.df, COL1)
# print result
print(my.temp.df)
```

```
##          COL1       COL2         G          B        COL3
## 1 0.08513597 0.4296715 0.3580500 0.83613414 0.5148075
## 2 0.30676851 0.2745305 0.5677378 0.05190332 0.5812990
## 3 0.42690767 0.2723051 0.1135090 0.26417767 0.6992127
## 4 0.50747820 0.2254366 0.6516557 0.42880942 0.7329148
## 5 0.69310208 0.6158293 0.5959253 0.39879073 1.3089314
##         COL4
## 1 0.9206575
## 2 1.1966514
## 3 1.4743226
## 4 1.5976360
## 5 1.6645001
```

Using `dplyr` functions for `dataframe` manipulations offers a simple interface and, sometimes, can be less verbose than the native functions. You'll most likely be using them within a pipeline operation, as described next.

9.5.2 The Pipeline Operator (%>%)

An important feature of package `dplyr` is the *pipeline* operator, first proposed by Bache and Wickham (2014) and defined by symbol %>%. It allows data operations to be performed in a sequential fashion, as in a pipeline, facilitating the optimization and readability of the resulting code. For example, we could write a `dataframe` manipulation procedure with the following code:

```
# example of using the pipeline operator
my.temp.df.pipeline <- my.df %>%
  select(COL1, COL2) %>%
  filter(COL1 > 0.25, COL2 < 0.75) %>%
  mutate(COL3 = COL1 + COL2,
         COL4 = COL3 + runif(length(COL1)) ) %>%
  arrange(COL1)

print(my.temp.df.pipeline)
```

```
##         COL1      COL2      COL3      COL4
## 1 0.3067685 0.2745305 0.5812990 1.4195867
## 2 0.4269077 0.2723051 0.6992127 0.9388019
## 3 0.5074782 0.2254366 0.7329148 1.4395617
## 4 0.6931021 0.6158293 1.3089314 2.0797029
```

In the code, we use symbol %>% in the end of each line to link the operations. The result from each line is passed to the next in a sequential fashion. That way, there is no need for creating intermediate objects. It makes the code prettier and more readable. You can also link the data manipulation stage with the creation of figures. We will discuss this possibility in chapter 8. Whenever possible, I strongly recommended the use of *pipelines*.

9.5.3   Simple Group Operations with dplyr

To illustrate the use of the functions group_by and summarise, we will execute the example of describing stock prices in previous sections. This time, however, we will use the structure of package dplyr to perform these calculations using the pipeline operator. Consider the following code:

```
library(dplyr)

# load data
load('data/SP500-Stocks-WithRet.RData')

# group data and calculate stats
my.tab <- my.df %>%
          group_by(ticker) %>%
          summarise(mean.price = mean(price.adjusted),
                    max.price = max(price.adjusted),
                    min.price = min(price.adjusted),
                    max.ret = max(ret),
                    min.ret = min(ret))

# print result
print(my.tab)

## # A tibble: 471 × 6
##    ticker mean.price max.price min.price    max.ret
##     <chr>      <dbl>     <dbl>     <dbl>      <dbl>
## 1       A   33.05298  48.18046 18.329764 0.11763059
## 2     AAL   23.42431  54.66265  3.893684 0.17316703
## 3     AAP  103.23486 199.99451 38.418693 0.16557581
```

```
## 4      AAPL   75.02859 127.96609 24.881912 0.08874137
## 5      ABC    58.40506 112.10088 23.307129 0.09532090
## 6      ABT    32.12158  49.33589 18.430625 0.06496596
## 7      ACN    70.61981 125.40000 31.589890 0.07989349
## 8      ADBE   55.25822 110.81000 22.690001 0.12780138
## 9      ADI    42.36350  73.90623 21.600676 0.10146155
## 10     ADM    33.77152  50.48857 20.866785 0.07298599
## # ... with 461 more rows, and 1 more variables:
## #   min.ret <dbl>
```

Explaining it, the first step in using `dplyr` is to group the data with function `group_by`. Here, we are grouping based on column `ticker`. This means we intend to perform a certain calculation for each stock in our database. Using `group_by` command is very flexible, allowing group operations with multiple columns, e.g., more than one factor.

After we group the data, we feed this object to the `summarise` function. It processes the data in blocks defined by the formation of groups in function `group_by`. Note each argument in `summarise` turns into a column in the output: `mean.price`, `max.price`, `min.price`, `max.ret`, `min.ret`. Each of the previous arguments is doing a different calculation based on the columns of `my.df`. If we wanted, we could add several other calculations with different columns by simply expanding the input arguments in `summarise`.

Using `dplyr` is highly recommended when you have to group the data based on more than one factor. Let's consider grouping stock data by ticker and the day of the week (Monday, Tuesday, ...). First, let's use function `weekday` to create a column called `week.day` in `my.df`.

```
# set new col week.day
my.df$week.day <- weekdays(my.df$ref.date)
```

```
# print it
print(head(my.df$week.day))
```

```
## [1] "Tuesday"   "Wednesday" "Thursday"  "Friday"
## [5] "Monday"    "Tuesday"
```

Now, we proceed by adding column `week.day` in `group_by`.

```
# group by ticker and weekday, calculate stats
my.tab <- my.df %>%
          group_by(ticker, week.day) %>%
          summarise(mean.price = mean(price.adjusted),
                    max.price = max(price.adjusted),
                    min.price = min(price.adjusted),
```

```
                    max.ret = max(ret),
                    min.ret = min(ret))
```

```
# print result
print(my.tab)
```

```
## Source: local data frame [2,355 x 7]
## Groups: ticker [?]
##
##     ticker  week.day mean.price max.price min.price
##      <chr>     <chr>      <dbl>     <dbl>     <dbl>
## 1       A     Friday   33.02034  47.88207 18.370543
## 2       A     Monday   33.11657  48.18046 18.458895
## 3       A   Thursday   33.03899  47.87212 18.696768
## 4       A    Tuesday   33.05971  48.02132 18.329764
## 5       A  Wednesday   33.03401  48.17052 18.744342
## 6     AAL     Friday   23.30720  54.66265  3.913153
## 7     AAL     Monday   23.63982  54.24885  4.137040
## 8     AAL   Thursday   23.27089  54.38582  4.283053
## 9     AAL    Tuesday   23.48269  52.86867  3.942356
## 10    AAL  Wednesday   23.43472  53.06473  3.893684
## # ... with 2,345 more rows, and 2 more variables:
## #   max.ret <dbl>, min.ret <dbl>
```

And that's it! To group the data to a new `factor`, all we need to do is add it in `group_by`.

Using `dplyr` to do simple group calculations is straightforward. The resulting code is efficient, self-contained, and elegant.

9.5.4 Complex Group Operations with `dplyr`

The previous example shows a simple case of group calculations. We can say it was simple because all argument operations in **summarise** had one value as the result. We had a mean for ticker X in weekday Z, another mean for ticker Y in weekday L, and so on.

Package `dplyr` also supports more complex operations, where the output is not a single value, but a complex object. This is useful in data processing tasks, as you can manipulate the data in the same tabular structure you usually think. We can estimate a different model for each ticker in our sample of financial data and store the whole result as a more complex table, where an element may not be a single value.

Let's look at the following example, where we use stock returns to calculate their accumulated value over time and store it as a whole vector.

```
library(dplyr)

# load data
load('data/SP500-Stocks-WithRet.RData')

# get acum ret of stoks
my.tab <- my.df %>%
  group_by(ticker) %>%
  do(acum.ret = cumprod(1+.$ret)) %>%
  mutate(last.cumret = acum.ret[length(acum.ret)],
         min.cumret = min(acum.ret))

print(head(my.tab))
```

```
## # A tibble: 6 × 4
##    ticker       acum.ret last.cumret min.cumret
##     <chr>         <list>       <dbl>      <dbl>
## 1       A <dbl [1,761]>    2.141724  0.8616613
## 2     AAL <dbl [1,761]>   10.033208  0.8385743
## 3     AAP <dbl [1,761]>    4.269025  0.9697870
## 4    AAPL <dbl [1,761]>    4.159118  0.8973880
## 5     ABC <dbl [1,761]>    3.233432  0.9677057
## 6     ABT <dbl [1,761]>    1.771201  0.8553816
```

Notice how column `acum.ret` is not a single value but an atomic vector containing several values. In fact, `acum.ret` is a list-column, meaning it can store any kind of object. We achieved this result by using function `do` in the previous code. As for the other columns, `last.cumret` and `min.cumret` are simple manipulations of `acum.ret`. An important observation is we used symbol `.$` to access the columns of `my.df` in the call to `do`. Whenever you use the `do` function, you must use this notation.

The greatest advantage of using complex group operations with `dplyr` is you can keep the same tabular representation. We can read the object `my.tab` as "for each stock, define a vector of accumulated returns". Using function `dplyr::do` is particularly interesting in the estimation of several models from the data. We will cover this topic in chapter 10.

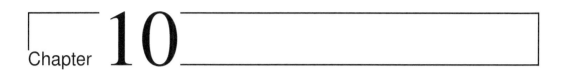

Chapter 10

Financial Econometrics with R

The modelling tools from financial econometrics allow the researcher to simulate stochastic processes, such as price series, make predictions, and test a particular hypothesis about the data. The number of possible empirical applications of financial models is enormous. Briefly, we estimate a model to learn something from the data. This model can later provide quantitative insights that will help the decision making process.

The variety of models used in financial econometrics is huge. It would be impossible to cover all possible models and their particularities. However, some types are used more often than others. In this chapter, we will deal with the following types of models and their applications:

- Linear models (OLS)
- Generalized linear models (GLS)
- Panel data models
- Arima models (Integrated Autoregressive Moving Averages)
- Garch models (generalized autoregressive conditional heteroskedasticity).
- Regime switching models

Here, we will not present a full description of the underlying theory behind the representation, estimation, and possible tests related to each type of model. The focus of this chapter is to present the main motivation and the computational details of working with these models in R, including the packages. While we will give quantitative context, providing examples with simulated and real data, these will not be deep. This chapter should be studied alongside the main literature of financial econometrics (Campbell et al., 1997, Brooks (2014), Hamilton (1994b), Greene (2003)). As a suggestion, more complete material on using R for Econometrics is found in Kleiber and Zeileis (2008).

10.1   Linear Models (OLS)

A linear model is, without a doubt, one of the most used econometric models in R and finance. Whenever you need to estimate a linear relationship from the data, you will likely use a linear model of the OLS (*ordinary least squares*) type. Its main advantage is simplicity and quick estimation. Since the model is estimated using a closed formula, its estimation, even for large amounts of data, is blazing fast.

In finance, the most direct and popular use of linear models is in the estimation of beta coefficients and factor models. Beta is a measure of systematic risk in the market, and it is estimated using stock returns as dependent variable and the returns on a market index, such as SP500 and FTSE, as the explanatory variable in a linear model. It is a measure of the strength of the relationship of a stock with the overall market. If the stock has a high value of beta, it strongly follows the market and has a high systematic risk. Later, we will look at an example of estimating the beta for a stock. Another example of using a linear regression in a research setup is available in section 11.3.2. For now, let's study a general case of a linear model.

A linear model with N explanatory variables can be represented as follows:

$$y_t = \alpha + \beta_1 x_{1,t} + \beta_2 x_{2,t} + ... + \beta_N x_{N,t} + \epsilon_t$$

The left side of the equation, (y_t), is the dependent (or explanatory) variable. This is the vector of information we are trying to explain and create predictions. Variables y_t and $x_{i,t}$ with $i = 1..N$ are the vectors with data. In R, they are the information we use as input in the estimation function. When we estimate the model, we find the values of α and β_i that minimize the sum of squared errors. We find the parameters that give the highest possible accuracy when predicting real data.

10.1.1   Simulating a Linear Model

Consider the following equation:

$$y_t = 0.5 + 2x_t + \epsilon_t$$

We can use R to simulate *1000* observations for y_t. We first define x_t and the model's error, ϵ_t, as random variables from the Normal distribution with zero mean and variance equal to one. The full simulation of y_t is performed with the following code:

```
set.seed(50)

# number of obs
nT <- 1000

# set x as Normal (0, 1)
x <- rnorm(nT)

# set coefficients
my.alpha <- 0.5
my.beta <- 2

# build y
y <- my.alpha + my.beta*x + rnorm(nT)
```

Using `ggplot`, we can create a scatter plot to visualize the correlation between objects x and y.

```
library(ggplot2)

# set temp df
temp.df <- data.frame(x, y)

# plot it
p <- ggplot(temp.df, aes(x = x, y = y))
p <- p + geom_point(size=0.5)

print(p)
```

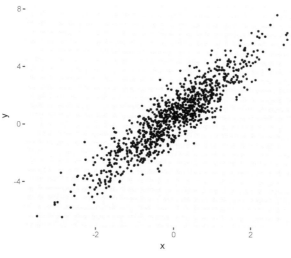

Clearly, there is a positive linear correlation; an upward straight line would be a good approximation for the relationship between these variables. We can check this result with the calculation of the correlation coefficient with command `cor(temp.df$x, temp.df$y)`. Here, the correlation between `y` and `x` is 0.901.

10.1.2   Estimating a Linear Model

In R, the main function for estimating a linear model is `lm`. Let's use it to estimate a model from the previous simulated data.

```
# set df
lm.df <- data.frame(x, y)

# estimate linear model
my.lm <- lm(data = lm.df, formula = y ~ x)
print(my.lm)


##
## Call:
## lm(formula = y ~ x, data = lm.df)
##
## Coefficients:
## (Intercept)              x
##      0.5083         1.9891
```

The `formula` argument defines the shape of the linear model. If we had another column, called `x2`, and wanted to include it in the model, we could write `formula=y ~ x1 + x2`. Notice the intercept (α) is, by default, included in the estimation. If we needed to omit the intercept, we could write `formula=y ~ 0 + x1` or `formula=y ~ -1 + x1`.

Argument `formula` allows other custom options, including interactions between the explanatory variables. Let's create another artificial dataset and look at some of these options:

```
set.seed(15)

# set simulated dataset
N <- 100
df <- data.frame(x = runif(N),
                 y = runif(N),
                 z = runif(N),
                 group = sample(LETTERS[1:3],
                                N,
```

```
                                    replace = TRUE ))

# Vanilla formula
#
# example: y ~ x + z
# model: y(t) = alpha + beta(1)*x(t) + beta(2)*z(t) + error(t)
my.formula <- y ~ x + z
print(lm(data = df,
         formula = my.formula))


##
## Call:
## lm(formula = my.formula, data = df)
##
## Coefficients:
## (Intercept)              x             z
##     0.44971        0.14223      -0.03781
# vannila formula with dummies
#
# example: y ~ group + x + z
# model: y(t) = alpha + beta(1)*D_1(t)+beta(2)*D_2(t) +
#                 beta(3)*x(t) + beta(4)*z(t) + error(t)
# D_i(t) - dummy for group i
my.formula <- y ~ group + x + z
print(lm(data = df,
         formula = my.formula))


##
## Call:
## lm(formula = my.formula, data = df)
##
## Coefficients:
## (Intercept)         groupB         groupC              x
##     0.48309       -0.06397        0.01144        0.13511
##           z
##    -0.05156
# Without intercept
#
# example: y ~ -1 + x + z
# model: y(t) = beta(1)*x(t) + beta(2)*z(t) + error(t)
my.formula <- y ~ -1 + x + z
```

```
print(lm(data = df,
         formula = my.formula))
```

```
##
## Call:
## lm(formula = my.formula, data = df)
##
## Coefficients:
##      x        z
## 0.5183  0.3133
```

```
# Using combinations of variables
# example: y ~ x*z
# model: y(t) = alpha + beta(1)*x(t) + beta(2)*z(t) +
#               beta(3)*x(t)*z(t) + error(t)
my.formula <- y ~ x*z
print(lm(data = df,
         formula = my.formula))
```

```
##
## Call:
## lm(formula = my.formula, data = df)
##
## Coefficients:
## (Intercept)            x            z          x:z
##     0.39827      0.22970      0.05129     -0.15464
```

```
# Interacting variables
# example: y ~ x:group + z
# model: y(t) = alpha + beta(1)*z(t) + beta(2)*x(t)*D_1(t) +
#               beta(3)*x(t)*D_2(t) + beta(4)*x(t)*D_3(t) +
#               error(t)
# D_i(t) - dummy for group i
my.formula <- y ~ x:group + z
print(lm(data = df,
         formula = my.formula))
```

```
##
## Call:
## lm(formula = my.formula, data = df)
##
## Coefficients:
## (Intercept)            z     x:groupA     x:groupB
##     0.45995     -0.05105      0.16573      0.06271
```

```
##      x:groupC
##      0.20025
```

The different options in the `formula` input allow a diversified range of linear models. Using common mathematical operations, such as `log(x)`, is also possible. More details about advanced uses of `formula` input is available in the manual.

The output of function `lm` is an object similar to a `list`. Therefore, its elements can be accessed using the `$` operator. Let's print all available names:

```
# print names in model
print(names(my.lm))
```

```
##  [1] "coefficients"  "residuals"     "effects"
##  [4] "rank"          "fitted.values" "assign"
##  [7] "qr"            "df.residual"   "xlevels"
## [10] "call"          "terms"         "model"
```

As you can see, there is a slot, called `coefficients`. Let's check its contents.

```
print(my.lm$coefficients)
```

```
## (Intercept)            x
##   0.5083045    1.9890616
```

All coefficients are stored in `my.lm$coefficients`. Its content is a simple atomic vector that increases in length, according to the number of explanatory variables in the model.

In our example of using `lm` with simulated data, the estimated coefficients are close to the actual values of 0.5 and 2. Remember, in the previous code, we set these values as `my.alpha <- 0.5` and `my.beta <- 2`.

Experienced researchers have probably noted, from the econometric point of view, using function `print` in the output of `lm` results in little information. Besides the values of the coefficients, many other aspects of a linear model must be analyzed. In R, to obtain more information about the previously estimated model, we use function `summary`. See next.

```
print(summary(my.lm))
```

```
##
## Call:
## lm(formula = y ~ x, data = lm.df)
##
## Residuals:
##     Min      1Q  Median      3Q     Max
## -3.0444 -0.6906 -0.0244  0.6807  3.2892
```

```
##
## Coefficients:
##               Estimate Std. Error t value Pr(>|t|)
## (Intercept)    0.50830    0.03107   16.36   <2e-16 ***
## x              1.98906    0.03031   65.61   <2e-16 ***
## ---
## Signif. codes:
## 0 '***' 0.001 '**' 0.01 '*' 0.05 '.' 0.1 ' ' 1
##
## Residual standard error: 0.9824 on 998 degrees of freedom
## Multiple R-squared:  0.8118, Adjusted R-squared:  0.8116
## F-statistic:  4305 on 1 and 998 DF,  p-value: < 2.2e-16
```

The estimated coefficients have high T values, and the model has a outstanding fit of the data, with an adjusted R^2 value of 0.8116. This positive result is not surprising. The data was simulated in a linear process, and the correlation was introduced artificially.

Additional information is available in the resulting object from **summary**. Let's look at the names of the output:

```
my.summary <- summary(my.lm)
print(names(my.summary))
```

```
## [1] "call"          "terms"        "residuals"
## [4] "coefficients"  "aliased"      "sigma"
## [7] "df"            "r.squared"    "adj.r.squared"
## [10] "fstatistic"   "cov.unscaled"
```

Each of these elements contains information that can be reported in a estimation table. We could export the values of coefficients, T statistics, and others to a spreadsheet tool and create a custom table to report the results. This, however, is not suggested. In section 10.8, we will discuss the best ways of reporting a model using specialized packages.

Now, let's move to an example with real data. For that, we will estimate the beta coefficient of a randomly selected stock. The beta specification, also called market model, is given by:

$$R_t = \alpha + \beta R_{M,t} + \epsilon_t$$

First, let's load the stock and SP500 data.

```
# load stock data
load('data/SP500-Stocks-WithRet.RData')
```

```
# select rnd asset and filter data
set.seed(10)
my.asset <- sample(my.df$ticker,1)
my.df.asset <- my.df[my.df$ticker == my.asset, ]

# load SP500 data
df.sp500 <- read.csv(file = 'data/SP500.csv',
                     colClasses = c('Date','numeric'))

# calculate return
df.sp500$ret <- calc.ret(df.sp500$price)

# print datasets
print(nrow(my.df.asset))
```

```
## [1] 1761
```

```
print(nrow(df.sp500))
```

```
## [1] 1801
```

You can see the number of rows of the dataset for stock JEC doesn't match the rows of the SP500 index. The dates of the different `dataframes` are not synchronized. So, the first step is to add a column in `my.df` with the returns of the market index. For that, we use function `match` to find the indices that synchronize the dates.

```
# find location of dates in df.sp500
idx <- match(my.df.asset$ref.date, df.sp500$date)

# create column in my.df with sp500 returns
my.df.asset$ret.sp500 <- df.sp500$ret[idx]
```

As a start, let's create the scatter plot with the returns of the stock and the market index, adding a linear trend.

```
library(ggplot2)

p <- ggplot(data = my.df.asset, aes(x=ret.sp500, y=ret))
p <- p + geom_point()
p <- p + geom_smooth(method = 'lm')
print(p)
```

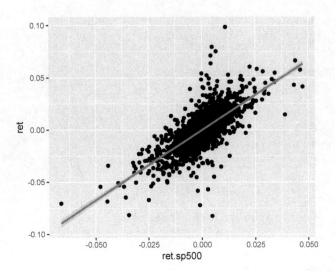

The figure shows a clear linear tendency; the returns from the market index are a good predictor of the returns of the stock. Now, let's estimate the linear model.

```
# estimate beta model
my.beta.model <- lm(data = my.df.asset, formula = ret ~ ret.sp500)

# print it
print(summary(my.beta.model))
```

```
##
## Call:
## lm(formula = ret ~ ret.sp500, data = my.df.asset)
##
## Residuals:
##       Min        1Q    Median        3Q       Max
## -0.088660 -0.006393 -0.000273  0.006384  0.083767
##
## Coefficients:
##               Estimate Std. Error t value Pr(>|t|)
## (Intercept) -0.0001985  0.0002920   -0.68    0.497
## ret.sp500    1.3406720  0.0298163   44.96   <2e-16 ***
## ---
## Signif. codes:
## 0 '***' 0.001 '**' 0.01 '*' 0.05 '.' 0.1 ' ' 1
##
## Residual standard error: 0.01224 on 1759 degrees of freedom
## Multiple R-squared:  0.5348, Adjusted R-squared:  0.5345
## F-statistic:  2022 on 1 and 1759 DF,  p-value: < 2.2e-16
```

Previous output shows stock JEC has a beta equal to 1.34. This means this is an aggressive stock with high sensitivity to market movements.

10.1.3   Statistical Inference in Linear Models

After estimating a model with function `lm`, the next step is to test some hypothesis about the coefficients. The F test verifies the most basic condition for a model to justify its existence – it tests the assumption that all coefficients, excluding the intercept, are equal to zero. When function `summary` is applied to a `lm` output, the F-test is provided by default in the last line of the text output. The null hypothesis of the test is that all slopes are equal to zero. Let's try it:

```
##
## Call:
## lm(formula = y ~ x.1 + x.2, data = df)
##
## Residuals:
##      Min       1Q    Median       3Q       Max
## -0.43125 -0.20631 -0.01184  0.18659   0.51744
##
## Coefficients:
##               Estimate Std. Error t value Pr(>|t|)
## (Intercept)   0.449997   0.075048   5.996 3.46e-08 ***
## x.1          -0.004976   0.092259  -0.054    0.957
## x.2          -0.006775   0.088308  -0.077    0.939
## ---
## Signif. codes:
## 0 '***' 0.001 '**' 0.01 '*' 0.05 '.' 0.1 ' ' 1
##
## Residual standard error: 0.2621 on 97 degrees of freedom
## Multiple R-squared:  8.477e-05,  Adjusted R-squared:  -0.02053
## F-statistic: 0.004112 on 2 and 97 DF,  p-value: 0.9959
```

In this example, the F statistic is 0.0041119. The associated p-value is higher than 10%, indicating a strong statistical evidence in line with the null hypothesis. We failed to reject the hypothesis that the parameters attached to `x.1` and `x.2` are equal to zero. The association between the explained variable and these vectors is almost null. For an example with the rejection of the null hypothesis of the F test, see the estimation of a model with artificial data in section 10.1.2.

Another type of test automatically executed by the `lm` and `summary` function is the T test. While the F statistics test the joint hypothesis that all coefficients are zero, the T statistic tests it for individual parameters. It verifies the hypothesis that a specific parameter is equal to zero. Each coefficient has its own T test.

In the practice of research, it is likely that both tests, T and F, will suffice in most cases. They will give you information about the statistical relationships in the data. However, you can also test custom hypothesis, such as the sum or product of parameters equal to a particular value, using package car (Fox and Weisberg, 2011). The tested hypotheses are usually provided from a theoretical model or analysis. For example, in section 11.3.2, we will study the performance of a forecasting algorithm. We will test the performance of the forecasts by estimating a linear model with the actual values of the variable as dependent and the forecasts as independent (explanatory). If the forecasting model works well, the intercept from the resulting model should be zero, and the slope should be equal to one. We can jointly test this hypothesis and calculate a p-value associated with it.

As a simple example, let's test a linear hypothesis for a simulated model. Here, we will create artificial data and test the formal hypothesis that the estimated coefficients are equal to the actual values provided in the simulation.

```
set.seed(10)

# number of time periods
nT <- 1000

# set parameters
my.intercept <- 0.5
my.beta <- 1.5

# simulate
x <- rnorm(nT)
y <- my.intercept + my.beta*x + rnorm(nT)

# set df
df <- data.frame(y, x)

# estimate model
my.lm <- lm(data = df,
            formula = y ~ x )
```

After the estimation of the model, we use function LinearHypothesis from package car (Fox and Weisberg, 2011) to implement our formal test. Before using it, we need to understand its input. The first input, model, is the estimated model from the previous chunk. Inputs hypothesis.matrix and rhs determine the linear hypothesis of the test in a matrix format. The object in hypothesis.matrix will be multiplied in matrix notation by a vertical vector of the coefficients from the model.

The `rhs` (right hand side) determines the hypothesised result from this calculation. In our case, the resulting matrix operation is:

$$\underbrace{\begin{bmatrix} 1 & 0 \\ 0 & 1 \end{bmatrix}}_{hypothesis.matrix} \begin{bmatrix} \alpha \\ \beta \end{bmatrix} = \underbrace{\begin{bmatrix} 0.5 \\ 1.5 \end{bmatrix}}_{rhs}$$

With this matrix operation, we test the joint hypothesis that the intercept is equal to 0.5 and the slope is equivalent to 1.5. Notice that using matrices gives flexibility to the user. We could test many other linear hypotheses by changing the shape of `hypothesis.matrix` and `rhs`. The actual R code that implements the test is given next.

```
library(car)

# set test matrix
test.matrix <- matrix(c(my.intercept,   # alpha test value
                        my.beta))  # beta test value

# hypothesis matrix
hyp.mat <- matrix(c(1,0,
                    0,1),nrow = 2)

# do test
my.waldtest <- linearHypothesis(my.lm,
                                hypothesis.matrix = hyp.mat,
                                rhs = test.matrix)

# print result
print(my.waldtest)

## Linear hypothesis test
##
## Hypothesis:
## (Intercept) = 0.5
## x = 1.5
##
## Model 1: restricted model
## Model 2: y ~ x
##
##   Res.Df    RSS Df Sum of Sq      F Pr(>F)
## 1   1000 1089.1
## 2    998 1086.8  2    2.3766 1.0912 0.3362
```

As we can see, the test fails to reject the null hypothesis. This means our simulation worked, and the parameters are correctly estimated as expected.

Another family of tests commonly applied to linear models is related to its assumptions. Every linear model of type OLS assumes several conditions to its errors, including: 1) independence, 2) homoscesdasticity (constant variance), and 3) adherence to the Normal distribution. If these assumptions are not true, the model may be inefficient or biased, meaning some modification or use of robust estimates is required. More details about why these assumption must be true and possible workarounds are found in any Econometric textbook, such as Greene (2003) and Maddala (2001).

In R, we can use package `lmtest` (Zeileis and Hothorn, 2002) to test for independence with the Breush-Godfrey and Durbin Watson test. The Shapiro-Wilk test for normality is available in package `stats`. Next, we provide an example of usage for the previously estimated model with random data.

```
library(lmtest)


# Breush Pagan test 1 - Serial correlation
# Null Hypothesis: No serial correlation in residual
print(bgtest(my.lm, order = 5))


# Breush Pagan test 2 - Homocesdasticity of residuals
# Null Hypothesis: homocesdasticity
#                  (constant variance of residuals)
print(ncvTest(my.lm))


# Durbin Watson test - Serial correlation
# Null Hypothesis: No serial correlation in residual
print(dwtest(my.lm))


# Shapiro test  - Normality
# Null Hypothesis: Data is normally distributed
print(shapiro.test(my.lm$residuals))
```

```
##
##  Breusch-Godfrey test for serial correlation of order
##  up to 5
##
## data:  my.lm
## LM test = 4.2628, df = 5, p-value = 0.5122
##
## Non-constant Variance Score Test
```

```
## Variance formula: ~ fitted.values
## Chisquare = 1.54328     Df = 1      p = 0.2141302
##
##  Durbin-Watson test
##
## data:  my.lm
## DW = 2.092, p-value = 0.9271
## alternative hypothesis: true autocorrelation is greater than 0
##
##
##  Shapiro-Wilk normality test
##
## data:  my.lm$residuals
## W = 0.99803, p-value = 0.2964
```

As expected, the model with artificial data passed all tests.

Another interesting approach for validating linear models is to use package `gvlma` (Pena and Slate, 2014). It provides a top level function that can execute all sorts of tests in linear models, including the ones described before. The main advantage is that it outputs all tests in a single function call. Let's try it:

```
library(gvlma)

# global validation of model
gvmodel <- gvlma(my.lm)

# print result
summary(gvmodel)
```

```
##
## Call:
## lm(formula = y ~ x, data = df)
##
## Residuals:
##     Min      1Q  Median      3Q     Max
## -3.2703 -0.6898  0.0063  0.7346  3.8266
##
## Coefficients:
##              Estimate Std. Error t value Pr(>|t|)
## (Intercept)  0.51510    0.03300   15.61   <2e-16 ***
## x            1.54658    0.03329   46.46   <2e-16 ***
## ---
## Signif. codes:
```

```
## 0 '***' 0.001 '**' 0.01 '*' 0.05 '.' 0.1 ' ' 1
##
## Residual standard error: 1.044 on 998 degrees of freedom
## Multiple R-squared:  0.6838, Adjusted R-squared:  0.6835
## F-statistic:  2159 on 1 and 998 DF,  p-value: < 2.2e-16
##
##
## ASSESSMENT OF THE LINEAR MODEL ASSUMPTIONS
## USING THE GLOBAL TEST ON 4 DEGREES-OF-FREEDOM:
## Level of Significance =  0.05
##
## Call:
##  gvlma(x = my.lm)
##
##                     Value p-value                Decision
## Global Stat         3.6404  0.4569 Assumptions acceptable.
## Skewness            1.7814  0.1820 Assumptions acceptable.
## Kurtosis            0.1738  0.6767 Assumptions acceptable.
## Link Function       0.6628  0.4156 Assumptions acceptable.
## Heteroscedasticity 1.0224  0.3119 Assumptions acceptable.
```

The output of `gvlma` shows several tests performed in the model. The result is also positive, as the decision from the model is that the OLS assumptions are acceptable. If a model did not pass the tests, one solution is to use robust estimates of standard errors. Package `sandwich` (Zeileis, 2004) offers function `NeweyWest` for this purpose.

10.2   Generalized Linear Models (GLM)

The generalized linear model (GLM) is a flexible alternative to a linear model. It allows the user to change the distribution of the error and the link function, a systematic way that quantifies how the explained variable will be affected by the response variable. GLM models are best suited when the OLS assumptions, such as normality of residuals, don't hold. For example, when you have a binary variable that takes only two values and you want to write a model for it, the residual is not normally distributed, given the limits of the explained variable.

We can write a general univariate GLM specification as:

$$E\left(y_t\right) = g\left(\alpha + \sum_{i=1}^{N} \beta_i x_{i,t}\right)$$

The main difference of a GLM model and a OLS model is the use of a link function

$g()$ and a custom distribution assumption for the error term. Function $g()$ can take many shapes. For example, if we are modelling a binary variable, we can use $g()$ as the *logit* function:

$$g(x) = \frac{\exp(x)}{1 + \exp(x)}$$

Notice, in this case, function $g()$ ensures any value of x will result in a number between 0 and 1. The response of the explained variable to the explanatory will be non linear.

10.2.1 Simulating a GLM Model

As an example, let's simulate the following GLM model, where the response vector y_t is a Bernoulli variable that takes value 1 with probability p_t. The probabilities are calculated from the non linear transformation of x_t:

$$p_t = \frac{\exp(2 + 5x_t)}{1 + \exp(2 + 5x_t)}$$

In R, we use the following code to build the response vector.

```
set.seed(15)

# set number of obs
nT <- 500

# set x
x = rnorm(nT)

my.alpha <- 2
my.beta <- 5

# set probabilities
z = my.alpha + my.beta*x
p = exp(z)/(1+exp(z))

# set response variable
y = rbinom(n = nT, size = 1, prob = p)
```

Function `rbinom` creates a vector of 1s and 0s, based on the probabilities of input `prob`. Let's plot the simulated series over time with `ggplot`.

```
library(ggplot2)

# set df for ggplot
df = data.frame(y, x)

# plot GLM sim
p <- ggplot(data = df, aes(x=seq_along(y) ,y=y))
p <- p + geom_point(size=0.5)
print(p)
```

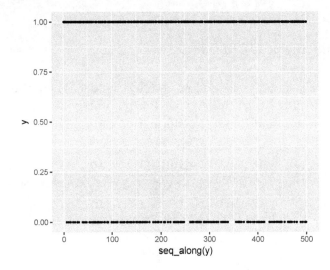

Object y contains zeros and ones, as expected.

10.2.2   Estimating a GLM Model

In R, the estimation of GLM models is accomplished with function glm. It works similarly to lm but contains several extra arguments that control the details of the models, such as the link function and the distribution of the residuals.

First, let's use the previously simulated data to estimate a logit model:

```
# estimate GLM
my.glm <- glm(data=df,
              formula = y~x ,
              family= binomial(link = "logit"))

# print it with summary
print(summary(my.glm))
```

```
## 
## Call:
## glm(formula = y ~ x, family = binomial(link = "logit"), data = df)
## 
## Deviance Residuals:
##      Min        1Q    Median        3Q       Max
## -2.99392  -0.13689   0.04087   0.23250   2.91383
## 
## Coefficients:
##             Estimate Std. Error z value Pr(>|z|)
## (Intercept)   2.1488     0.2622   8.197 2.47e-16 ***
## x             4.9050     0.5110   9.598  < 2e-16 ***
## ---
## Signif. codes:
## 0 '***' 0.001 '**' 0.01 '*' 0.05 '.' 0.1 ' ' 1
## 
## (Dispersion parameter for binomial family taken to be 1)
## 
##     Null deviance: 634.18  on 499  degrees of freedom
## Residual deviance: 214.14  on 498  degrees of freedom
## AIC: 218.14
## 
## Number of Fisher Scoring iterations: 7
```

The estimated coefficients are close to what we set in `my.alpha` and `my.beta`. As expected, the model has a good fit of the data, with both parameters being statistically significant at 1%.

Function `glm` offers many options for setting a customized model. From the help files, we have the following alternatives for the distribution and link function and their corresponding inputs:

Family	Default Link Function
binomial	link = "logit"
gaussian	link = "identity"
Gamma	link = "inverse"
inverse.gaussian	link = "1/mu^2"
poisson	link = "log"
quasi	link = "identity", variance = "constant"
quasibinomial	link = "logit"
quasipoisson	link = "log"

The first step in using a GLM model is to identify the distribution and link function that best suits your data. After that, you can use the previous table to set the input of function `glm`.

As an example with real data from financial markets, let's randomly select a stock and estimate a model for the probability of a positive return with the probit model (`link='probit'`). We will use the returns of the SP500 as the explanatory variable. We want to test whether the market index influences the chance that a stock has a positive return, an alternative version of the market model.

```
set.seed(15)

# select stock
my.stock <- sample(unique(my.df$ticker), 1)
my.df.asset <- my.df[my.df$ticker == my.stock, ]

# find location of dates in df.sp500
idx <- match(my.df.asset$ref.date, df.sp500$date)

# create column in my.df with sp500 returns
my.df.asset$ret.sp500 <- df.sp500$ret[idx]

# set column with dummy variable
my.df.asset$D_ret <- my.df.asset$ret > 0

# estimate model
my.glm <- glm(data=my.df.asset,
              formula = D_ret~ret.sp500 ,
              family= binomial(link = "probit"))

print(summary(my.glm))
```

```
##
## Call:
## glm(formula = D_ret ~ ret.sp500, family = binomial(link = "probit"),
##     data = my.df.asset)
##
## Deviance Residuals:
##     Min       1Q    Median       3Q      Max
## -2.7100  -1.0391    0.2688   1.0161   2.5873
##
## Coefficients:
##               Estimate Std. Error z value Pr(>|z|)
## (Intercept) -0.005122   0.032334  -0.158    0.874
## ret.sp500   78.567162   4.616749  17.018   <2e-16 ***
```

```
## ---
## Signif. codes:
## 0 '***' 0.001 '**' 0.01 '*' 0.05 '.' 0.1 ' ' 1
##
## (Dispersion parameter for binomial family taken to be 1)
##
##       Null deviance: 2439.8  on 1760   degrees of freedom
## Residual deviance: 2038.9  on 1759   degrees of freedom
## AIC: 2042.9
##
## Number of Fisher Scoring iterations: 5
```

The parameter for the market index is positive and significant. This result implies the probability that stock MJN has a positive return is affected by the changes in the SP500. When the index increases its prices, a positive return in the stock is more likely.

10.3 Panel Data Models

Panel data models are advised when the modelled data is multidimensional, covering information about individuals or companies that spawn over time. A dataset with financial information about several companies for many years is a classic case of panel data. We have a column identifying the company, another column for the time, and one or more columns identifying the financial indicators. In a cross section of time, we have several companies and several financial ratios. The dataset can be further categorized as balanced, where all companies have information in all dates, and unbalanced, where not all companies have data for all dates.

The main motivation to use panel data models is to allow common effects within the groups. If a standard OLS estimation is used for each group, such as companies, we implicitly assume the models are independent. If the assumption of independence is not true, our econometric analysis is jeopardized by a possible bias. Using panel data models allows for more flexible representations. Some parameters can be individual to each group, while others are shared. Using panel data models requires careful thought about how the model is identified. Many statistical tests are available for this purpose.

We can represent the simplest case of a panel data model as:

$$y_{i,t} = \alpha_i + \beta x_{i,t} + \epsilon_{i,t}$$

Notice we now use index i in the dependent and independent variables. This index controls for the groups, such as different companies. In our specific model, all i cases have different intercepts, but share the same beta. Depending on the assumptions about the intercept, the previous equation can represent a panel data model of type *fixed* or *random effects* . There are many other ways to customize a panel data model and set dynamic effects, such as lagged terms. You can find more details in Hsiao (2014).

10.3.1   Simulating Panel Data Models

Let's simulate a balanced panel data with fixed effects for twelve different firms and five time periods. This is a classic case of panel data, with large N and small T. Each company will have a explanatory variable, called **x**, that varies over different dates. The following code uses matrix operations to simulate all cases. Notice the many uses of the **sapply** function. After creating the multivariate data, we stack it in single vectors and save it in a **dataframe**.

```
set.seed(25)

# number of obs for each case
nT <- 5

# set number of groups
N <- 12

# set possible cases
possible.cases <- LETTERS[1:N]

# set parameters
my.alphas <- seq(-10,10,length.out = N)
my.beta <- 1.5

# set indep var (x) and dates
indep.var <- sapply(rep(nT,N), rnorm)
my.dates <- Sys.Date() + 1:nT

# create response matrix (y)
response.matrix <- matrix(rep(my.alphas,nT),
                          nrow = nT,
                          byrow = TRUE) +
   indep.var*my.beta + sapply(rep(nT,N),rnorm, sd = 0.25)

# set df
```

```
sim.df <- data.frame(G = as.character(sapply(possible.cases,
                                             rep,
                                             times=nT )),
                     dates = rep(my.dates, times=N),
                     y = as.numeric(response.matrix),
                     x = as.numeric(indep.var),
                     stringsAsFactors = FALSE)

# print result
print(str(sim.df))

## 'data.frame':    60 obs. of  4 variables:
##  $ G    : chr  "A" "A" "A" "A" ...
##  $ dates: Date, format: "2017-05-06" ...
##  $ y    : num  -10.68 -11.55 -11.74 -9.84 -11.96 ...
##  $ x    : num  -0.212 -1.042 -1.153 0.322 -1.5 ...
## NULL
```

The result is a `dataframe` object with 60 rows and 4 columns. We can look at the scatter plot of x and y for each firm using `ggplot2`:

```
library(ggplot2)

p <- ggplot(sim.df, aes(x=x, y=y))
p <- p + geom_point()
p <- p + facet_wrap(~G)

print(p)
```

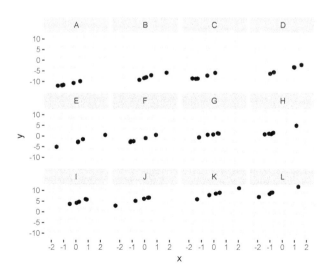

The figure shows the strong linear relationship shared between x and y in the different groups. If we estimated a linear model from this data, we would have to allow a different intercept for each group we find in column `cases`.

10.3.2   Estimating Panel Data Models

With the artificial data simulated in the previous step, let's estimate the model using package `plm` (Croissant and Millo, 2008). This is a great package that offers a comprehensive set of tools in testing and estimating panel data models. The interface of function `plm` is similar to `lm`. However, we need to define the panel data model in argument `model` and the names of columns that define the groups and time reference in input `index`.

```
library(plm)

# estimate panel data model with fixed effects
my.pdm <- plm(data = sim.df,
              formula = y ~ x,
              model = 'within',
              index = c('G','dates'))

# print result
print(summary(my.pdm,))

## Oneway (individual) effect Within Model
##
## Call:
## plm(formula = y ~ x, data = sim.df, model = "within", index = c("G",
##     "dates"))
##
## Balanced Panel: n=12, T=5, N=60
##
## Residuals :
##    Min. 1st Qu.  Median 3rd Qu.     Max.
##  -0.440  -0.148  -0.033   0.154    0.479
##
## Coefficients :
##    Estimate Std. Error t-value  Pr(>|t|)
## x 1.479366   0.035854  41.261 < 2.2e-16 ***
## ---
## Signif. codes:
## 0 '***' 0.001 '**' 0.01 '*' 0.05 '.' 0.1 ' ' 1
```

```
##
## Total Sum of Squares:    106.87
## Residual Sum of Squares: 2.871
## R-Squared:       0.97313
## Adj. R-Squared: 0.96627
## F-statistic: 1702.44 on 1 and 47 DF, p-value: < 2.22e-16
```

As expected, the parameters were correctly retrieved from the data, with a small difference from the actual value defined in `my.beta`. Notice the different intercepts were not printed in the `summary` output. We can retrieve them using function `fixef`:

```
print(fixef(my.pdm))
```

```
##            A            B            C            D            E
## -10.0934047  -8.2435523  -6.3253831  -4.6552624  -2.8087407
##            F            G            H            I            J
##  -0.9794636   0.9609360   2.7568233   4.4134081   6.2113577
##            K            L
##   8.1880249  10.0337231
```

Again, the simulated intercept values are close to the ones obtained from the estimation.

As an example with real data, let's use the dataset from Grunfeld (1958). This research paper studied the components of corporate investments using data for ten companies for twenty years. The data is available with package `plm`, and we can load it with function `data`. Let's import it and look in its content.

```
library(plm)
```

```
# data from Grunfeld
data("Grunfeld")
```

```
# print it
print(str(Grunfeld))
```

```
## 'data.frame':    200 obs. of  5 variables:
##  $ firm   : int  1 1 1 1 1 1 1 1 1 1 ...
##  $ year   : int  1935 1936 1937 1938 1939 1940 1941 1942 1943 1944 ...
##  $ inv    : num  318 392 411 258 331 ...
##  $ value  : num  3078 4662 5387 2792 4313 ...
##  $ capital: num  2.8 52.6 156.9 209.2 203.4 ...
## NULL
```

The `Grunfeld` dataset contains company information about gross investment, market value, and capital (plant and equipment). The `dataframe` is in the long format and ready to be used. In the model, column `inv` is set as the dependent variable. Columns `firm` and `year` are the index of panel data estimation. The remaining columns, `value` and `capital`, are explanatory variables. You can find more details about the Grunfeld data, including information about different versions of the dataset and its historical usage, in Kleiber and Zeileis (2010).

A note here is important; given its high number of time periods in proportion to the number of firms, the Grunfeld data is best suited for a more advanced econometric model of type SUR (seemly unrelated regression). For educational purposes of learning R, we will explore other types of panel models with this dataset . See Greene (2003) for more details.

First, let's explore the raw data by estimating a different OLS model for each firm. This is also called the pooled model. We can use function `by` with a custom function for this purpose (see chapter 9 for details).

```
my.fct <- function(df) {
  # Estimates a linear model from Grunfeld data
  #
  # Args:
  #    df - dataframe from Grunfeld
  #
  # Returns:
  #    lm object

  my.model <- lm(data = df,
                 formula = inv ~  value + capital)

  return(my.model)
}


# estimate model for each firm
my.l <- by(Grunfeld,
           INDICES = Grunfeld$firm,
           FUN = my.fct)

# print result
my.coefs <- sapply(my.l, coef)
print(my.coefs)
```

```
##                         1             2            3
## (Intercept) -149.7824533  -49.1983219  -9.95630645
## value          0.1192808    0.1748560   0.02655119
## capital        0.3714448    0.3896419   0.15169387
```

```
##                             4             5           6          7
## (Intercept) -6.18996051 22.707116014 -8.68554338 -4.4995344
## value         0.07794782  0.162377704  0.13145484  0.0875272
## capital       0.31571819  0.003101737  0.08537427  0.1237814
##                             8           9          10
## (Intercept) -0.50939018 -7.72283708 0.161518567
## value         0.05289413  0.07538794 0.004573432
## capital       0.09240649  0.08210356 0.437369190
```

The results show a great discrepancy between the coefficients obtained for each firm. This is especially true for the intercept value. It ranges from -149.8 to 22.71. This result shows evidence it might be more realistic to assume different coefficients for the different firms. We can formally test this hypothesis with function `polltest` from `plm`. It tests the null hypothesis that all coefficients are the same across the cases, against the alternative hypothesis they are not. Let's use it.

```
# test if all coef are the same across firms
my.pooltest <- pooltest(inv~value+capital,
                        data = Grunfeld,
                        model = "pooling")

# print result
print(my.pooltest)
```

```
##
##   F statistic
##
## data:  inv ~ value + capital
## F = 27.749, df1 = 27, df2 = 170, p-value < 2.2e-16
## alternative hypothesis: unstability
```

The high F test and small p-value suggest the rejection of the null hypothesis. The evidence that the same coefficients can be applied to all firms is minimal. The motivation for using panel data models for the Grunfeld dataset is justified by the statistical test.

Before estimating the model, we need to understand which kind of panel data model is best suited for the data. For simplicity, let's assume only two possible choices, fixed or random effects. In both models, each group has unobserved individual effects but share the same impact (beta) of the observed explanatory variables. The difference between the models is how the unobserved individual effect is perceived. Individual effects are correlated to the explanatory variables in the fixed effect model, while in the random effects, they are random variables. The correct estimation of the model and econometric analysis will change according to the underlying correlation structure. See Greene (2003) for more technical details about the difference between fixed and random effects models.

We can test the model specification using package `plm`. Function `phtest` executes the Hausman test (Hausman, 1978), a statistical procedure that tests the null hypothesis that the best model is the random effects and not the fixed effect. Let's try it for our data.

```
# set options for Hausman test
my.formula <- inv ~ value + capital
my.index <- c('firm','year')

# do Hausman test
my.hausman.test <- phtest(x = my.formula,
                          data = Grunfeld,
                          model = c('within', 'random'),
                          index = my.index)

# print result
print(my.hausman.test)

##
##   Hausman Test
##
## data:  my.formula
## chisq = 2.3304, df = 2, p-value = 0.3119
## alternative hypothesis: one model is inconsistent
```

The p-value of 31.19% is higher than an acceptable threshold of 10%. Therefore, we fail to reject the null hypothesis that the most efficient panel data model is the random effects. We have strong statistical evidence that a random effect model is better suited than a fixed effect type for the Grunfeld dataset.

After identifying the model, let's estimate it using function `plm`.

```
# set panel data model with random effects
my.model <- 'random'
my.formula <- inv ~ value + capital
my.index <- c('firm','year')

# estimate it
my.pdm.random <- plm(data = Grunfeld,
                     formula = my.formula,
                     model = my.model,
                     index = my.index)
```

```
# print result
print(summary(my.pdm.random))
```

```
## Oneway (individual) effect Random Effect Model
##     (Swamy-Arora's transformation)
##
## Call:
## plm(formula = my.formula, data = Grunfeld, model = my.model,
##     index = my.index)
##
## Balanced Panel: n=10, T=20, N=200
##
## Effects:
##                  var std.dev share
## idiosyncratic 2784.46   52.77 0.282
## individual    7089.80   84.20 0.718
## theta:  0.8612
##
## Residuals :
##    Min. 1st Qu.  Median 3rd Qu.    Max.
## -178.00  -19.70    4.69   19.50  253.00
##
## Coefficients :
##               Estimate Std. Error t-value Pr(>|t|)
## (Intercept) -57.834415  28.898935 -2.0013  0.04674 *
## value         0.109781   0.010493 10.4627  < 2e-16 ***
## capital       0.308113   0.017180 17.9339  < 2e-16 ***
## ---
## Signif. codes:
## 0 '***' 0.001 '**' 0.01 '*' 0.05 '.' 0.1 ' ' 1
##
## Total Sum of Squares:    2381400
## Residual Sum of Squares: 548900
## R-Squared:      0.7695
## Adj. R-Squared: 0.76716
## F-statistic: 328.837 on 2 and 197 DF, p-value: < 2.22e-16
```

As expected, the coefficients are significant at 1%. The adjustment of the model is also high, with an adjusted R-Squared equal to 0.77. This means a great proportion of the variation in the data was explained by the model. The results from the panel data model indicate the value of the firms and their current assets are positively related to the amount of investments. Firms with higher market value and capital tend to invest more.

As a last example of using R in panel models with the `Grunfeld` data, let's estimate a SUR (seemingly unrelated regression) model, which is best suited for this data. The SUR specification assumes the different models for each group can be estimated individually, with a correlation between the disturbances across models. It is best suited when we have many time periods and few groups, such as in the `Grunfeld` data.

Package `systemfit` offers a function with the same name for the estimation of the SUR model. The first step in using `systemfit` is to allocate the `Grunfeld` data to a specific `data.frame` format with function `plm::pdata.frame`. Let's try it.

```
library(systemfit)

# set pdataframe
p.Grunfeld <- pdata.frame(Grunfeld, c( "firm", "year" ))

# estimate sur
my.SUR <- systemfit(formula = inv ~value + capital,
                    method =  "SUR",
                    data = p.Grunfeld)
print(my.SUR)
```

```
##
## systemfit results
## method: SUR
##
## Coefficients:
##  1_(Intercept)        X1_value       X1_capital 10_(Intercept)
##   -135.6061364       0.1138135        0.3861235      1.9893500
##       X10_value      X10_capital  2_(Intercept)       X2_value
##      -0.0161291       0.3768475     -10.9059829      0.1627658
##      X2_capital  3_(Intercept)        X3_value      X3_capital
##       0.3406261     -15.8959008       0.0349626      0.1257302
##   4_(Intercept)        X4_value       X4_capital  5_(Intercept)
##       1.8043270       0.0678437        0.3075528     26.4673602
##        X5_value      X5_capital  6_(Intercept)       X6_value
##       0.1274473       0.0119871      -6.1934512      0.1333107
##      X6_capital  7_(Intercept)        X7_value      X7_capital
##       0.0540052      -9.7701305       0.1134649      0.1281802
##   8_(Intercept)        X8_value       X8_capital  9_(Intercept)
##       3.1490972       0.0537015        0.0433622     -3.1568643
##        X9_value      X9_capital
##       0.0765949       0.0654245
```

The output object `my.SUR` contains the estimation of all equations, firm by firm. Using `print` is limited in this case; it only shows the estimated coefficients. Function `summary` provides more information, including the correlation structure between the disturbances. But, its output is extensive and would fill several pages of this book. We leave it as an exercise.

10.4 Arima Models

Using time series models is common in financial research. Arima is a special model that uses the past of a time series to explain its own future. Estimating an Arima model for stock returns can tell how the returns today are related to past returns. In a forecasting horse race, we can compare predictive performance of forecasting candidates against an Arima model. If the proposed model works well, it should provide forecasts with higher accuracy.

A simple example of an Arima model is defined by the following equation:

$$y_t = 0.5y_{t-1} - 0.2\epsilon_{t-1} + \epsilon_t$$

In this example, we have an ARIMA(AR = 1, D = 0, MA = 1) model without the intercept. This specific notation informs the configuration of the model and the number of used parameters. The first value in (1, 0, 1) indicates the maximum *lag* used in y_t in the right hand side of the equation. The second value indicates the degree of differentiation of the time series (Hamilton, 1994b). If $D = 1$, we use the first difference of y_t as the dependent variable. The third component, *MA*, shows the maximum *lag* used for the error of the model. This identification process can be arbitrary or not. A common procedure is to search for the combination of AR, D, and MA terms that maximizes an adjustment function, as shown in section 10.4.2.

10.4.1 Simulating Arima Models

First, let's simulate an Arima model using function `arima.sim` from `stat`. This package is loaded by default, and we need not source it with `library`.

```
set.seed(1)

# set number of observations
my.n <- 5000

# set model's parameters
my.model <- list(ar = 0.5, ma = -0.1)
```

```
my.sd <- 1

# simulate model
my.ts <- arima.sim(n = my.n,
                    model = my.model ,
                    sd = my.sd)
```

We can look at the result of the simulation by creating a plot with the artificial time series:

```
library(ggplot2)

# set df
temp.df <- data.frame(y = unclass(my.ts),
                      date = Sys.Date() + 1:my.n)

p <- ggplot(temp.df, aes(x = date, y = y))
p <- p + geom_line(size=0.5)

print(p)
```

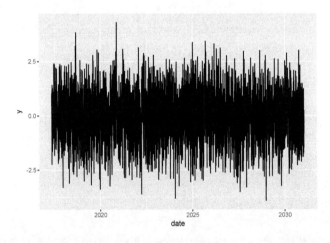

The graph shows a time series with an average close to zero and strong instability. These are typical properties of an Arima model.

10.4.2 Estimating Arima Models

To estimate a Arima model, we use function **arima** from the same package. Let's estimate a model for our simulated data.

```
# estimate arima model
my.arima <- arima(my.ts, order = c(1,0,1))

# print result
print(coef(my.arima))

##            ar1          ma1      intercept
##   0.482547196 -0.077376754 -0.007458499
```

As expected, the estimated parameters are close to the simulated values, with *ar1* equal to 0.4825 and *ma1* equal to -0.07738. As we did for a `lm` and `plm` model, we can also use function `summary` to get more information from the estimation of the Arima model. Let's look at all elements available in `summary(my.arima)`:

```
print(summary(my.arima))

##                Length Class  Mode
## coef           3      -none- numeric
## sigma2         1      -none- numeric
## var.coef       9      -none- numeric
## mask           3      -none- logical
## loglik         1      -none- numeric
## aic            1      -none- numeric
## arma           7      -none- numeric
## residuals   5000      ts     numeric
## call           3      -none- call
## series         1      -none- character
## code           1      -none- numeric
## n.cond         1      -none- numeric
## nobs           1      -none- numeric
## model         10      -none- list
```

We have the adjustment criteria in `aic`, residuals in `residuals`, coefficients in `coef`, covariance matrix of estimated coefficients in `var.coef`, and many more.

The identification of the Arima model, defining values AR, D, MA in Arima (AR, D, MA), can also be performed automatically. Package `forecast` (Hyndman and Khandakar, 2007) offers function `auto.arima` that automates this process by choosing the best model according to an adjustment criterion, such as AIC (*Akaike information criteria*) and BIC (*Bayesian information criteria*). This is a very useful function. We allow the data to speak for itself, avoiding a possible bias in the identification of the model.

In the next example, we use function `auto.arima` to find the best model for the daily returns of the SP500 index. First, we load the data from file `SP500.csv` and add a column for the returns using function `calc.ret`, first presented in chapter 9.

```
# read file
my.f <- 'data/SP500.csv'
df.SP500 <- read.csv(my.f)

calc.ret <- function(P) {
  # calculates arithmetic returns from a vector of prices
  #
  # Args:
  #   P - vector of prices (numeric)
  #
  # Returns:
  #   A vector of returns

  my.length <- length(P)
  ret <- c(NA, P[2:my.length]/P[1:(my.length - 1)] - 1)
  return(ret)
}

# set return column
df.SP500$ret <- calc.ret(df.SP500$price)
```

Before estimating the model, we need to check the stationarity of the return data. If the data is not stationary, it might be necessary to use the first differences of the original series (Maddala, 2001). Since we are modelling returns, the raw data of prices was already differentiated (see return equation in chapter 5). It is worth testing this property of the data before estimating the Arima model. Package `tseries` (Trapletti and Hornik, 2017) provides a function called `adf.test` that will check if the data has unit root (not stationary). The null hypothesis of the test is the non-stationarity of the data, i.e, the existence of unit roots.

```
library(tseries)
print(adf.test(na.omit(df.SP500$ret)))


##
##   Augmented Dickey-Fuller Test
##
## data:  na.omit(df.SP500$ret)
## Dickey-Fuller = -12.188, Lag order = 12, p-value =
## 0.01
## alternative hypothesis: stationary
```

The result of the test shows a small p-value that strongly suggests the rejection of the null hypothesis. The evidence indicates that the return vector can be considered stationary. For curiosity, let's also try the test on the price series:

```
print(adf.test(df.SP500$price))
```

```
##
##  Augmented Dickey-Fuller Test
##
## data:  df.SP500$price
## Dickey-Fuller = -2.9396, Lag order = 12, p-value =
## 0.1806
## alternative hypothesis: stationary
```

This time, we easily fail to reject the null hypothesis with a large p-value. The test strongly suggests the price series is not stationary. From the econometric point of view, we are correct in estimating an Arima model for returns, not prices.

Function `forecast::auto.arima` estimates na Arima model with automatic identification of the best model. Let's try it with its default options:

```
library(forecast)
```

```
# estimate arima model with automatic identification
my.autoarima <- auto.arima(x = df.SP500$ret)
```

```
# print result
print(my.autoarima)
```

```
## Series:
## ARIMA(1,0,0) with non-zero mean
##
## Coefficients:
##           ar1     mean
##       -0.0499   5e-04
## s.e.   0.0235   2e-04
##
## sigma^2 estimated as 9.373e-05:  log likelihood=5794.03
## AIC=-11582.06    AICc=-11582.05   BIC=-11565.58
```

The result tells us the best model for the returns of the SP500 index is an Arima (1,0,0). This result implies the return series of the financial index has a low memory and only the previous return has predictable power over the current returns. In this case, since we find a negative coefficient, a positive return is more likely to be followed by a negative return.

10.4.3   Forecasting Arima Models

We can obtain the forecasts of an Arima model with function `forecast`, also from package `forecast`. The forecast is of the static type; only information up to time t is used to make forecasts in $t+k$. In the following example, we calculate the forecasts for 5 periods ahead, with their corresponding confidence interval.

```
# forecast model
print(forecast(my.autoarima, h = 5))
```

```
##         Point Forecast        Lo 80       Hi 80        Lo 95
## 1802     0.0006066170  -0.01180036  0.01301359  -0.01836821
## 1803     0.0004481322  -0.01197427  0.01287054  -0.01855030
## 1804     0.0004560393  -0.01196641  0.01287848  -0.01854245
## 1805     0.0004556448  -0.01196680  0.01287809  -0.01854285
## 1806     0.0004556645  -0.01196678  0.01287811  -0.01854283
##               Hi 95
## 1802 0.01958145
## 1803 0.01944656
## 1804 0.01945453
## 1805 0.01945414
## 1806 0.01945416
```

10.5   Garch Models

Garch models relate to the seminal work of Engle (1982) and Bollerslev (1986). The main innovation in this class of models is that the variance of the residual can change . This variation is modelled using a specific autoregressive process. Garch models became very popular mainly because they replicate characteristics of financial asset returns, such as the existence of fat tails in their distribution and the clustering of volatile periods, where extreme price movements happen within the same time. Garch models are mostly used where risk is being assessed and managed.

A GARCH model is modular. In its simplest format, you have two main equations: a process that sets the conditional mean, and another that defines the variance of the error. See the following example for an ARIMA(1,0,0)-GARCH(1,1) model:

$$y_t = \mu + \theta y_{t-1} + \epsilon_t$$
$$\epsilon_t \sim N(0, h_t)$$
$$h_t = \omega + \alpha \epsilon_{t-1}^2 + \beta h_{t-1}$$

The y_t equation sets the process for the conditional mean, an AR model with one lag.

This is the actual observed value of the time series. Variable h_t defines the variance of the error, the instability of the model. Different Garch models will use different equations for h_t and different distributions of the error term. In its simplest case, the one presented here, we use the Normal distribution. It is important to understand this basic notation for Garch models, because R functions that handle this model follow the same structure.

10.5.1 Simulating Garch Models

R has no native function to simulate and estimate models of Garch. There are two main packages related to Garch models. The first is package `fGarch` (Wuertz et al., 2016) and the second is `rugarch` (Ghalanos, 2015). Both have great features and are optimized for agile estimations. You will be well served in choosing either of them. For simplicity, we will give preference to package `fGarch`, with an interface similar to the one used with Arima models in the previous section.

In `fGarch`, we simulate a model using function `garchSim`. The first step is to load package `fGarch` and create the model specification:

```
library(fGarch)
```

```
# set list with model spec
my.model = list(omega=0.001,
                alpha=0.15,
                beta=0.8,
                mu=0.02,
                ar = 0.1)
```

```
# set garch spec
spec = garchSpec(model = my.model)
```

```
# print it
print(spec)
```

```
##
## Formula:
##  ~ ar(1) + garch(1, 1)
## Model:
##  ar:    0.1
##  mu:    0.02
##  omega: 0.001
##  alpha: 0.15
##  beta:  0.8
```

```
## Distribution:
##   norm
## Presample:
##   time            z        h              y
## 1      0 0.1145392 0.02 0.02222222
```

The previous code defines a Garch model equivalent to the following equations.

$$y_t = 0.02 + 0.1y_{t-1} + \epsilon_t$$
$$\epsilon_t \sim N\left(0, h_t\right)$$
$$h_t = 0.001 + 0.15\epsilon_{t-1}^2 + 0.8h_{t-1}$$

To simulate *1000* observations of this model, we use function `garchSim`:

```
set.seed(20)
# simulate garch model
sim.garch = garchSim(spec, n = 1000)
```

We can visualize the artificial time series generated by creating a plot with `ggplot`:

```
# set df for ggplot
temp.df <- data.frame(sim.ret = sim.garch$garch,
                      idx=seq_along(sim.garch$garch))


library(ggplot2)
p <- ggplot(temp.df, aes(x=idx, y=sim.ret))
p <- p + geom_line()
print(p)
```

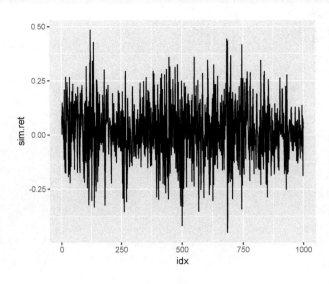

The behaviour of the simulated series is similar to the return series of the stocks presented in chapter 8. It is difficult to set one apart from the other based solely on visual inspection. Unlike other models, where the instability is constant, a Garch model can portray a return series more realistically by assuming a time changing volatility.

10.5.2 Estimating Garch Models

The estimation of the parameters from a GARCH model is usually achieved using a technique called *maximum-likelihood*. This procedure finds the parameters that make the distribution of the model as close as possible to the distribution of the time series of interest. It involves a numerical optimization process that requires a reasonable amount of processing time. Fortunately, package `fGarch` provides a function, called `garchFit`, that performs the whole operation.

In the following example we estimate a Garch model for the artificial data created in the previous section. We set option `trace = FALSE` to prevent the presentation of the details of the optimization process, as they are extensive and would occupy several pages of this book.

```
# estimate garch model
my.garchfit <- garchFit(data = sim.garch,
                        formula = ~ arma(1,0) + garch(1,1),
                        trace = FALSE)
```

To learn more about the estimated model, we can present it on the screen with the command `print`:

```
print(my.garchfit)
```

```
##
## Title:
##  GARCH Modelling
##
## Call:
##  garchFit(formula = ~arma(1, 0) + garch(1, 1), data = sim.garch,
##     trace = FALSE)
##
## Mean and Variance Equation:
##  data ~ arma(1, 0) + garch(1, 1)
## <environment: 0x000000001e4106b0>
##  [data = sim.garch]
##
## Conditional Distribution:
```

```
##   norm
##
## Coefficient(s):
##         mu         ar1       omega      alpha1       beta1
## 0.0164569   0.0695426   0.0010592   0.1292775   0.8175425
##
## Std. Errors:
##   based on Hessian
##
## Error Analysis:
##           Estimate  Std. Error  t value Pr(>|t|)
## mu       0.0164569   0.0039213    4.197 2.71e-05 ***
## ar1      0.0695426   0.0327651    2.122   0.0338 *
## omega    0.0010592   0.0004267    2.482   0.0131 *
## alpha1   0.1292775   0.0282136    4.582 4.60e-06 ***
## beta1    0.8175425   0.0405741   20.149  < 2e-16 ***
## ---
## Signif. codes:
## 0 '***' 0.001 '**' 0.01 '*' 0.05 '.' 0.1 ' ' 1
##
## Log Likelihood:
##   604.1894    normalized:  0.6041894
##
## Description:
##   Fri May 05 14:18:40 2017 by user: marcelo
```

The resulting parameters from the estimation are close to the values defined arbitrarily in the call to garchSpec. We can achieve higher accuracy by increasing the number of observations in the simulated model. Function summary also works for Garch models. Due to the large amount of information on the prompt, we leave it as an exercise for the reader.

Now, as an example with real data, let's estimate a Garch model for the SP500 index. The data is loaded from section 10.4.2, so we can use it directly. First, let's execute the LM Arch test (Engle, 1982; Tsay, 2005) to verify if the returns of the market index have the Arch effect. Function ArchTest from FinTS (Graves, 2014) can perform this task.

```
library(FinTS)

# test for Arch effects
my.arch.test <- ArchTest(x = df.SP500$ret, lags = 5)

# print result
```

```
print(my.arch.test)
```

```
##
##   ARCH LM-test; Null hypothesis: no ARCH effects
##
## data:  df.SP500$ret
## Chi-squared = 357.05, df = 5, p-value < 2.2e-16
```

The evidence is strong for Arch effects in SP500 returns. The null hypothesis of the test is the non-existence of the Arch effects, and we can easily reject it at 1%. Let's estimate a Arma(1,0)-Garch(1,1) for the returns.

```
# set object for estimation
df.est <- as.timeSeries(na.omit(df.SP500))

# estimate garch model for SP500
my.garchfit.sp500 <- garchFit(data = df.est ,
                              formula = ret ~ arma(1,0) + garch(1,1),
                              trace = FALSE)
```

```
print(my.garchfit.sp500)
```

```
##
## Title:
##   GARCH Modelling
##
## Call:
##   garchFit(formula = ret ~ arma(1, 0) + garch(1, 1), data = df.est,
##       trace = FALSE)
##
## Mean and Variance Equation:
##   ret ~ arma(1, 0) + garch(1, 1)
##   [data = df.est]
##
## Conditional Distribution:
##   norm
##
## Coefficient(s):
##           mu            ar1         omega        alpha1
##   7.7257e-04   -4.4142e-02   4.1689e-06    1.5308e-01
##        beta1
##   8.0207e-01
##
```

```
## Std. Errors:
##   based on Hessian
##
## Error Analysis:
##            Estimate  Std. Error  t value Pr(>|t|)
## mu        7.726e-04   1.749e-04    4.416 1.00e-05 ***
## ar1      -4.414e-02   2.616e-02   -1.687   0.0915 .
## omega     4.169e-06   7.535e-07    5.533 3.15e-08 ***
## alpha1    1.531e-01   2.029e-02    7.544 4.55e-14 ***
## beta1     8.021e-01   2.220e-02   36.126  < 2e-16 ***
## ---
## Signif. codes:
## 0 '***' 0.001 '**' 0.01 '*' 0.05 '.' 0.1 ' ' 1
##
## Log Likelihood:
##   6040.208     normalized:  3.355671
##
## Description:
##   Fri May 05 14:18:41 2017 by user: marcelo
```

As expected, all Garch coefficients are significant at 1%. As for the mean equation, we again find a negative value for ar1, but its significance is not strong, with a p-value close to 10%. We could use the previously estimated Garch model to simulate future returns and prices of the SP500 index.

10.5.3 Forecasting Garch Models

Forecasting Garch models involves two elements: a forecast for the conditional mean (see the first equation in the Garch formula) and a forecast for future values of conditional volatility (see the second equation). While the first sets the forecast of the next values of the analysed series, the second quantifies the uncertainty of this forecast.

In package fGarch, both forecasts are calculated using function predict that, just like summary, is a generic function that can be used for different models. Consider the following example, where we forecast the next values and the future volatilities of the Garch model fitted with the SP500 returns.

```
# static forecast for garch
my.garch.forecast <- predict(my.garchfit.sp500, n.ahead = 3)


# print df
print(my.garch.forecast)
```

```
##    meanForecast    meanError standardDeviation
## 1 0.0008860155 0.005145661       0.005145661
## 2 0.0007334607 0.005432390       0.005427639
## 3 0.0007401948 0.005688981       0.005683925
```

The first column of the previous result is the forecast of the conditional mean; the second presents the expected error of the previous forecast, and the third indicates the expected volatility in standard deviation (root of the variance). All forecasts are the static type. Information up to time t is used to make forecasts for $t+k$.

10.6   Regime Switching Models

Markov regime switching models are a specification in which the selling point is the flexibility in handling processes driven by heterogeneous states of the world (Hamilton, 1994a). In financial markets, we can have two regimes for volatility (uncertainty), one regime where volatility is high and other where it is low. We can justify these regimes as time periods with greater or lesser amount of new information and uncertainty. Each regime can have its own characteristics. As a modeller, we need to understand how to identify these regimes and estimate the parameters from our models separately.

As a way to motivate the model, consider the following econometric process:

$$y_t = \mu_{S_t} + \epsilon_t$$

where $S_t = 1..k$ and ϵ_t follows a Normal distribution with zero mean and variance given by $\sigma^2_{S_t}$. This is the simplest case of a model with a switching dynamic. If there are k states of the world, there will be k values for the conditional mean and conditional variance. If there is only one state of the world ($k=1$), the previous formula becomes a simple linear regression model under general conditions.

Now, let's assume the previous model has two states ($k=2$). An alternative representation is:

$$y_t = \mu_1 + \epsilon_t \qquad \text{for State 1}$$
$$y_t = \mu_2 + \epsilon_t \qquad \text{for State 2}$$

where:

$$\epsilon_t \sim (0, \sigma_1^2) \qquad \text{for State 1}$$
$$\epsilon_t \sim (0, \sigma_2^2) \qquad \text{for State 2}$$

This representation implies two processes for the dependent variable. When the state of the world for time t is 1, the expectation of the dependent variable is μ_1 and the volatility of the innovations is σ_1^2. Likewise, when the state is 2, the mean and volatility take other values.

As an example in finance, the dependent variable y_t can represent a vector of log returns. The value of μ_1 is the expected return on a bull market state, which implies a positive trend for financial prices and consequently a positive log return. The lower, and possibly negative, value of μ_2 measures the expected log return for the bear market state, where asset prices have a tendency to go down.

The different volatilities represent the higher uncertainty regarding the predictive power of the model in each state of the world. We can expect the bear market state is more volatile than the bull market. This implies prices go down faster than they go up. The usual explanation for this effect is that traders react faster to bad news when comparing to good news. This can also be explained by limit loss orders, which will sell at market prices once a particular threshold in the prices has been breached. When used by a significant amount of traders and at different threshold levels, these limit loss orders will create a cascade effect, accelerating the downfall of prices. This means we can expect the volatility in state 2 (bear market) to be higher than the volatility in state 1 (bull market).

The changes of the states in the model can be set in a deterministic way. We could've set state 1 to be true for time t when another time series is higher or lower than a known threshold. This greatly simplifies the model as each state is observable; therefore, we can treat the model as a regression with dummy variables. Function `lm` could be used for the estimation of this model.

A special regime switching model is markov switching. Its main difference from the regression with dummy variables is the identification of states is part of the estimation process. The model learns it from the data. The transition of states in a markov switching model is not deterministic; it is stochastic. This means one is never sure whether there will be a switch of state. But, the dynamics behind the switching process are known and driven by a transition matrix. This matrix, also estimated from the data, will control the probabilities of making a switch from one state to the other. It can be represented as:

$$P = \begin{bmatrix} p_{11} & \cdots & p_{1k} \\ \vdots & \ddots & \vdots \\ p_{k1} & \cdots & p_{kk} \end{bmatrix}$$

In the previous matrix, row i, column j controls the probability of a switch from state j to state i. Consider that, for some time t, the state of the world is 2. This means the probability of a switch from state 2 to state 1 between time t and $t+1$ will be given by p_{12}. Likewise, the probability of staying in state 2 is determined by p_{22}. This is one of the central points of the structure of a markov regime switching model: the switching of states is a stochastic process.

10.6.1 Simulating Regime Switching Models

In R, two packages are available for handling univariate markov regime switching models, MSwM (Sanchez-Espigares and Lopez-Moreno, 2014) and fMarkovSwitching (Perlin, 2014). The last one also includes functions for simulating a time series. Before using it, let's install fMarkovSwitching from the R-Forge repository. Be aware this package is not available in CRAN.

```
install.packages("fMarkovSwitching",
                 repos="http://R-Forge.R-project.org")
```

Once it is installed, let's look at its functions:

```
library(fMarkovSwitching)
print(ls('package:fMarkovSwitching'))
```

```
## [1] "dim.MS_Model"     "MS_Regress_Fit"    "MS_Regress_For"
## [4] "MS_Regress_Lik"   "MS_Regress_Simul"  "plot.MS_Model"
## [7] "plot.MS_Simul"    "print.MS_Model"    "print.MS_Simul"
```

The package includes functions for simulating, estimating, and forecasting an univariate markov switching model. As an example, let's simulate the regime switching model from the following equations:

$$y_t = +0.5x_t + \epsilon_t \qquad \text{State 1}$$
$$y_t = -0.5x_t + \epsilon_t \qquad \text{State 2}$$
$$\epsilon_t \sim N(0, 0.25) \qquad \text{State 1}$$
$$\epsilon_t \sim N(0, 1) \qquad \text{State 2}$$

The transition matrix will be given by:

$$P = \begin{bmatrix} 0.90 & 0.2 \\ 0.10 & 0.8 \end{bmatrix}$$

This model has two states with different volatilities. In each state, the impact of the explanatory variable will be different. From package `fMarkovSwitching`, we can use function `MS_Regress_Simul` to simulate this model. Look at the following code, where we simulate the model from the previous equations.

```
set.seed(10)
library(fMarkovSwitching)

# number of obs
nr <- 500

# distribution of residuals
distrib <- "Normal"

# number of states
k <- 2

# set transition matrix
P <- matrix(c(.9 ,.2,
              .1 ,.8),
            nrow = 2,
            byrow = T)

# set switching flag
S <- c(0,1)

# set parameters of model (see manual for details)
nS_param <- matrix(0)
S_param <- matrix(0,sum(S),k)
S_param[,1] <-  .5
S_param[,2] <- -.5

# set variance of model
sigma <- matrix(0,1,k)
sigma[1,1] <- sqrt(0.25)   # state 1
sigma[1,2] <- 1            # state 2

# build list
Coeff <- list(P = P                    ,
```

```
                  S = S                    ,
                  nS_param = nS_param ,
                  S_param = S_param   ,
                  sigma = sigma           )

# simulate model
my.ms.simul <- MS_Regress_Simul(nr,Coeff,k,distrib)
```

In the simulation function, argument `nS_param` sets the non switching parameters. These are the coefficients in the right hand side of the econometric equation that will not switch states. We use a value of zero, as our simulated model has no non-switching coefficients. Even if not used, we need to set this argument in `MS_Regress_Simul`; otherwise, the function will return an error. The elements in `S_param` define the coefficients in each state for the switching parameters. In our example, we have a positive effect of x_t in y_t in state one and a negative effect in state two. Finally, the `sigma` input defines the volatility (standard deviation) of the residual in each regime.

Once the model is simulated and available, let's plot the time series of artificial values. A note here is important; the output from `my.ms.simul` is a S3 object was custom designed to interact with the common functions `print` and `plot`. To access its elements, we use @ instead of $.

```
library(ggplot2)
df.to.plot <- data.frame(y = my.ms.simul@dep,
                         x = Sys.Date()+1:my.ms.simul@nr,
                         states = my.ms.simul@trueStates[,1])

p <- ggplot(data = df.to.plot, aes(y=y, x=seq_along(y)))
p <- p + geom_line()
p <- p + labs(x='Time', y = 'Simulated time series')
print(p)
```

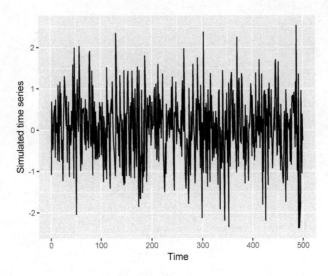

We can also look at the simulated states:

```
library(ggplot2)
df.to.plot <- data.frame(y = my.ms.simul@dep,
                         x = Sys.Date()+1:my.ms.simul@nr,
                         states = my.ms.simul@trueStates[,1])

p <- ggplot(data = df.to.plot, aes(y=states, x=x))
p <- p + geom_line()
p <- p + labs(y='Probability of state 1')
print(p)
```

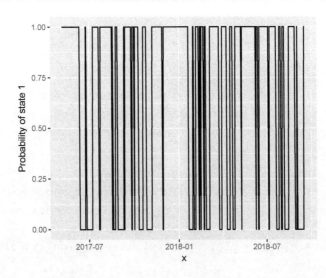

As expected, the model is switching from one state to the other. Either state is strongly predominant over time, but state one seems to have a longer duration than state two. This property is controlled by the transition probabilities set in object P.

10.6.2   Estimating Regime Switching Models

We can estimate a univariate markov switching model with function `MS_Regress_Fit`. Let's try it for the previously simulated time series.

```
# set dep and indep
dep <- my.ms.simul @dep
indep <- my.ms.simul@indep

# set switching parameters and distribution
S <- c(0,1)
k <- 2
distIn <- "Normal"

# estimate the model
my.MS.model <- MS_Regress_Fit(dep,indep,S,k)   # fitting the model
```

Argument `dep` and `indep` sets the variables in the estimation, left and right side of the econometric equation. Input `S` only takes values zero and one. It defines where the switching effect will occur. Since we only have two independent variables where the first does not switch states, we use `S <- c(0,1)`. Object `k` sets the number of states in the model, in this case two. After finishing the estimation, let's look at the output.

```
# print estimation output
print(my.MS.model)
```

```
##
##
## ***** Numerical Optimization for MS Model Converged *****
##
## Final log Likelihood: -544.5191
## Number of parameters: 7
## Distribution Assumption -> Normal
##
## ***** Final Parameters *****
##
## ---> Non Switching Parameters <---
##
##   Non Switching Parameter at Indep   Column  1
##        Value:      -0.0333
```

```
##        Std error: 0.0266 (0.21)
##
## --->    Switching Parameters     <---
##
##    State 1
##        Model Standard Deviation: 0.5082
##        Std Error:               0.0235 (0.00)
##    State 2
##        Model Standard Deviation: 0.9584
##        Std Error:               0.0613 (0.00)
##
##    Switching Parameters for Indep  Column  2
##
##    State  1
##       Value:       0.5471
##       Std error:   0.0313 (0.00)
##    State  2
##       Value:      -0.4563
##       Std error:   0.0979 (0.00)
##
## ---> Transition Probabilities Matrix <---
##
##        0.90    0.21
##        0.10    0.79
##
## ---> Expected Duration of Regimes <---
##
##        Expected duration of Regime #1: 10.52 time periods
##        Expected duration of Regime #2: 4.81 time periods
```

The estimated coefficients are close to the ones from the simulation. The estimation recognized the parameters from the simulated data. The output object from MS_Regress_Fit can also be used with plot for a custom figure. Have a look.

```
plot(my.MS.model)    # plotting output
```

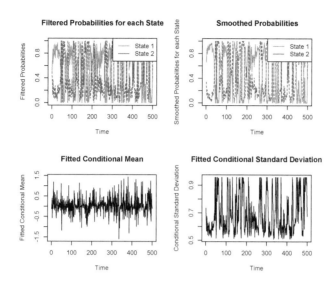

As an example with real data, let's estimate the same markov regime switching model for the SP500 returns.

```
# read file
my.f <- 'data/SP500.csv'
df.SP500 <- read.csv(my.f,
                     colClasses = c('Date','numeric'))

# set calc.ret
calc.ret <- function(P) {
  return(c(NA, P[2:length(P)]/P[1:(length(P) - 1)] - 1))
}

# set return column
df.SP500$ret <- calc.ret(df.SP500$price)

# set input objects to MS_Regress_Fit
ret <- na.omit(df.SP500$ret)
dep <- matrix(ret, nrow = length(ret))
indep <- matrix(rep(1, length(dep)),nrow = length(dep))

S <- c(1)    # where to switch (in this case in the only indep)
k <- 2       # number of states
distIn <- "Normal" #distribution assumption

my.SP500.MS.model <- MS_Regress_Fit(dep,indep,S,k)  # fitting the model
```

And now, we check the result.

```
# printing output
print(my.SP500.MS.model)
```

```
##
##
## ***** Numerical Optimization for MS Model Converged *****
##
## Final log Likelihood: 6033.029
## Number of parameters: 6
## Distribution Assumption -> Normal
##
## ***** Final Parameters *****
##
## ---> Non Switching Parameters <---
##
## There was no Non Switching Parameters. Skipping this result
##
## --->    Switching Parameters    <---
##
##    State 1
##        Model Standard Deviation: 0.0055
##        Std Error:                0.0002 (0.00)
##    State 2
##        Model Standard Deviation: 0.0140
##        Std Error:                0.0005 (0.00)
##
##    Switching Parameters for Indep  Column  1
##
##    State  1
##        Value:      0.0011
##        Std error:  0.0002 (0.00)
##    State  2
##        Value:      -0.0006
##        Std error:  0.0006 (0.30)
##
## ---> Transition Probabilities Matrix <---
##
##        0.96   0.06
##        0.04   0.94
##
## ---> Expected Duration of Regimes <---
```

```
##
##          Expected duration of Regime #1: 27.61 time periods
##          Expected duration of Regime #2: 17.24 time periods
```

The model identified two volatility regimes from the SP500 returns. In the first, low volatility regime, the standard deviation of the returns is 0.548%. In the second state with high uncertainty, the value of the standard deviation is 1.4%. As we expected, the high volatility state has a negative mean of -0.0569% and the low volatility state has a positive mean of 0.109%. The information from the model is that the SP500 index goes down faster than it goes up. More interesting information is related to the expected duration of the states. A bull market, with positive average returns, tends to last approximately 28 days, while a bear market cycle lasts 17 days. In the US market, equity prices go up slowly and fall fast.

A common figure in the analysis of markov switching models is the price dynamic in different states. It is a time series plot with overlapped information. Let's try it. First, we create a `factor` object assuming a state threshold of 50%; if the probability of state one in time t is higher than 50%, we will assume state one is true. We then use the resulting `factor` as a color property in a `ggplot` figure.

```
library(dplyr)

# get smooth probs of states
smooth.prob = as.numeric(my.SP500.MS.model@smoothProb[,1])

# build df to plot
df.to.plot <- data.frame(smooth.prob = smooth.prob,
                         ref.date = df.SP500$date[2:nrow(df.SP500)],
                         price = df.SP500$price[2:nrow(df.SP500)])

# create factor from probs
df.to.plot$States <- ifelse(df.to.plot$smooth.prob > 0.5,
                            'State 1','State 2')

# plot with ggplot
p <- ggplot(df.to.plot,
            aes(y=price, x =ref.date, color=States)) +
  geom_point()

# plot it!
print(p)
```

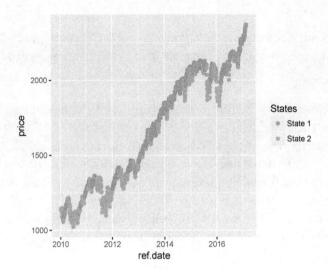

The figure shows how the price increases in state 1 and decreases in state 2. From 2013 to 2015, it is clearly a bull market trend for the SP500 prices.

10.6.3   Forecasting Regime Switching Models

Package MS_Regress provides function MS_Regress_For for statically forecasting an univariate markov switching model. Its inputs are: a model estimated with MS_Regress_Fit, argument myModel, and the set of new explanatory variables in input newIndep. Let's use it to forecast the next day return of the SP500. In our case, since the regime switching model only had an intercept, we set newIndep = 1.

```
# make static forecast of regime switching model
newIndep <- 1

my.for <- MS_Regress_For(my.SP500.MS.model, newIndep)

# print output
print(my.for)

## $condMean
##                  [,1]
## [1,] 0.0009647028
##
## $condStd
##                  [,1]
## [1,] 0.006140928
```

The model predicts, the day after the last date available in the SP500 data (2017-

02-28), the stock market index will increase its value in 0.096%, with a volatility of 0.61%.

10.7   Dealing with Several Models

In the practice of research, it is likely we will estimate more than one model. We might want to test different models, have different study cases, or run a robustness test by estimating the same model in different time periods. Learning how to manage different models efficiently in R is important. This issue become more important when the scale of the research increases. More data and more models require an efficient computational structure.

In chapter 9, we learned we can use functions from the `apply` family or package `dplyr` to do iterative data tasks. We can use it to estimate several models from the data. Let's start with an example. Here, we will estimate an Arima model for the returns of four stocks selected randomly. The extra information to be included in the code from section 10.4.2 is the vector with the stock's tickers. First, let's load the data.

```
set.seed(10)

# set number of stocks
n.stocks <- 4

# load data from .RData
load('data/SP500-Stocks-WithRet.RData')

# select tickers
my.tickers <- sample(unique(my.df$ticker), n.stocks)

# set my.df
my.df.stocks <- my.df[my.df$ticker %in% my.tickers, ]

# renew factors in ticker
my.df.stocks$ticker <- as.factor(as.character(my.df.stocks$ticker))
```

Now, what we want to do with this data is separate the returns by ticker and use function `arima` to estimate a model for each stock. One solution is to use function `tapply`:

```
my.l <- tapply(X = my.df.stocks$ret,
               INDEX = my.df.stocks$ticker,
```

```
             FUN = arima,
             order = c(1,0,0))
```

Each model is available in `my.l`. To retrieve all coefficients, we can use `sapply` and function `coef`:

```
print(sapply(X = my.l, FUN = coef))
```

```
##                    DOW            GPC           JEC
## ar1        0.0087664911  -0.0292559871  0.0241489275
## intercept  0.0006910872   0.0007219031  0.0003833143
##                    OKE
## ar1        0.0517872000
## intercept  0.0009778744
```

A limitation is, by using `tapply`, we are restricted to using a single column of `my.df`. Notice how input `X` of `tapply` only accepts one vector. To use more columns of the `dataframe` in a group type operation, we can use function `by`. This function will break a `dataframe` into several smaller ones, based on a factor or character object. We then pass a function to be applied to each smaller `dataframe`.

For an example of estimating several models with function `by`, let's calculate the beta coefficient for all stocks in our database. First, let's load the index data and add a new column in `my.df` with the returns of the SP500 index.

```
# load SP500 data
df.sp500 <- read.csv(file = 'data/SP500.csv',
                     colClasses = c('Date','numeric'))


# calculate return
df.sp500$ret <- calc.ret(df.sp500$price)



# find location of dates in df.sp500
idx <- match(my.df$ref.date, df.sp500$date)

# create column in my.df with sp500 returns
my.df$ret.sp500 <- df.sp500$ret[idx]
```

The next step is to create a function that will take a `dataframe` as input, use the returns of the asset and the returns of the SP500 index to output the beta. Have a look:

```
estimate.beta <- function(df) {
  # Function to estimate beta from dataframe of stocks returns
```

```
  #
  # Args:
  #   df - Dataframe with columns ret and ret.sp500
  #
  # Returns:
  #   The value of beta

  my.model <- lm(data = df, formula = ret ~ ret.sp500)

  return(coef(my.model)[2])
}
```

Now, we can use the previous function with `by`.

```
# calculate beta for each stock
my.betas <- by(data = my.df,
               INDICES = my.df$ticker,
               FUN = estimate.beta)
```

The values of the different `betas` are available in object `my.betas`. Let's look at the distribution of our betas using a histogram:

```
library(ggplot2)

df.to.plot <- data.frame(betas = as.numeric(my.betas))

p <- ggplot(df.to.plot, aes(x=betas)) +
  geom_histogram()

print(p)
```

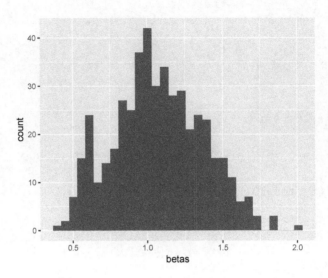

For the SP500 data, we find no negative value of beta. Given the market portfolio is built as an average of the stocks, not surprisingly, the average beta equals one.

Another way of storing and managing several models is to use the capabilities of list-columns with `dplyr`. Look at the next example of code, where we replicate the previous procedure of estimating an Arima model for several stocks using functions from `dplyr`.

```
library(dplyr)

my.tab <- my.df %>%
  group_by(ticker) %>%
  do(my.model = arima(x = .$ret, order = c(1,0,0)))

print(head(my.tab))

## # A tibble: 6 × 2
##    ticker     my.model
##     <chr>       <list>
## 1       A <S3: Arima>
## 2     AAL <S3: Arima>
## 3     AAP <S3: Arima>
## 4    AAPL <S3: Arima>
## 5     ABC <S3: Arima>
## 6     ABT <S3: Arima>
```

We have a list-column, called `my.model`, storing the objects with each result from the estimation. We can also use `mutate` to get information about the model. Look at the next code, where we present the coefficients of the model in the same object.

```
my.model.tab <- my.df %>%
  group_by(ticker) %>%
  do(my.model = arima(x = .$ret, order = c(1,0,0))) %>%
  mutate(alpha = coef(my.model)[2],
         ar1 = coef(my.model)[1])

print(head(my.model.tab))
```

```
## # A tibble: 6 × 4
##   ticker     my.model      alpha            ar1
##    <chr>       <list>      <dbl>          <dbl>
## 1      A <S3: Arima> 0.0006101093 -0.010115360
## 2    AAL <S3: Arima> 0.0017778322  0.006841853
## 3    AAP <S3: Arima> 0.0009725565 -0.026065447
## 4   AAPL <S3: Arima> 0.0009459582  0.022077870
## 5    ABC <S3: Arima> 0.0007552257 -0.049711324
## 6    ABT <S3: Arima> 0.0003933039  0.001729130
```

Another trick in handling models with `dplyr` is to use package `broom` (Robinson, 2017) to access the estimated coefficients. In the previous use of `mutate`, we added two columns in `my.tab` with the *alpha* and *ar1* coefficients. A simpler, more direct way of accessing information for all coefficients is to use function `tidy` from `broom`. Have a look:

```
library(broom)
```

```
# get coefs with tidy
my.coef.tab <- my.model.tab %>%
  tidy(my.model)
```

```
# print result
print(head(my.coef.tab))
```

```
## Source: local data frame [6 x 6]
## Groups: ticker, alpha, ar1 [3]
##
##   ticker       alpha          ar1      term     estimate
##    <chr>       <dbl>        <dbl>     <chr>        <dbl>
## 1      A 0.0006101093 -0.010115360       ar1 -0.0101153599
## 2      A 0.0006101093 -0.010115360 intercept  0.0006101093
## 3    AAL 0.0017778322  0.006841853       ar1  0.0068418534
## 4    AAL 0.0017778322  0.006841853 intercept  0.0017778322
## 5    AAP 0.0009725565 -0.026065447       ar1 -0.0260654469
```

```
## 6     AAP 0.0009725565 -0.026065447 intercept   0.0009725565
## # ... with 1 more variables: std.error <dbl>
```

Notice how function `tidy` included the estimated errors from the model. If we had more coefficients, they would also be reported in `my.coef.tab`. As for general information about the model, we can use function `glance`:

```
# get info on models
my.info.models <- my.model.tab %>%
  glance(my.model)


print(head(my.info.models))
```

```
## Source: local data frame [6 x 7]
## Groups: ticker, alpha, ar1 [6]
##
##    ticker        alpha           ar1       sigma    logLik
##     <chr>        <dbl>         <dbl>       <dbl>     <dbl>
## 1       A 0.0006101093 -0.010115360 0.01875836 4503.189
## 2     AAL 0.0017778322  0.006841853 0.03069869 3635.755
## 3     AAP 0.0009725565 -0.026065447 0.01720277 4655.637
## 4    AAPL 0.0009459582  0.022077870 0.01649846 4729.252
## 5     ABC 0.0007552257 -0.049711324 0.01320499 5121.377
## 6     ABT 0.0003933039  0.001729130 0.01162294 5346.108
## # ... with 2 more variables: AIC <dbl>, BIC <dbl>
```

It includes information about coefficients and statistics about each model, such as log-likelihood, AIC (Akaike Informatino Criteria), and BIC (Bayesan Information Criteria).

10.8   Reporting Models with `texreg`

After creating many models, the next step is to report the results in a visually appealing fashion. One solution is to retrieve information from the models and manually build customized tables to be included in the final document. Luckily for R users, there are packages that facilitate the construction and customization of estimation tables. The most popular ones are `xtable`, `texreg` and `stargazer`.

As an example, let's use package `texreg` to report the results from calculating beta of four stocks. We will use function `screenreg`, which outputs a text representation of the estimation table, including all the bells and whistles we usually expect. Have a look:

```
library(texreg)
library(dplyr)

set.seed(20)

# get tickers
my.tickers <- sample(unique(my.df$ticker), 4)
df.stocks <- my.df[my.df$ticker %in% my.tickers, ]

# estimate betas
beta.tab <- df.stocks %>%
  group_by(ticker) %>%
  do(beta.model = lm(data=., ret ~ ret.sp500))

# report result
est.table <- screenreg(l = beta.tab$beta.model,
                       custom.model.names = beta.tab$ticker,
                       custom.coef.names = c('Alpha', 'Beta'),
                       digits = 2)

# print it
print(est.table)
```

```
##
## ==============================================================
##                DRI           K            RHT           TJX
## --------------------------------------------------------------
## Alpha          0.00         0.00         0.00          0.00 *
##               (0.00)       (0.00)       (0.00)        (0.00)
## Beta           0.83 ***     0.49 ***     1.24 ***      0.80 ***
##               (0.03)       (0.02)       (0.04)        (0.03)
## --------------------------------------------------------------
## R^2            0.28         0.23         0.35          0.34
## Adj. R^2       0.28         0.23         0.35          0.34
## Num. obs.   1761          1761         1761          1761
## RMSE           0.01         0.01         0.02          0.01
## ==============================================================
## *** p < 0.001, ** p < 0.01, * p < 0.05
```

In the previous code, we use a list of models from `beta.tab$beta.model`, defined custom names of models using input `custom.model.names`, coefficient names with `custom.coef.names`, and the number of digits with input `digits`. Package `texreg` offers many more options to the user. You can customize your estimation table in many ways. Exporting to other formats, such as latex and html, is possible and recommended. For Microsoft Office users, function `htmlreg` also allows to export a table to a Word file. You can do that by setting input `file` as a *.doc* file. If you work with estimation tables on a day-to-day basis, package `texreg` will save you a lot of time.

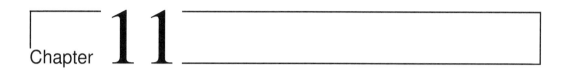

## Chapter 11

Writing Research Scripts

In previous chapters, we learned how to use R for many different tasks. Here we will discuss best practices in structuring and organizing a research script. Three practical and replicable cases of data analysis in finance are presented. All the knowledge learned in previous chapters will be used to provide examples of the full cycle of research, from the acquisition of the data, to the reporting of results.

11.1 Structure of a Research Script

Doing research with R will generally involve a set of steps. Each stage of a data processing script evolves in a recursive fashion. The data processing stage depends on the code that imports and cleans the raw data. We can organize a research script in four consecutive steps:

1. **Importation of data**: At this stage, the raw (original) data is imported from a source, internet or a local file. When the origin of the data is not obvious, it is important to use comments to register where the data is coming and its last update.

2. **Cleaning and structuring the data**: The dataset imported in the previous step is further cleaned and structured according to the need of the research. Abnormal records and errors in observations can be removed or treated. In R, as already mentioned in the previous chapters, it is advised to structure all the data in a single `dataframe`, guided by lines (*long* format).

3. **Modelling and hypothesis testing**: After cleansing and structuring the data, the script should continue with the implementation of the main procedure of the research, hypothesis testing. Here, you can use models or direct

statistical tests. This is the *heart* of the research and the part that is most likely to take more development time.

4. **Reporting the results**: The final stage of a research script is reporting the results. This step is related to exporting tables and figures to a text processing software such as Latex, Writer (LibreOffice) or Word (Microsoft).

Each of the mentioned steps can be structured in a single .R file or in several separate files. The use of multiple files is preferable when the first steps of the research demand a significant amount of processing time. For example, in importing and organizing a large volume database, it is worth the trouble to separate the procedures in different files.

A practical example would be the analysis of a large dataset of financial transactions. Importing and cleansing the data takes too much computer time. A smart organization of the work would be to insert these primary data procedures in a .R file and save the final objects of this stage in an external storage file. This local archive serves as a bridge to the next step. In the next stage, hypothesis testing, the previously created file with clean data is imported. Every time a change is made to the hypothesis testing script, it is not necessary to rebuild the whole dataset. This simple organization of files saves a lot of time. The underlying logic is simple, isolate the parts of the script that demand more computational time and less development, and connect them to the rest of the code using external data files. This way you'll be able to work more efficiently.

If you are working with multiple files, one suggestion is to create a naming structure that informs the steps of the research in an intuitive way. An example would be to name the data importing code `1-Import-and-clean-data.R`, the modeling code as `2-build-report-models.R` and so on. The practical effect is that the use of a number in the first letter of the filenames makes the order of execution clear. We can also create a *master* script called `0-run-it-all.R` or `0-main.R` that runs (`source`) all other scripts. So, every time we make an update to the original data, we can simply run `0-run-it-all.R` and will have the new results, without the need to run each script individually.

11.2   Folder Structure

A proper, thought out, folder structure also benefits the reproducibility and organization of research. In simple scripts, with a small database and a low number of procedures, it is not necessary to spend much time thinking about the organization of files. This is certainly the case for most of the code in this book. More complex programs, with several stages of data cleansing, hypothesis testing, and several sources of data, organizing the file structure is essential.

A suggestion for an effective folder structure is to create a single directory with the title of the research and, within it, create subdirectories for each input and output element. For example, you can create a subdirectory called `data`, where all the original data will be stored, a directory `fig` and `tables`, where figures and tables with final results will be exported. If you are using many custom written functions in the scripts, you can also create a directory called `R-Fcts` and save all files with function definitions at this location. As for the root of the directory, you should only find the main research scripts there. An example of a file structure that summarizes this structure is:

```
/My Research about capital markets/
    /data/
        datafile1.csv
        datafile2.csv
        datafile2.csv
    /fig/
        MyImpressiveFigure.png
    /table/
        Table_with_publishable_results.tex
        DescriptiveTable.tex
    /R-Fcts/
        estimate_model.R
        get_results.R
        read_my_files.R
    0-run-it-all.R
    1-import-and-clean-data.R
    2-run-research.R
```

The research code should also be self-contained, with all files available within a subfolder of the root directory. If you are using many different R packages, it is advisable to add a comment in the first lines of `0-run-it-all.R` that indicates which packages are necessary to run the code. The most friendly way to inform this is adding a commented line that install all required packages, as in `#install.packages('pkg1', 'pkg2', ...)`. So, when someone receives the code for the first time, all he (or she) needs to do is uncomment the line and execute it. External dependencies and steps for their installation should also be informed.

The benefits of this directory format are clear. If you need to share the code with other researchers, simply compress the directory to a format such as *.zip* and send the file to the recipient. After uncompressing the file, the structure of the folder immediately informs the user where to change the original data, the order of execution of the scripts, and where the outputs are saved. The same benefit goes when you reuse your code in the future. By working smarter, you will produce faster and spend less time with repetitive and unnecessary steps.

An example of the contents of file `0-run-it-all.R` would be:

```
# Example script for executing a research
#
# Output:
#   Figure in folder fig, tables in folder table
#
# Author: Mr R programmer
# Date: 01/01/2017



#install.packages(c('BatchGetSymbols', 'plm'))

# clean up workspace
rm(list=ls())

# close all figure windows created with x11()
graphics.off()

# change directory
my.d <- 'My Dir here!'
setwd(my.d)

# load all functions
my.R.files <- list.files(path='R-Fcts',
                         pattern = '*.R',
                         full.names=TRUE)


# source all function file
sapply(my.R.files,source)

# run all steps of research
my.R.files <- list.files(path='',
                         pattern = '*.R',
                         full.names=TRUE)


# source all main scripts
sapply(my.R.files,source)
```

Notice that to run the above code on another computer, all you need to do is change the directory in `my.d`. The installation of the packages used in the research may also be required. We could also automate the copy of figure and table files used in the report with `file.copy`. From there, you can create a link in the text for each figure file. As an example, in LaTeX you can include a figure file with the command `\includegraphics{filenamehere}`. You can also create a direct link for the figure file in the research folder, although this method is not recommended, since it creates an external dependency to the written report. Either way, whenever the main code is executed, all research figures will be automatically updated in the text. As previously mentioned in chapter 4, you can also produce table files in different formats using packages `xtable` and `texreg`.

11.3 Examples of Research Scripts

Here we will present three elaborate examples of financial research with R. Every script provided here is reproducible. You can download the code and replicate all results. Each research script is saved in a single *.Rmd* file and is available in the book repository, folder `Research Scripts`.

The first example of research is the analysis of the historical performance of several international stock indices using data from Yahoo Finance and Quandl. In the second example we investigate the forecasting accuracy of `prophet`, a open source forecasting algorithm from the Facebook team. In the last and final example, we present a simple study about importing and dealing with high frequency trade data from the Brazilian exchange.

11.3.1 The performance of international investments

One of the most popular subjects in Finance is the historical analysis of performance in the financial markets. The possibility of earning money in capital markets is real and instigates a systematic curiosity about how different investments performed historically. This topic is also popular in academic research. Financial theory predicts that financial instruments with greater risk are those which, on average, would offer greatest return. This premise is part of the main theoretical models of asset pricing. The topic of investment performance, therefore, attracts the attention of practitioners and academics.

In this example of research, we will analyze the long term performance of international market indices from the point of view of an investor that operates in dollar. This choice is justified by the fact that market indices are priced in local currencies. Using dollar adjusted prices removes the effect of local inflation. Since the US exchange (dollar) is one of the most liquid assets, it becomes easier to find data about local exchange rates and make the conversion from local currency to dollar. While we could use derivatives contracts to hedge currency risk, using adjusted indices is a simpler and a more data intensive approach, which suits our needs.

11.3.1.1   The Data

The first step of the study is to identify the indices used in the research. For that, we look into all assets available at the Yahoo Finance World Indices page. We select equity indices according to the following rules:

- The index must be composed of stocks. No volatility index is allowed.
- Data about about the local exchange rate to dollar must be available in Quandl (see section 7.1.7).
- There must be at least 10 year of data about local currency and index price.

After verifying these conditions for all assets in the list of tickers from Yahoo, we save the information about those that fit the criteria in a *.csv* file. We add a column that includes information about the local exchange rate and also the Quandl symbol related to the conversion to dollar. This file was manually built and is available in data/MktIndices_and_Symbols.csv. Let's use R to have a look in its content.

```
# load indices data
# last update: 2017-04-04
# data manually built with:
#   Yahoo Finance: https://finance.yahoo.com/world-indices
#   Quandl: https://www.quandl.com/

my.f <- 'data/MktIndices_and_Symbols.csv'
df.indices <- read.csv(file = my.f, colClasses = 'character')

# print df
print(df.indices)
```

```
##          ticker                    name currency
## 1         ^GSPC              S&P 500      USD
## 2         ^FTSE             FTSE 100      GPB
## 3        ^GDAXI                  DAX      EUR
## 4         ^FCHI               CAC 40      EUR
## 5     ^STOXX50E        ESTX50 EUR P      EUR
## 6          ^BFX              BEL 20      EUR
## 7         ^N225          Nikkei 225      JPY
## 8          ^HSI     HANG SENG INDEX      HKD
## 9     000001.SS   SSE Composite Index    CNY
## 10         ^STI            STI Index      SGD
## 11      ^GSPTSE S&P/TSX Composite index  CAD
## 12         ^MXX                  IPC      MXN
##          quandl.symbol
## 1
```

```
## 2   FED/RXI_US_N_B_UK
## 3   FED/RXI_US_N_B_EU
## 4   FED/RXI_US_N_B_EU
## 5   FED/RXI_US_N_B_EU
## 6   FED/RXI_US_N_B_EU
## 7      FED/RXI_N_B_JA
## 8      FED/RXI_N_B_HK
## 9      FED/RXI_N_B_CH
## 10     FED/RXI_N_B_SI
## 11     FED/RXI_N_B_CA
## 12     FED/RXI_N_B_MX
```

The data is composed of European, North American and Asian stock indices. We will use column `ticker` to import price data from Yahoo Finance and column `quandl.symbol` to import exchange rate data from Quandl.

The first part of our research script is to clean the memory, change the working directory and close all graphical windows:

```
# clean workspace
rm(list=ls())

# change dir
my.d <- dirname(rstudioapi::getActiveDocumentContext()$path)
setwd(my.d)

# close all graphics
graphics.off()
```

Let's also set the options of the research script. These are the main information used for the rest of the code. It includes the dates of the data, the api key of Quandl and the name of the file with the raw data about ticker and quandl symbols. The variables defined here will be used throughout the rest of the code. In this study, we will use daily data from **2000-01-01** to **2016-12-31**.

```
# set dates
first.date <- as.Date('2000-01-01')
last.date <- as.Date('2016-12-31')

# set api key (will not work for you, do change it!)
my.api.key <- 'Esv1Ac7zuZzJSCGxynyV'
my.f <- 'data/MktIndices_and_Symbols.csv'
```

Given the structure of the raw data about international indices, we will need do process each row of `df.indices` individually. For every line, we download data from Yahoo Finance, data from Quandl and merge it using the dates as reference. After that, we calculate the dollar adjusted values of the international indices and add it as a new column.

The easiest way to organize our code is to first write a function that takes a input a ticker and quandl symbol, downloads the data from both sources, merge it and output a `dataframe` with the desired dataset and new columns. The first and last dates are also used as inputs in order to retrieve the correct time period. The adjustment of the price series is accomplished by multiplying the original value by the exchange rate of the dollar to the local currency.

A particularity of the exchange rate data from the US Federal Reserve database in Quandl is that, sometimes, the exchange rate is quoted as the local currency by the dollar and not the usual, dollar by the local exchange. However, this information is available in the Quandl symbol. Whenever the symbol has the text `US`, it is the dollar to the local currency exchange. If it does not have that symbol, it provides the inverse. This is important because we need to know the direction of the exchange rate in order to properly calculate the dollar adjusted values of index prices. In the code, we use an `if` statement together with function `stringr::str_detect` to control the cases and properly adjust prices.

Another control that must be made in the code is the case of the SP500. There is no need to download exchange data for it since prices are already in dollar. We control it in the code with another `if` statement. When the function receives the ticker of SP500 (^GSPC), it simply returns the raw data and a vector of dollar adjusted prices equal to the value of the index. The whole R function is defined by the following code:

```
get_and_clean_data <- function(ticker,
                               quandl.symbol,
                               first.date,
                               last.date) {
  # gets price data from yahoo and exchange
  # data from Quandl and adjusts it to dollar.
  #
  # Args:
  #   ticker - a ticker symbol from Yahoo finance
  #   quandl.symbol - the symbol of the exchange
  #                   rate in quandl
  #   first.date - first date of data
  #   last.date - last date of data
  #
  # Returns:
  #   A dataframe with dollar adjusted values of asset price
```

```r
require(Quandl)
require(BatchGetSymbols)
require(stringr)


cat(paste0('\nGetting data for ',ticker))
cat(paste0('\n\tDownloading price data from Yahoo Finance'))

# get data from yahoo finance
df.ticker <- BatchGetSymbols(tickers = ticker,
                             first.date = first.date,
                             last.date = last.date)$df.tickers

# remove uninteresting info and rename cols
cols.to.keep <- c("price.adjusted",
                  "ref.date",
                  "ticker" )

df.ticker <- df.ticker[, cols.to.keep]
colnames(df.ticker) <- c("price",
                         "ref.date",
                         "ticker" )

# get data from quandl
cat(paste0('\n\tDownloading FX data from Quandl'))

# case of SP500 (no need for exchange data)

if (ticker == '^GSPC') {
  df.ticker$forex <- 1
  df.ticker$price.USD <- df.ticker$price/df.ticker$forex
  df.ticker$quandl.symbol <- quandl.symbol
  return(df.ticker)
}

# register api key
Quandl.api_key(my.api.key)

df.currency <- Quandl(code = quandl.symbol,
                      type = 'raw',
                      start_date = first.date,
```

```
                         end_date = last.date)

  # fix names
  df.currency$quandl.symbol <- quandl.symbol
  colnames(df.currency) <- c('ref.date','forex','quandl.symbol')

  # merge datasets
  df.ticker <- merge(x = df.ticker,
                     y = df.currency,
                     by = 'ref.date')

  # calculated USD value of index
  if (str_detect(quandl.symbol,'US')) {
    df.ticker$price.USD <- df.ticker$price*df.ticker$forex
  } else {
    df.ticker$price.USD <- df.ticker$price/df.ticker$forex
  }

  return(df.ticker)

}
```

Now that we have our function to download data for each asset, let's use it in a loop and process all cases.

```
n.rows <- nrow(df.indices)

my.df <- data.frame()
for (i in seq(1,n.rows)) {
  ticker.now <- df.indices$ticker[i]
  quandl.code.now <- df.indices$quandl.symbol[i]

  df.temp <- get_and_clean_data(ticker = ticker.now,
                                quandl.symbol = quandl.code.now,
                                first.date=first.date,
                                last.date=last.date)

  my.df <- rbind(my.df, df.temp)
}
```

For every iteration of the loop, we incremented object my.df with the information from df.temp. The data from the previous code is available in file ../data/AdjustedPrices-InternacionalIndices.RDATA. Now, let's have a look in the resulting `dataframe`.

```
## 'data.frame':    50063 obs. of  6 variables:
##  $ price        : num   1455 1399 1402 1403 1441 ...
##  $ ref.date     : Date, format: "2000-01-03" ...
##  $ ticker       : chr   "^GSPC" "^GSPC" "^GSPC" "^GSPC" ...
##  $ forex        : num   1 1 1 1 1 1 1 1 1 1 ...
##  $ price.USD    : num   1455 1399 1402 1403 1441 ...
##  $ quandl.symbol: chr   "" "" "" "" ...
## NULL
```

As expected, we have a new column called `price.USD` with the dollar adjusted values of the stock market indices.

11.3.1.2 Calculating annual returns

The next step in the research is to calculate the annual returns for each asset. The annual return is the percentage value that an investor would earn if he bought the instrument at the end of previous year and sold it at the end of the following year. At this stage, for simplicity, we ignore the effects of income tax on investment in different instruments.

The imported data available in `my.df` is in the daily frequency. We can easily calculate yearly returns with package `dplyr`. The first step is to create a new column in `my.df` with the year of the data. After that, we use function `group_by` to group the data by ticker and year. The last step is to find the last price of each year and calculate the return vector. This set of steps is executed with the following code:

```
library(dplyr)

my.ret <- my.df %>%
  mutate(year = format(ref.date, '%Y')) %>%
  group_by(ticker, year) %>%
  summarise(last.price = price.USD[length(price.USD)]) %>%
  mutate(ret = c(0, last.price[2:length(last.price)]/
                 last.price[1:(length(last.price)-1)]-1))
```

A small difference here from the previous code is that we use a value of zero as the first observation in the calculation of returns. We do that because we will soon calculate accumulated returns and, by setting the first value of the return vector equal to zero, the first accumulated return will be 1.

Let's have a look in the yearly returns of the different assets over time:

```
library(ggplot2)
p <- ggplot(my.ret, aes(x=as.numeric(year),
                        y=ret,
                        color=ticker))
p <- p + geom_line(size=1.5)
p <- p + labs(x='Year', y = 'Annual Return')
p <- p + theme(legend.position="bottom")
p <- p + theme(legend.title=element_blank())
print(p)
```

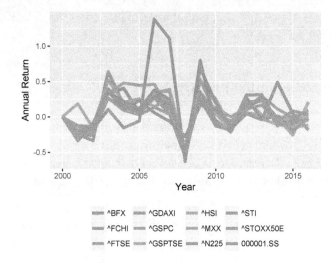

The yearly returns of the different investments are mostly positive. It is interesting to see the impact of the 2008 financial crisis. All indices had an extreme loss of value at that year. However, in the following year, 2009, there was a systematic recovery for all stock markets in our sample. The figure also shows a clear correlation in between the indices. Let's have a look at its correlation matrix:

```
library(tidyr)

# turn long df to wide and remove year col
ret.wide <- my.ret %>%
  select(year, ticker,ret) %>%
  spread(key = ticker, value = ret, drop = TRUE) %>%
  select(-year)

# turn to matrix
ret.mat <- as.matrix(ret.wide)

# print summary of cor matrix
```

```
summary(cor(ret.mat))
```

```
##       ^BFX              ^FCHI             ^FTSE
## Min.   :0.5547    Min.   :0.5760    Min.   :0.5951
## 1st Qu.:0.7892    1st Qu.:0.8211    1st Qu.:0.8447
## Median :0.8388    Median :0.8728    Median :0.8979
## Mean   :0.8329    Mean   :0.8596    Mean   :0.8683
## 3rd Qu.:0.9263    3rd Qu.:0.9403    3rd Qu.:0.9322
## Max.   :1.0000    Max.   :1.0000    Max.   :1.0000
##       ^GDAXI            ^GSPC             ^GSPTSE
## Min.   :0.5590    Min.   :0.4502    Min.   :0.4852
## 1st Qu.:0.7979    1st Qu.:0.7605    1st Qu.:0.7595
## Median :0.8425    Median :0.8131    Median :0.8062
## Mean   :0.8319    Mean   :0.7819    Mean   :0.7952
## 3rd Qu.:0.9021    3rd Qu.:0.8528    3rd Qu.:0.8643
## Max.   :1.0000    Max.   :1.0000    Max.   :1.0000
##       ^HSI              ^MXX              ^N225
## Min.   :0.6485    Min.   :0.4579    Min.   :0.1938
## 1st Qu.:0.7726    1st Qu.:0.6411    1st Qu.:0.6423
## Median :0.8815    Median :0.7258    Median :0.7616
## Mean   :0.8500    Mean   :0.7157    Mean   :0.7067
## 3rd Qu.:0.9044    3rd Qu.:0.8001    3rd Qu.:0.8038
## Max.   :1.0000    Max.   :1.0000    Max.   :1.0000
##       ^STI              ^STOXX50E         000001.SS
## Min.   :0.6236    Min.   :0.6092    Min.   :0.1938
## 1st Qu.:0.7801    1st Qu.:0.8071    1st Qu.:0.4784
## Median :0.8313    Median :0.8789    Median :0.5675
## Mean   :0.8276    Mean   :0.8605    Mean   :0.5765
## 3rd Qu.:0.9035    3rd Qu.:0.9398    3rd Qu.:0.6255
## Max.   :1.0000    Max.   :1.0000    Max.   :1.0000
```

As expected, the matrix of returns has a strong correlation in between the columns. In practice, when one market goes up in dollar values, the others tend to follow. The economic reasoning is that, given the effects of international commerce and globalization, when an economic shock is seen in one market, it tends to spread to others. The use of the same exchange rate to normalize prices can also explain the positive correlations.

Another way of analyzing the appreciation of value in the indices is to look at the accumulated returns over the years. This mimics the total return an investor would have each year by keeping the asset in his portfolio. In R, we can add a column in the existing `my.ret` object using functions `tapply` and `unlist`.

```
# calculate accumulated returns
my.l <- tapply(X = my.ret$ret,
               INDEX = my.ret$ticker,
               FUN = function(x) cumprod(c(x+1)))

# sorts my.l by ticker and add new column in my.ret
my.l <- my.l[unique(my.ret$ticker)]
my.ret$acum.ret <- unlist(my.l)
```

Previous code calculates the cumulative return for each share using arithmetic returns from column `ret`. These cumulative returns are stored in `my.l`. Soon after, we use the command `my.l <- my.l[unique(my.ret$ticker)]` to order the elements in `my.l`. Remember that function `tapply` orders its output alphabetically, which is not what we need. Finally, we add column `acum.ret` with the `unlist` command.

Now, let's plot the result.

```
p <- ggplot(my.ret, aes(x = as.numeric(year),
                        y = acum.ret,
                        color = ticker))
p <- p + geom_line(size=1)
p <- p + labs(x = 'Year',
              y = 'Accumulated Return')
p <- p + theme(legend.position = "bottom",
               legend.title = element_blank())
print(p)
```

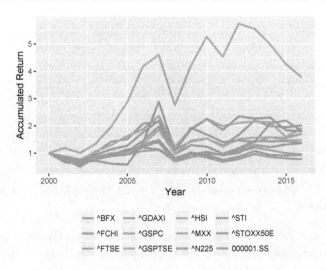

It is interesting to see how an investment in ^MXX, the Mexican stock market index, provided the highest accumulated return in the period of 16 years. However, analyzing performance is not just about maximizing raw returns. We also need to understand the risk of theses investments and whether it is proportional to the returns.

There are many ways we can quantify risk. In a simple analysis that is coherent to financial theory, risk can be represented as the standard deviation of annual returns. This measure of volatility quantifies the expected uncertainty about future returns. For example, if an asset always yields returns that are close to its average, it is reasonable to expect that future returns will also be close to the historical average. The certainty about future returns increases as the standard deviation of returns decreases.

The following code will use object `my.ret` to calculate the average and standard deviation of returns in the investments. We also add a column with the sharpe ratio, the average return divided by the standard deviation. This simple measure indicates how much return is provided by the asset for every unit of risk. The higher the sharpe ratio, the better the investment.

```
my.tab <- my.ret %>%
  group_by(ticker) %>%
  summarise(mean.ret = mean(ret),
            sd.ret = sd(ret),
            sharpe = mean.ret/sd.ret) %>%
  arrange(-sharpe)

print(my.tab)

## # A tibble: 12 × 4
##        ticker   mean.ret     sd.ret      sharpe
##         <chr>      <dbl>      <dbl>       <dbl>
## 1         ^MXX 0.11534289 0.2773979 0.41580299
## 2        ^GDAXI 0.07885876 0.2817598 0.27987934
## 3       ^GSPTSE 0.07216617 0.2633533 0.27402798
## 4         ^GSPC 0.04709950 0.1731060 0.27208473
## 5          ^STI 0.07164052 0.2803992 0.25549471
## 6     000001.SS 0.13116395 0.5189561 0.25274574
## 7          ^HSI 0.05467892 0.2566677 0.21303389
## 8          ^BFX 0.05166544 0.2496124 0.20698266
## 9         ^N225 0.03468718 0.1847752 0.18772641
## 10        ^FCHI 0.02143972 0.2273614 0.09429797
## 11        ^FTSE 0.01879847 0.2016375 0.09322904
## 12    ^STOXX50E 0.01154059 0.2300936 0.05015605
```

Object `my.tab` shows the descending values of sharpe ratio. The best asset in terms of return by risk is again the Mexican stock index. It not only offers a high average of returns, but also a low volatility. The previous result can be analyzed visually, with the so-called mean-variance chart. This is a scatter plot with the horizontal axis as the risk of investment and the vertical axis as the expected return. Let's create it with `ggplot2`.

```
p <- ggplot(my.tab, aes(x=sd.ret, y=mean.ret))
p <- p + geom_point(size=3)
p <- p + annotate('text', x = my.tab$sd.ret-0.007,
                  y = my.tab$mean.ret+0.01,
                  label = my.tab$ticker)
p <- p + labs(x='Risk', y='Expected Return')
print(p)
```

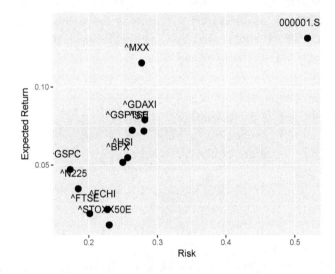

The graph confirms the results about the high performance of the Mexican market. Its ticker, ^MXX, is located at the top left of the chart, with a high return and low risk. In the other side we have 000001.SS, the Chinese market index. It offers a higher average return but with excessive volatility.

Now, let's build a portfolio using the previous data. It makes sense to spread the total capital in different assets in order to obtain the benefits of diversification. Here, we want to find the portfolio weights that maximize our sharpe ratio. Package `fPortfolio` offer several functions for this purpose. First, we need to make sure that our matrix of returns is positive-definite and has no `NA` values. If this is not true, we won't be able to run the optimization procedure. Let's test it:

```
library(matrixcalc)

# check if ret matrix is positive definite
```

```
print(is.positive.definite(cov(ret.mat)))
```

```
## [1] TRUE
```

```
# check for na
print(any(is.na(ret.mat)))
```

```
## [1] FALSE
```

As we can see, the return matrix is positive definite and without `NA` values. We can now proceed to the estimation of our efficient portfolio. For that, we use function `fPortfolio::tangencyPortfolio` that takes as input a matrix of returns in the `timeSeries` class.

```
library(fPortfolio)
```

```
# convert to timeSeries
ret.mat <- as.timeSeries(ret.mat)
```

```
# get port composition for max sharpe ratio
eff.port <- tangencyPortfolio(ret.mat)
```

```
# print result
print(eff.port)
```

```
##
## Title:
##  MV Tangency Portfolio
##  Estimator:         covEstimator
##  Solver:            solveRquadprog
##  Optimize:          minRisk
##  Constraints:       LongOnly
##
## Portfolio Weights:
##      ^BFX      ^FCHI      ^FTSE     ^GDAXI      ^GSPC    ^GSPTSE
##    0.0000     0.0000     0.0000     0.0000     0.0964     0.0000
##      ^HSI       ^MXX      ^N225       ^STI  ^STOXX50E  000001.SS
##    0.0000     0.8172     0.0000     0.0000     0.0000     0.0864
##
## Covariance Risk Budgets:
##      ^BFX      ^FCHI      ^FTSE     ^GDAXI      ^GSPC    ^GSPTSE
##    0.0000     0.0000     0.0000     0.0000     0.0412     0.0000
##      ^HSI       ^MXX      ^N225       ^STI  ^STOXX50E  000001.SS
##    0.0000     0.8559     0.0000     0.0000     0.0000     0.1029
```

```
##
## Target Returns and Risks:
##   mean    Cov   CVaR    VaR
## 0.1101 0.2608 0.4200 0.4200
##
## Description:
##  Fri May 05 14:19:03 2017 by user: marcelo
```

Not surprisingly, the optimized portfolio invested a significant proportion in ^MXX. The American and Chinese market, with symbols ^GSPC and ^00001.SS, were left with approximately 10% of the portfolio. We can find out the exact sharpe ratio of this portfolio with the following code:

```
# get weights of efficient port
my.w <- eff.port@portfolio@portfolio$weights

# change to vector
my.w <- matrix(my.w, nrow = length(my.w))

# calculate vector with portfolio returns
my.port <- as.matrix(ret.mat)%*%my.w

# get sharpe ratio
my.sharpe <- mean(my.port)/sd(my.port)

# print it
print(my.sharpe)
```

```
## [1] 0.4222147
```

The value of the resulting sharpe ratio is slightly higher than investing all capital in the Mexican market index. Exploring even more the functions from package fPortfolio, we can also plot the efficient frontier in our mean-variance graph with function tailoredFrontierPlot:

```
# get eff frontier
my.pf <- portfolioFrontier(data = ret.mat)

# plot it
tailoredFrontierPlot(object = my.pf,
                     risk = 'Sigma',
                     twoAssets = FALSE,
                     sharpeRatio = FALSE)
```

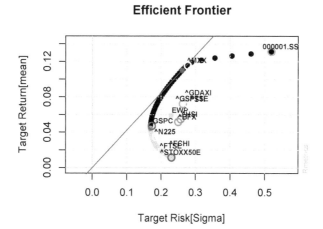

The figure shows the investment opportunities of each stock individually and also the efficient frontier, the portfolios that offer the highest expected return for each value of risk. The efficient frontier represents the best possible investments in the mean/variance world. The red point to the left is the portfolio with the minimum variance. The blue point is the portfolio with highest sharpe ratio.

The efficient frontier clearly shows how an investor can benefit from diversification. Every point in this curve has superior sharpe ratio than any other at the same level of risk. In other words, allocating all capital in ^FTSE or ^FCHI is a bad investment choice as better opportunities for the same level of risk are available. An investor should set a risk target and choose a portfolio from the efficient frontier.

In this study we analyzed the historical performance of several international, dollar adjusted, market indices. Our results shows a strong correlation between the yearly returns of the different assets. We also find that the index with the best performance, measured by the sharpe ratio, is the Mexican stock index (^MXX). When building a optimized portfolio, we are able to marginally improve the sharpe ratio by investing 82% of the portfolio in ^MXX, and the rest of capital split in SP500 (^GSPC) and the Chinese SSE Composite Index (^000001.SS). The efficient frontier shows exactly where an investor should allocate his capital for every value of risk. As for future performance, the big question is whether history will repeat itself and this optimized portfolio will continue to offer high returns for low risk. This clearly could be the question of another, more complex, research.

The written code in this research is reproducible and easily expandable. If one desires to include more assets, all that is necessary is to add new rows in file data/MktIndices_and_Symbols.csv. This addition should include information about tickers and quandl symbols for local currencies. The dates of the research are also easy to modify with options `first.date` and `last.date`. We could also add other types of returns and risk estimates by creating a custom function and using it in the analysis.

11.3.2 Can we predict stock's returns with Prophet?

Facebook recently released an API package allowing access to its forecasting model called prophet:

> "It's not your traditional ARIMA-style time series model. It's closer in spirit to a Bayesian-influenced generalized additive model, a regression of smooth terms. The model is resistant to the effects of outliers, and supports data collected over an irregular time scale (ingliding presence of missing data) without the need for interpolation. The underlying calculation engine is Stan; the R and Python packages simply provide a convenient interface."

— Facebook Core Data Science team

Given its open source format, the prophet algorithm and package was well received by the community. In finance, there is a large amount of work dedicated in forecasting financial markets. So, a natural application for Prophet is the attempt to forecast returns in the stock market. Here, we ask the question, **can we predict stock's returns based on prophet?** This research problem was inspired by one of my blog posts, with a significant extension of the original content.

Before describing the code and results, it is noteworthy to point out that forecasting stock returns is really hard! There is a significant body of literature trying to forecast prices and to prove (or not) that financial markets are efficient in pricing publicly available information, including past prices. This is the so called efficient market hypothesis. The variation in prices is due to random factors that cannot be anticipated. The explanation is simple, prices move according to investor's expectation from available information. Every time that new (random) information, true or not, reaches the market, investor's update their beliefs and trade accordingly. So, unless, new information or market expectation have a particular pattern, price changes will be mostly random.

The role of practitioners is also important to point out. Economically speaking, there is a high payoff in being able to forecast financial markets. Even a small advantage can lead to huge gains. For example, if someone can predict a 1% change in a stock index, he (or she) can trade derivative contracts and leverage significantly his total returns by taking a financial position according to his prediction. Since every shock in the order flow can change the price of the contract, we can expect that such predictable patterns are short lived. As more investors learn it, it disappears over time. However, for educational purposes of learning R in a research setup, the investigation is certainly interesting.

11.3.2.1 The Data

For this research exercise, we will use the database of prices of all stocks that belong to the SP500 index, file data/SP500-Stocks-WithRet.RData. We will not restrict the sample and all 471 assets are going to be used.

Before applying the model to the data, we need to understand how package `prophet` works. From the manual we see that the default estimation is straightforward. In order to use the modelling function `prophet`, only one input is necessary: a `dataframe` with the time series itself (column `y`) and a vector with the corresponding dates (column `ds`). A downside of using `prophet` in a large scale is that the function is verbose, giving several messages in the prompt. While this is OK for one estimation, it fills the screen with clutter when estimating many models. Soon you'll see that we will need to silence the output messages of `prophet` using function `capture.output`.

Let's try a simple example of estimating and forecasting a model with `prophet` for the returns of one of the assets in the database.

```
library(prophet)

# get ret data from df
my.stock <- unique(my.df$ticker)[1]
temp.df <- my.df[my.df$ticker %in% my.stock , ]

# set df for estimation
df.est <- data.frame(y = temp.df$ret,
                     ds = temp.df$ref.date)

# estimate and print model
my.prophet <- prophet(df = df.est)

## Initial log joint probability = -42.58
## Optimization terminated normally:
##    Convergence detected: absolute parameter change was below tolerance
# create forecasts
df.pred <- predict(my.prophet,
                   make_future_dataframe(my.prophet,
                                         periods = 10,
                                         include_history = FALSE))
```

```
# print result
print(head(df.pred))
```

```
##              ds        t              trend   yhat_lower  yhat_upper
## 1 2016-12-31 1.000392 -0.0003055182 -0.01717911 0.01158751
## 2 2017-01-01 1.000784 -0.0003053772 -0.01768187 0.01184872
## 3 2017-01-02 1.001176 -0.0003052362 -0.01540638 0.01466073
## 4 2017-01-03 1.001568 -0.0003050952 -0.01416107 0.01573194
## 5 2017-01-04 1.001960 -0.0003049542 -0.01357974 0.01602591
## 6 2017-01-05 1.002352 -0.0003048131 -0.01388536 0.01675243
##      trend_lower    trend_upper seasonal_lower seasonal_upper
## 1 -0.0003055182 -0.0003055182  -0.0024148818  -0.0024148818
## 2 -0.0003053772 -0.0003053772  -0.0025166442  -0.0025166442
## 3 -0.0003052362 -0.0003052362   0.0007601026   0.0007601026
## 4 -0.0003050952 -0.0003050952   0.0009337965   0.0009337965
## 5 -0.0003049542 -0.0003049542   0.0015559184   0.0015559184
## 6 -0.0003048131 -0.0003048131   0.0011263063   0.0011263063
##           weekly  weekly_lower  weekly_upper        yearly
## 1 -0.0027603338 -0.0027603338 -0.0027603338  3.454520e-04
## 2 -0.0027603338 -0.0027603338 -0.0027603338  2.436896e-04
## 3  0.0006238955  0.0006238955  0.0006238955  1.362071e-04
## 4  0.0009091033  0.0009091033  0.0009091033  2.469318e-05
## 5  0.0016449048  0.0016449048  0.0016449048 -8.898637e-05
## 6  0.0013291257  0.0013291257  0.0013291257 -2.028195e-04
##    yearly_lower  yearly_upper      seasonal          yhat
## 1  3.454520e-04  3.454520e-04 -0.0024148818 -0.0027204000
## 2  2.436896e-04  2.436896e-04 -0.0025166442 -0.0028220213
## 3  1.362071e-04  1.362071e-04  0.0007601026  0.0004548664
## 4  2.469318e-05  2.469318e-05  0.0009337965  0.0006287014
## 5 -8.898637e-05 -8.898637e-05  0.0015559184  0.0012509643
## 6 -2.028195e-04 -2.028195e-04  0.0011263063  0.0008214931
```

The usage is straightforward, we input a `dataframe` containing the data and dates to function `prophet`. We make predictions using output `my.prophet` with the `predict` function. The number of forecasts is set with argument `periods` in `make_future_dataframe`.

Now that we understand how `prophet` works, the next step is to think about how to structure a function for our research problem. Our study has two steps, first we will set a training (in-sample) period, estimate the model and make forecasts. After that, we use the *out-of-sample* data to test the accuracy of the model. The whole procedure of estimating and forecasting will be encapsulated in a single R function that will accept as input a `dataframe` with our data and output another `dataframe` with the predictions and real values of returns. For each asset, we will break the whole time series of returns in half. The first half is used to estimate the model and the rest is used to test its predictive performance. So, if one asset has a vector with 1000 returns, we use rows 1 to 500 to estimate the model with `prophet` and rows 501 to 1000 to test the predictions. Here's the function definition:

```r
est.model.and.forecast <- function(df.in){
  # Estimates a model using prophet and forecast it
  #
  # Args:
  #   df.in - A dataframe with columns ret and ref.date
  #
  # Returns:
  #   A dataframe with forecasts and errors

  require(prophet)
  require(dplyr)

  my.ticker <- as.character(unique(df.in$ticker[1]))

  cat('\nProcessing ', my.ticker)

  # get total number of rows in df.in
  n.row <- nrow(df.in)

  # remove uninteresting columns
  df.in <- select(df.in, ref.date, ret)
  names(df.in) <- c('ds', 'y')

  # get half the sample for estimation
  idx <- floor(nrow(df.in)/2)

  df.est <- df.in[1:idx, ]
  df.for <- df.in[(idx + 1):nrow(df.in), ]

  # estimate a (silent) prophet model
  capture.output(
    m <- prophet(df = df.est)
  )

  # calculate number of forecasts needed to match data
  n.forecasts <- length(seq(from = min(df.for$ds),
                            to = max(df.for$ds),
```

```
                                         by = '1 day'))

  # make predictions
  df.pred <- predict(m,
                     make_future_dataframe(m,
                                           periods = n.forecasts,
                                           include_history = FALSE))

  # merge y and yhat
  df.for <- merge(df.for, df.pred, by = 'ds')
  df.for <- select(df.for, ds, y, yhat)

  # set ticker
  df.for$ticker <- my.ticker

  return(df.for)
}
```

With the previous function ready, we can use `by` to apply it to each stock in our sample. All results are later combined in a single `dataframe` with function `do.call`. Be aware that the next chunk of code is time demanding. The estimation of the model for each asset is computer intensive and, when running it for all assets in our database, a long waiting period is required. As way of saving time, object `my.result` was saved in file data/prophet-models-AllSP500Stocks.Rdata. You can download it from the book repository.

```
out.l <- by(data = my.df,
            INDICES = my.df$ticker,
            FUN = est.model.and.forecast)

# merge results
my.result <- do.call(rbind, out.l)
```

After estimating the models and creating the forecasts, let's have a look in the resulting `dataframe`:

```
print(str(my.result))
```

```
## 'data.frame':    413913 obs. of  4 variables:
##  $ ds    : Date, format: "2013-07-05" ...
##  $ y     : num   0.02455 0.00294 0.00541 0.01592 0.00905 ...
##  $ yhat  : num  -0.00393 -0.00575 -0.00399 -0.00494 -0.00385 ...
##  $ ticker: chr  "A" "A" "A" "A" ...
## NULL
```

In this object we find the forecasts (**yhat**), the actual values (**y**) and the ticker symbols. Now that we have the information about forecasts and real values, let's assess whether the predictions are accurate and have economic significance.

11.3.2.2   The Encopassing Test

A simple and powerful test for verifying the accuracy of a prediction algorithm is the encompassing test. The idea is to estimate a linear model with the real values of the predictive variable as the dependent variable and the predictions as the explanatory. We learned how to estimate a linear model in R in chapter 10. The econometric model is given by the following equation.

$$y_t = \alpha + \beta \hat{y}_t + \epsilon_t$$

If the predictive model provides good forecasts, we can expect that the intercept of the previous equation is equal to zero (no bias) and the slope is equal to 1. If both conditions are true, we have a prediction that, in average, is equal to the real value. In other words, our forecasting model provides an unbiased estimator of the predicted variable. With this setup, we can check if both conditions are true for our estimated model using a test of linear hypothesis, also called Wald test (see section 10.1.3).

First, let's find the result of the encompassing test for all stocks, i.e., the full `dataframe`.

```
# do encompassing test for all data
lm.model <- lm(formula = y ~ yhat,
               data = my.result)

# print result
summary(lm.model)

##
## Call:
## lm(formula = y ~ yhat, data = my.result)
##
## Residuals:
##      Min       1Q    Median       3Q       Max
## -0.39229 -0.00766   0.00007   0.00780   0.40346
##
## Coefficients:
##              Estimate Std. Error t value Pr(>|t|)
## (Intercept) 5.458e-04  2.704e-05   20.184  < 2e-16 ***
```

```
## yhat          2.458e-02   6.955e-03    3.535 0.000408 ***
## ---
## Signif. codes:
## 0 '***' 0.001 '**' 0.01 '*' 0.05 '.' 0.1 ' ' 1
##
## Residual standard error: 0.01641 on 413911 degrees of freedom
## Multiple R-squared: 3.019e-05,  Adjusted R-squared:  2.777e-05
## F-statistic:  12.5 on 1 and 413911 DF,  p-value: 0.0004081
```

The result is far from good! the value of the intercept is 0.000546 and the slope is 0.0246. While the intercept is close to zero, the slope is far from being equal to one. On the positive side, the slope presented statistical significance at 5%, meaning that there is a positive correlation between the forecasts and the real returns. Now, let's use a more formal approach with the Wald test, which will verify the joint hypothesis that the intercept and the slope are equal to 0 and 1, respectively. Package `car` provides function `linearHypothesis` for this purpose.

```
library(car)

# set test matrix
my.rhs <- matrix(c(0,     # alpha test value
                   1))    # beta test value

# hypothesis matrix
hyp.mat <- matrix(c(1,0,
                    0,1),nrow = 2)

# do wald test
my.waldtest <- linearHypothesis(lm.model,
                                hypothesis.matrix = hyp.mat,
                                rhs = my.rhs)

# print result
print(my.waldtest)

## Linear hypothesis test
##
## Hypothesis:
## (Intercept) = 0
## yhat = 1
##
## Model 1: restricted model
## Model 2: y ~ yhat
```

```
##
##    Res.Df    RSS Df Sum of Sq       F    Pr(>F)
## 1 413913 116.91
## 2 413911 111.41  2     5.5072 10231 < 2.2e-16 ***
## ---
## Signif. codes:
## 0 '***' 0.001 '**' 0.01 '*' 0.05 '.' 0.1 ' ' 1
```

The results show that the joint hypothesis of a coefficient vector equal to `c(0,
1)` is easily rejected at 1%, meaning that there is a very small evidence that our
forecasting model is unbiased and accurate. However, it might be the case that the
performance is better when looking at stocks individually. Let's try the same test
for each stock by using a custom function with `dplyr`:

```r
library(dplyr)
```

```r
do.wald.test <- function(lm.model) {
  # Tests the joint hypothesis that alpha equals 0 and beta equals 1
  #
  # Args:
  #   lm.model - a model estimated with lm()
  #
  # Returns:
  #   The pvalue of the test

  require(car)
  wald.test<-linearHypothesis(lm.model,
                              hypothesis.matrix = matrix(c(1,0,0,1),
                                                         nrow = 2),
                              rhs = matrix(c(0,1)))

  p.value <- wald.test$`Pr(>F)`[2]

  return(p.value)

}

# do wald test for each stock
my.tab <- my.result %>%
  group_by(ticker) %>%
  do(model = lm(formula = y ~yhat, data = .)) %>%
  mutate(p.value = do.wald.test(model))
```

Now that we have the p-value of the Wald test for each stock, let's calculate how many cases we fail to reject the null hypothesis at 10%:

```
n.fail.to.reject <- sum(my.tab$p.value>0.1)
print(n.fail.to.reject)
```

```
## [1] 3
```

So, in only 3 stocks we have evidence of prophet's positive performance in the encompassing test, which is very low proportion of the 471 stocks in the sample. In terms of accuracy, the results are clear cut: in aggregate, Prophet does a bad job at forecasting returns from the stock market.

11.3.2.3   Directional Forecasts and a Timing Strategy

When looking at performance in a trading application, it might not be of interest to forecast actual returns. If you are trading according to these forecasts, you are probably more worried about the direction of the forecasts and not its absolute error. A model can have bad forecasts, but be good in predicting the sign of the next price movement. If this is the case, you can still make money by following the predictions from the model, even though your model fails in the encompassing test.

In order to test if `prophet` is able to provide good directional forecasts, we calculate the proportion of correct directional forecasts. This is simply the proportion of times that the model was able to correctly predict the sign of the return. We can also check the total return of a timing strategy based on forecasts. This is accomplished by the following trading rules, applied for each asset individually:

- buy in end of day t if return forecast in $t+1$ is positive and sell at the end of $t+1$
- short-sell in the end of day t when return forecast for $t+1$ is negative and buy it back in the end of $t+1$

While the values of the proportion of correct sign predictions can be compared to simple chance (50%), the returns from the strategy must be compared to a proper benchmark. Here, we use a *buy&hold* strategy. We simulate a purchase of the asset in the beginning of the sample period and a sell at the end. The return from this naive approach is the total accumulated return from the stock. We analyze the performance of the strategy by calculating the difference between the return from the timing strategy and the total return from the *buy&hold* strategy. The result is called excess return.

The following R code will execute these calculations for each stock.

```
library(dplyr)

# check directional performance and trading strategy
my.tab <- my.result %>%
  group_by(ticker) %>%
  summarise(n.correct.dir = sum(sign(y)==sign(yhat))/n(),
            ret.strat = prod(1+sign(yhat)*y)-1,
            ret.naive = prod(1 + y)-1,
            ret.excess = ret.strat - ret.naive)
```

We can now analyze the results for all stocks using histograms:

```
library(ggplot2)

p <- ggplot(my.tab, aes(x=n.correct.dir))
p <- p + geom_histogram()
p <- p + geom_vline(aes(xintercept =  0.5),size=1)
print(p)

p <- ggplot(my.tab, aes(x=ret.excess))
p <- p + geom_histogram()
p <- p + geom_vline(aes(xintercept =  0.0),size=1)
print(p)
```

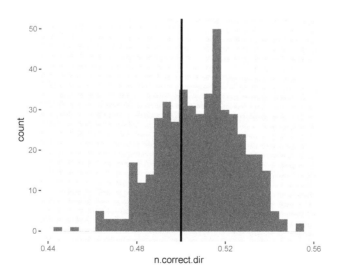

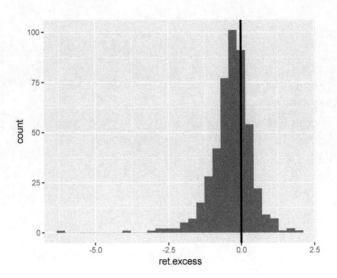

The visual results shows that the forecasting model has a relative good performance in forecasting direction of return. Out of 471 cases, 315 stocks (66.88%) presented a proportion of correct directional forecasts higher than 50%. While it is not a strong result, it is certainly not ignorable. However, when looking at excess return from the benchmark, only in 29.51% of the stocks we are able to find a positive excess return. While the model can predict the direction of the return, it mostly predicts small returns. In aggregate, the evidence that the model can outperform a simple *buy&hold* strategy is weak.

Let's confirm this result using a formal test. In package **rugarch** (see section 10.5.2) we find function **DACTest** that implements the directional accuracy test of Pesaran and Timmermann (1992) and the excess profitability test of Anatolyev and Gerko (2005). Its usage is straightforward, we input the forecasts in argument **forecast** and the real return values in **actual**. The choice of test is defined in input **test**. Let's implement the test for all tickers.

```
my.DAC.fct <- function(yhat, y, type.test) {
  # Tests for directional accuracy (PT) and excess profitability (AG)
  # Null hypothesis: PT - No directional accuracy
  #                  AG - No excess profitability
  # Args:
  #   yhat - vector of forecasted values
  #   y - vector of real values
  #   type.test - The option for test (PT or AG)
  #
  # Returns:
  #   The p-value from the test
```

```
require(rugarch)

test.out <- DACTest(forecast = yhat,
                    actual = y,
                    test = type.test)

return(test.out$p.value)

}

# use test for each stock
my.tab <- my.result %>%
  group_by(ticker) %>%
  summarise(p.value.PT = my.DAC.fct(yhat, y, 'PT'),
            p.value.AG = my.DAC.fct(yhat, y, 'AG'))

# plot histogram (PT)
p <- ggplot(my.tab, aes(x=p.value.PT)) +
    geom_histogram() +
    geom_vline(aes(xintercept =  0.1),size=1)

print(p)
```

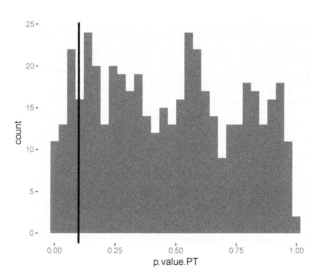

```
# plot histogram (AG)
p <- ggplot(my.tab, aes(x=p.value.AG)) +
    geom_histogram() +
    geom_vline(aes(xintercept =  0.1),size=1)
```

```
print(p)
```

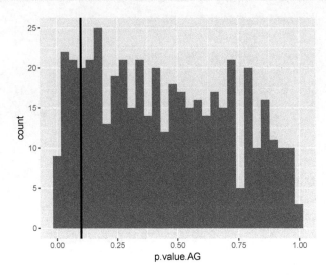

The results in `my.tab` show that only in 50 stocks (out of 471) we reject the null hypothesis of no directional accuracy. As for the test of excess profit, we find that only in 62 cases the null hypothesis is rejected. We used a threshold value of 10% in both analysis. When looking at the whole dataset, the statistical evidence of directional predictability is very weak.

The main results of the study are clear: `prophet` is particularly bad at point forecasts for returns but does a better job in directional predictions. Even though we find a positive correlation between forecast and real values, the formal Wald test clearly shows that the forecasting model is not able to provide an unbiased prediction of returns. In a trading setup, the results indicates that the model was not able to provide an over performance for the majority of the stocks. Both results were confirmed by formal statistical tests.

In line with the previous example of research script, the R code presented here can be easily used in other setups. Changing the raw dataset is very simple: just set a new `dataframe` with columns `ret` and `ref.date`. You can investigate the same research hypothesis for other financial markets without much effort. Function `est.model.and.forecast` could also be changed for other forecasting models.

11.3.3   An Analysis of High Frequency trade Data

In this final example of research script, we will provide two simple cases of manipulating high frequency trade data obtained with package `GetHFData`. Both examples are limited in research depth, but they do show the potential in using high frequency trade data. First, we download aggregate data from the Brazilian stock exchange and look into the shape of the intraday liquidity. In the second case, we use raw (tick by tick) trade data and package `highfrequency` (Boudt et al., 2017) to calculate measures of realized volatility for several assets. Both example are inspired in the work of Perlin and Ramos (2016).

11.3.3.1 Liquidity and the Time of the Day

In order to illustrate the usage of aggregated trade data, we will analyze the intraday *U* shaped pattern of liquidity in the equity market. The main problem is how liquidity varies during a typical trading day. This is specially important to liquidity takers such as intraday traders who want to minimize the impact of their trading orders by trading in the hours with the highest liquidity. This particular issue has been found and discussed in several papers from the literature such as Admati and Pfleiderer (1988), Back and Pedersen (1998) , Engle and Russell (1998), Groß-Klußmann and Hautsch (2011), among many others.

The data used in this empirical study is related to the six most traded assets in the thirty day period from the last available date in Bovespa ftp site at the time of the book compilation. The use of a short time period is not accidental. We chose to keep thirty days as it facilitates the replication of the example by decreasing the time needed to download the dataset by the user.

The first step is to select the liquid assets to run the empirical research. To do that, we need to find the six most traded assets in the last date available at the ftp:

```
library(GetHFData)

# set type of market (equity, options,BMF)
type.market <- 'equity'

# get available files from ftp
df.ftp <- ghfd_get_ftp_contents(type.market = type.market)

# get last available date
last.date <- max(df.ftp$dates)

# get 6 most traded
df.tickers <- ghfd_get_available_tickers_from_ftp(my.date = last.date,
                                                  type.market)
```

The last available date is 2017-04-07. Function `ghfd_get_available_tickers` will output a `dataframe` with the number of trades for each ticker found in the dataset.

As a robustness check, we can use package `ggplot2` to create a figure to illustrate the number of trades for each of the 25 most traded stocks in the date of 2017-04-07:

```
library(ggplot2)

# select tickers
temp.df <- df.tickers[1:25, ]

p <- ggplot(temp.df, aes(x = reorder(tickers, -n.trades), y = n.trades))
p <- p + geom_bar(stat = "identity")
p <- p + theme(axis.text.x=element_text(angle=90,hjust=1,vjust=0.5))
p <- p + labs(x = 'Tickers', y = 'Number of trades')
print(p)
```

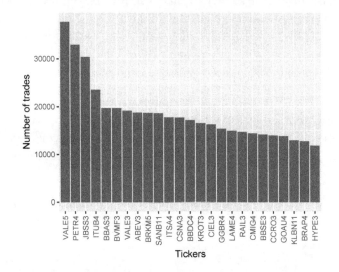

We can see that the six most traded assets in 2017-04-07 are VALE5, PETR4, JBSS3, ITUB4, BBAS3, BVMF3. A particular feature of the high frequency data from Brazil is that the liquidity is disperse and decreases rapidly across the assets. Even though we are only looking at trading data for one day, we can expect that the number of trades will also drop quickly in other time periods as well.

From the programming side, object `df.tickers` is already sorted by the number of trades. So, in order to select the six most traded assets, we select the first six elements of `df.tickers$tickers`.

```
n.assets <- 6
my.assets <- df.tickers$tickers[1:n.assets]

print(my.assets)

## [1] "VALE5" "PETR4" "JBSS3" "ITUB4" "BBAS3" "BVMF3"
```

We continue the empirical example using package `GetHFData` to download and aggregate the desired information for later analysis. The first step in this stage is to set the options. We use an initial intraday time period as 10:30:00 and the last as 16:30:00. Any data outside of this time interval will be ignored. We set these limits in order to avoid the trading noise from the opening and closing hours of the market. The options used with `GetHFData` are set as follows.

```
# intraday time thresholds
first.time <- '10:30:00'
last.time <- '16:30:00'

# type of market
type.market <- 'equity'

# dates of study
last.date <- max(df.ftp$dates)
first.date <- last.date-30

# type of output and aggregation
type.output <- 'agg'
agg.diff <- '15 min'
```

After setting the inputs, we now use function `ghfd_get_HF_data` to download and aggregate the financial data.

```
df.out.agg <- ghfd_get_HF_data(my.assets = my.assets,
                               type.market = type.market,
                               first.date = first.date,
                               last.date = last.date,
                               first.time = first.time,
                               last.time = last.time,
                               type.output = type.output,
                               agg.diff = agg.diff)
```

The previous code will take some time to finish as it has to download and read several large files from the ftp site. To save time, the result of the download and aggregation can be found in file data/HFData_equity_6_Assets_15 min_30days.RData, also available in the book repository. Let's have a look in the output object.

```
print(head(df.out.agg))
```

```
##   InstrumentSymbol SessionDate        TradeDateTime n.trades
## 1            BBAS3 2017-03-08 2017-03-08 10:30:00      611
## 2            BBAS3 2017-03-08 2017-03-08 10:45:00      735
## 3            BBAS3 2017-03-08 2017-03-08 11:00:00      443
```

```
## 4                  BBAS3   2017-03-08 2017-03-08 11:15:00        408
## 5                  BBAS3   2017-03-08 2017-03-08 11:30:00        658
## 6                  BBAS3   2017-03-08 2017-03-08 11:45:00        824
##    last.price weighted.price     period.ret period.ret.volat
## 1       34.14       34.26031 -0.0066918825      0.0002493388
## 2       34.15       34.04835  0.0002929115      0.0005046596
## 3       34.14       34.09116 -0.0005854801      0.0002855653
## 4       34.26       34.17656  0.0035149385      0.0003146822
## 5       34.20       34.25063 -0.0026246719      0.0002388978
## 6       34.28       34.24894  0.0023391813      0.0001692893
##    sum.qtd   sum.vol n.buys n.sells Tradetime
## 1   283200   9702501    232     379  10:30:00
## 2   362100  12328874    397     338  10:45:00
## 3   161300   5498896    266     177  11:00:00
## 4   152100   5198235    278     130  11:15:00
## 5   170100   5826022    409     249  11:30:00
## 6   219000   7500502    533     291  11:45:00
```

As described earlier, the object returned from `ghfd_get_HF_data` is a `dataframe` with several columns calculated from the raw data. The columns already have the correct class, which facilitates the future manipulation of the data.

Once the data is available, we proceed to the analysis of the intraday pattern of liquidity. To do so, we use the number of trades (column `n.trades`) as a proxy for liquidity. The analysis will be based on the visual examination of a figure that relates the distribution of number of trades to the time of the day (column `Tradetime`) . Since the number of trades are not comparable across assets, we plot the same figure for different stocks using `facet_wrap`. Have a look in the code and output.

```
p <- ggplot(df.out.agg, aes(x =  Tradetime, y = n.trades))
p <- p + geom_boxplot() + coord_cartesian(ylim = c(0, 2500))
p <- p  + theme(axis.text.x=element_text(angle=90,hjust=1,vjust=0.5))
p <- p + facet_wrap(~InstrumentSymbol)
p <- p + labs(y='Number of Trades', x = 'Time of Day')
print(p)
```

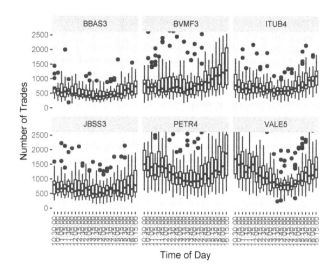

Previous figure shows the number of trades as a function of the time of the day. As expected, we find that the intraday shape of liquidity follows a U pattern. That is, the number of trades rises in the beginning and ending of the day, with the smallest value around 13:15:00. Such a pattern is found for the great majority of the assets.

This result is supported by previous findings in the literature (Engle and Russell, 1998, Groß-Klußmann and Hautsch (2011)). In the beginning of the trading day, a significant volume of overnight information is priced at the market, which justifies the increase of the number of trades. As for the end of the day, the higher volume of trades can be explained as an inventory strategy by the investors or market makers, which aims to finish the day with null portfolio positions in order to avoid the overnight risk. Since the decrease of portfolio size is achieved with more trades, we see a significant increase of negotiations at the end of the day.

11.3.3.2 Calculating Realized Volatility from Tick by Tick Data

One of the main innovations in the research field of pricing uncertainty is the possibility of estimating ex-post measures of volatility based on high frequency data, the so called realized volatility (Andersen et al., 2003, Barndorff-Nielsen and Shephard (2002)). Empirical studies have showed that these new estimators are more accurate than traditional measures calculated from datasets of lower frequencies such as daily returns (Andersen et al., 2003, Fleming et al. (2003), Barndorff-Nielsen and Shephard (2002)).

In this section we will present a simple example of calculating daily realized volatility from tick by tick data imported using `GetHFData`. In order to do so, we will use a popular R package designed to perform common operations in high frequency financial data, package `highfrequency` (Boudt et al., 2017). This is a very use-

ful package for a researcher in market microstructure, providing functions for the
organization and manipulation of trade and quote data. It also includes several
functions for the calculation of realized volatility measures, among other features.
Further details about this package can be found in its main website.

The first step in this empirical section is to import the raw dataset. We will use a
block of code similar to the previous example however, we set `type.output` as `raw`.
Next, we present the actual R code that downloads the dataset:

```
# set raw df, tick by tick
type.output <- 'raw'


# get data
df.out.raw <- ghfd_get_HF_data(my.assets = my.assets,
                               type.market = type.market,
                               first.date = first.date,
                               last.date = last.date,
                               first.time = first.time,
                               last.time = last.time,
                               type.output = type.output)
```

In this example of calculating realized volatility, we will use the simplest case available in package `highfrequency`, function `medRV`. From it own help manual:

> "The medRV belongs to the class of realized volatility measures in this
> package that use the series of high-frequency returns $r_{t,i}$ of a day t to produce an ex post estimate of the realized volatility of that day t. medRV
> is designed to be robust to price jumps. The difference between RV and
> medRV is an estimate of the realized jump variability."

> — Help file for `highfrequency::medRV`

Further inspection in the usage of `medRV` shows that it was designed to work with `xts`
objects. Also, function `medRV` only works in a stock-by-stock case. These elements
in the usage of `medRV` requires some adaptation since the `dataframe` output from
`getHFData` is not a `xts` object and it will include several stocks. A simple solution
is to build a wrapper function around `medRV` and use the capabilities of package
`dplyr` to calculate the realized volatility measure for all stocks, in all days.

The wrapper function works with the following steps: it takes as input a trade
price vector and its related date-time, change the input data to a `xts` object and,
finally, use the new format with function `medRV` to calculate the realized volatility
for the given inputs. Next, we present the actual R code that registers the wrapper
function.

```
my.RV.fct <- function(TradePrice, TradeDateTime){
  # Calculates realized volatility from vetor of prices and trade times
  #
  # Args:
  #    TradePrice - a trade price vector
  #    TradeDateTime - a date-time vector with trade times
  #
  # Returns:
  #    A single value of realized volatility

  require(highfrequency)

  temp.x <- xts(TradePrice, order.by = TradeDateTime)
  RV <- medRV(temp.x, makeReturns = T)

  return(as.numeric(RV))
}
```

Once the function is available, we use it together with the manipulation capabilities of `dplyr`. We calculate the daily realized volatility for all assets in our dataset with the following code.

```
library(dplyr)

RV.tab <- df.out.raw %>%
  group_by(InstrumentSymbol, SessionDate) %>%
  summarise(RV = my.RV.fct(TradePrice, TradeDateTime))
```

The result is a `dataframe` with three columns, the asset code (column `InstrumentSymbol`), the date (column `SessionDate`), and the realized volatility (column `RV`):

```
print(head(RV.tab))
```

```
## Source: local data frame [6 x 3]
## Groups: InstrumentSymbol [1]
##
##    InstrumentSymbol SessionDate          RV
##               <chr>      <date>       <dbl>
## 1            BBAS3  2017-03-08 0.0011887256
## 2            BBAS3  2017-03-09 0.0005225615
## 3            BBAS3  2017-03-10 0.0007449950
## 4            BBAS3  2017-03-13 0.0005331642
## 5            BBAS3  2017-03-14 0.0005755642
```

```
## 6              BBAS3    2017-03-15 0.0011781613
```

Once the processed data is ready, we illustrate the dynamics of the realized volatility for each asset in the next figure, which was generated with the following R code:

```
p <- ggplot(RV.tab, aes(x=SessionDate, y=RV))
p <- p + geom_line(size=1)
p <- p + facet_wrap(~InstrumentSymbol)
p <- p + labs(x='Date', y='Realized Volatility')
print(p)
```

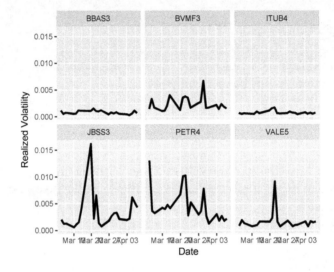

As expected, the realized volatility presents the clustering effect, where high/low values of volatility are followed by another high/low value. The custom function could be further extended to included an option for the type of volatility estimate.

Bibliography

Admati, A. R. and Pfleiderer, P. (1988). A theory of intraday patterns: Volume and price variability. *Review of Financial studies*, 1(1):3–40.

Anatolyev, S. and Gerko, A. (2005). A trading approach to testing for predictability. *Journal of Business & Economic Statistics*, 23(4):455–461.

Andersen, T. G., Bollerslev, T., Diebold, F. X., and Labys, P. (2003). Modeling and forecasting realized volatility. *Econometrica*, 71(2):579–625.

Bache, S. M. and Wickham, H. (2014). *magrittr: A Forward-Pipe Operator for R.* R package version 1.5.

Back, K. and Pedersen, H. (1998). Long-lived information and intraday patterns. *Journal of financial markets*, 1(3):385–402.

Barndorff-Nielsen, O. E. and Shephard (2002). Econometric analysis of realized volatility and its use in estimating stochastic volatility models. *Journal of the Royal Statistical Society Series B*, 64(2):253–280.

Baumer, B., Cetinkaya-Rundel, M., Bray, A., Loi, L., and Horton, N. J. (2014). R markdown: Integrating a reproducible analysis tool into introductory statistics. *arXiv preprint arXiv:1402.1894*.

Bollerslev, T. (1986). Generalized autoregressive conditional heteroskedasticity. *Journal of econometrics*, 31(3):307–327.

Boudt, K., Cornelissen, J., Payseur, S., Nguyen, G., and Schermer, M. (2017). *highfrequency: Tools for Highfrequency Data Analysis*. R package version 0.5.

Brooks, C. (2014). *Introductory econometrics for finance*. Cambridge university press.

Campbell, J. Y., Lo, A. W.-C., MacKinlay, A. C., et al. (1997). *The econometrics of financial markets*, volume 2. princeton University press Princeton, NJ.

Croissant, Y. and Millo, G. (2008). Panel data econometrics in R: The plm package. *Journal of Statistical Software*, 27(2).

Dowle, M., Srinivasan, A., Short, T., with contributions from R Saporta, S. L., and Antonyan, E. (2015). *data.table: Extension of Data.frame*. R package version 1.9.6.

Dragulescu, A. A. (2014). *xlsx: Read, write, format Excel 2007 and Excel 97/2000/XP/2003 files*. R package version 0.5.7.

Engle, R. F. (1982). Autoregressive conditional heteroscedasticity with estimates of the variance of united kingdom inflation. *Econometrica: Journal of the Econometric Society*, pages 987–1007.

Engle, R. F. and Russell, J. R. (1998). Autoregressive conditional duration: a new model for irregularly spaced transaction data. *Econometrica*, pages 1127–1162.

Fan, F. Y. (2016). *FinCal: Time Value of Money, Time Series Analysis and Computational Finance*. R package version 0.6.3.

Fleming, J., Kirby, C., and Ostdiek, B. (2003). The economic value of volatility timing using "realized" volatility. *Journal of Financial Economics*, 67(3):473–509.

Fox, J. and Weisberg, S. (2011). *An R Companion to Applied Regression*. Sage, Thousand Oaks CA, second edition.

Freitas, W. (2016). *bizdays: Business Days Calculations and Utilities*. R package version 1.0.1.

Garmonsway, D. (2017). *tidyxl: Read Untidy Excel Files*. R package version 0.2.1.

Ghalanos, A. (2015). *rugarch: Univariate GARCH models*. R package version 1.3-6.

Gohel, D. (2017). *ReporteRs: Microsoft Word and PowerPoint Documents Generation*. R package version 0.8.8.

Graves, S. (2014). *FinTS: Companion to Tsay (2005) Analysis of Financial Time Series*. R package version 0.4-5.

Greene, W. H. (2003). *Econometric analysis*. Pearson Education India.

Grolemund, G. and Wickham, H. (2011). Dates and times made easy with lubridate. *Journal of Statistical Software*, 40(3):1–25.

Groß-Klußmann, A. and Hautsch, N. (2011). When machines read the news: Using automated text analytics to quantify high frequency news-implied market reactions. *Journal of Empirical Finance*, 18(2):321–340.

Grunfeld, Y. (1958). The determinants of corporate investment, unpublished ph. d. *D thesis, The University of Chicago*.

Hamilton, J. (1994a). *Time Series Analysis*. Princeton University Press.

Hamilton, J. D. (1994b). *Time series analysis*, volume 2. Princeton university press Princeton.

Harrison, J. (2016). *RSelenium: R Bindings for Selenium WebDriver*. R package version 1.4.5.

Hausman, J. A. (1978). Specification tests in econometrics. *Econometrica: Journal of the Econometric Society*, pages 1251–1271.

Hsiao, C. (2014). *Analysis of panel data*. Number 54. Cambridge university press.

Hyndman, R. and Khandakar, Y. (2007). Automatic time series forecasting: The forecast package for r 7. 2008. *URL: https://www. jstatsoft. org/article/view/v027i03 [accessed 2016-02-24][WebCite Cache]*.

Ittelson, T. R. (1998). *Financial statements: A step-by-step guide to understanding and creating financial reports*. Career PressInc.

James, D. and Hornik, K. (2017). *chron: Chronological Objects which Can Handle Dates and Times*. R package version 2.3-50. S original by David James, R port by Kurt Hornik.

Kleiber, C. and Zeileis, A. (2008). *Applied econometrics with R*. Springer Science & Business Media.

Kleiber, C. and Zeileis, A. (2010). The grunfeld data at 50. *German economic review*, 11(4):404–417.

Lang, D. T. and the CRAN Team (2016). *XML: Tools for Parsing and Generating XML Within R and S-Plus*. R package version 3.98-1.4.

Lee, S. (2016). *finreportr: Financial Data from U.S. Securities and Exchange Commission*. R package version 1.0.1.

Leisch, F. (2002). Sweave: Dynamic generation of statistical reports using literate data analysis. In *Compstat*, pages 575–580. Springer.

Maddala, G. (2001). Introduction to econometrics.

Mirai Solutions GmbH (2016). *XLConnect: Excel Connector for R*. R package version 0.2-12.

Pena, E. A. and Slate, E. H. (2014). *gvlma: Global Validation of Linear Models Assumptions*. R package version 1.0.0.2.

Penman, S. H. and Penman, S. H. (2007). *Financial statement analysis and security valuation*. McGraw-Hill New York.

Perlin, M. (2014). *fMarkovSwitching: R Package for Estimation, Simulation and Forecasting of a Univariate Markov Switching Model*. R package version 1.0/r5838.

Perlin, M. (2016). *BatchGetSymbols: Downloads and Organizes Financial Data for Multiple Tickers*. R package version 1.0.

Perlin, M. and Ramos, H. (2016). *GetHFData: A R Package for Downloading and Aggregating High Frequency Trading Data from Bovespa*.

Pesaran, M. H. and Timmermann, A. (1992). A simple nonparametric test of predictive performance. *Journal of Business & Economic Statistics*, 10(4):461–465.

R Core Team (2015). *foreign: Read Data Stored by Minitab, S, SAS, SPSS, Stata, Systat, Weka, dBase, ...* R package version 0.8-66.

Robinson, D. (2017). *broom: Convert Statistical Analysis Objects into Tidy Data Frames*. R package version 0.4.2.

Ross, S. A., Westerfield, R., and Jordan, B. D. (2008). *Fundamentals of corporate finance*. Tata McGraw-Hill Education.

Ryan, J. A. (2015). *quantmod: Quantitative Financial Modelling Framework*. R package version 0.4-5.

Ryan, J. A. and Ulrich, J. M. (2014). *xts: eXtensible Time Series*. R package version 0.9-7.

Sanchez-Espigares, J. A. and Lopez-Moreno, A. (2014). *MSwM: Fitting Markov Switching Models*. R package version 1.2.

Team, R. C., Wuertz, D., Setz, T., Chalabi, Y., Maechler, M., and Byers, J. W. (2015). *timeDate: Rmetrics - Chronological and Calendar Objects*. R package version 3012.100.

Teetor, P. (2011). *R cookbook*. " O'Reilly Media, Inc.".

Thompson, K. (1968). Programming techniques: Regular expression search algorithm. *Communications of the ACM*, 11(6):419–422.

Trapletti, A. and Hornik, K. (2017). *tseries: Time Series Analysis and Computational Finance.* R package version 0.10-38.

Tsay, R. S. (2005). *Analysis of financial time series*, volume 543. John Wiley & Sons.

Venables, W. N., Smith, D. M., Team, R. D. C., et al. (2004). An introduction to r.

Wickham, H. (2007). Reshaping data with the reshape package. *Journal of Statistical Software*, 21(12):1–20.

Wickham, H. (2009). *ggplot2: elegant graphics for data analysis.* Springer Science & Business Media.

Wickham, H. (2014). *Advanced R.* CRC Press.

Wickham, H. (2015). *stringr: Simple, Consistent Wrappers for Common String Operations.* R package version 1.0.0.

Wickham, H. (2016a). *readxl: Read Excel Files.* R package version 0.1.1.

Wickham, H. (2016b). *rvest: Easily Harvest (Scrape) Web Pages.* R package version 0.3.2.

Wickham, H. (2016c). *tidyr: Easily Tidy Data with spread() and gather() Functions.* R package version 0.6.0.

Wickham, H. and Francois, R. (2016). *dplyr: A Grammar of Data Manipulation.* R package version 0.5.0.

Wickham, H., Francois, R., and Müller, K. (2017). *tibble: Simple Data Frames.* R package version 1.3.0.

Wickham, H., Hester, J., and Francois, R. (2016). *readr: Read Tabular Data.* R package version 1.0.0.

Wuertz, D., with contribution from Michal Miklovic, Y. C., Boudt, C., Chausse, P., and others (2016). *fGarch: Rmetrics - Autoregressive Conditional Heteroskedastic Modelling.* R package version 3010.82.1.

Xie, Y. (2015). *Dynamic Documents with R and knitr*, volume 29. CRC Press.

Xie, Y. (2016). *bookdown: Authoring Books and Technical Documents with R Markdown.* CRC Press.

Zeileis, A. (2004). Econometric computing with hc and hac covariance matrix estimators.

Zeileis, A. and Hothorn, T. (2002). Diagnostic checking in regression relationships. *R News*, 2(3):7–10.

Index

CPSIA information can be obtained
at www.ICGtesting.com
Printed in the USA
LVHW102044251218
601652LV00029B/1162/P